FEAR NO EVIL

The Pathwork Method
of Transforming The Lower Self

The Pathwork Series:
General Editor: Donovan Thesenga

The Pathwork of Self-Transformation. Eva Pierrakos.
Bantam/ 1990

Fear No Evil;
The Pathwork Method of Transforming The Lower Self.
Eva Pierrakos and Donovan Thesenga.

The Undefended Self. Susan Thesenga.

The Pathwork of Relationship. Eva Pierrakos and Judith Saly.

Published by **Pathwork Press**
Route 1, Box 86 • Madison, VA 22727 • Phone/Fax: 703-948-5508
President: Gene Humphrey. Design and Publicity: Karen Millnick

FEAR NO EVIL

The Pathwork Method
of Transforming The Lower Self

Compiled and edited by
Donovan Thesenga
from material channelled by
Eva Pierrakos

Pathwork Press
Madison, Virginia
1993

Library of Congress Catalog Card Number: 93-84262

ISBN   0-9614777-2-5   12.00

Cover Design: Karen Millnick and Donovan Thesenga.

Cover Painting: _Saint George and the Dragon (detail)_; RAPHAEL; National Gallery of Art, Washington; Andrew W. Mellon Collection.

Chapters 7, 8, and 18 appeared, in slightly different form, in _The Pathwork of Self-Transformation_, Bantam New Age, 1990.

PRINTED IN THE UNITED STATES OF AMERICA

AUTHORSHIP

The cover of this book lists the names of two human beings, but neither of us is truly the author. Most of the words in this volume were spoken by a discarnate being who came to be called "the Guide", and Eva Pierrakos was the channel through which the material was delivered. For over twenty five years Eva developed herself spiritually, thus deepening her capacity to be a channel for higher truth. However, the Guide did not ever "speak out" a volume called *Fear No Evil*. Nor did he ever arrange in one stream all of his comments about the transformation of the lower self. The idea of gathering together the Guide's teachings on this subject, the work of editing and assembling these teachings, and the choice of a title, were mine. Since the final choices as to which of the Guide's words to include and which to omit have been mine, any errors of omission or commission are also mine.

The editorial labors and suggestions of Judith Saly, John Saly, Susan Thesenga, and Jan Bresnick were indispensable; as was the technical assistance of Karen Millnick, Iris Markham, Hedda Koehler and Rebecca Daniels.

Fear No Evil was commissioned by The Pathwork Foundation.

Donovan Thesenga
Sevenoaks Center
Madison, Va.
October, 1991

Though I walk through the valley of the shadow of death, I will fear no evil.

Psalm XXIII

If a way to the better there be, it lies in taking a full look at the worst.

Thomas Hardy

ॐ

CONTENTS

ॐ

INTRODUCTION

I. You and I and Evil.

Human nature is capable of an infinite amount of evil. ... Today as never before it is important that human beings should not overlook the danger of the evil lurking within them. It is unfortunately all too real, which is why psychology must insist on the reality of evil and must reject any definition that regards it as insignificant or actually nonexistent.
                                    C. G. Jung [1]

When evil is understood to be intrinsically a divine energy flow, momentarily distorted due to specific wrong ideas, concepts, and imperfections, then it is no longer rejected in its essence.
                        "The Meaning of Evil and
                            Its Transcendence" [2]

You are not an evil person. I am not an evil person. Yet evil exists in the world. Where does it come from?

The evil things that are done on earth are done by human

beings. We can't blame the plants and animals, or an infectious disease, or evil influences from outer space. But if you and I are not evil, who is? Does evil reside only in other places such as Nazi Germany or the "evil empire" of the Stalinist Soviet Union? Or only in the hearts of criminals and drug lords, but not in the hearts of anyone we know?

Or is it possible that no one is evil, but only misguided? Can we really attribute the almost-unbelievable horror of the Holocaust, or the sadism of an Idi Amin, or the government-sanctioned torture being practiced right now in many countries of the world, to simple misguidedness? The word seems thin and insufficient as an explanation.

So where does evil reside? From whence does it arise?

The Pathwork teaches that evil resides in each and every human soul. Or, to put it another way: evil in the world is nothing more than the sum total of the evil that exists in all human beings.

"Evil" is a very strong word. Most people want to reserve it for the Hitlers and the criminals of the world, and do not want to apply it to themselves. Does it apply to you and to me?

The first definition of "evil" given by my dictionary is: "morally reprehensible, sinful, wicked". This definition makes it clear that it is an inappropriate use of the word to speak of "the evils of disease and death." Disease and death are painful aspects of human existence, but they are certainly not "morally reprehensible." On the other hand, it is a correct use of the word to speak of "the evil institution of slavery."

I have done things that are morally reprehensible, and I strongly suspect that so have you. We all have character flaws, we all are more or less egocentric, selfish and petty. And these character flaws have led me, many times, to be unloving, spiteful, jealous, and to act in ways that only add to the sum total of distress in the world. But does this make me *evil*?

You and I are certainly not evil in our totality, or in our essence, but we do have evil within us. Hence, the word "evil" can describe a continuum of behavior that goes all the way from simple pettiness and egocentricity on one end to the genocidal sadism of Nazism on the other. Those of us who predominantly inhabit the low end of the spectrum may wish to say we have nothing in common with the murderers at the high end; yet can it be true that we have *nothing* in common with them? To use the second of those dictionary synonyms, are we not all *sinners*?

Thirty or forty years ago the word "sin" was still in common use, but (save among the fundamentalists) it is scarcely ever used anymore. Now we are more likely to use the terminology of psychology, which talks instead about our human faults and failings, but usually in ways that put the blame elsewhere—on parents or society for making us the way we are. Personal change then happens when we understand the source of the negative programming others have done to us, feel all the feelings involved (primarily anger and grief), and then forgive the outer source of the negativity we still suffer from. And this is a crucial part of the transformation process.

"However, in the psychological view we have lost something that the old religious idea of sin gave to us. Namely that we are responsible for our own negativity, our personal acts of omission and commission. Being responsible is quite different from being guilty. It means simply acknowledging ourselves as sometimes the source of pain, injustice, and uncaring toward ourselves, others, and the world." [3]

If I can assent to this degree of self-responsibility—that I am not merely a victim of the evil in the world, but, in my own small way, an initiator of negativity—what then should I do about it? How can I go about transforming the evil in myself?

Traditional religion gives us moral precepts to live by, such as: "Do unto others as you would have them do unto you" and "Love thy neighbor as thyself." Surely we can all agree that if everyone abided by these golden rules the world would be a much more pleasant place in which to live. But we do not very often abide by them. I do not, and you do not. If we accept the principle as valid, why is it so hard to live up to? How do I go about changing my behavior? What do I need to do to become more loving? The answer of traditional religion too often seems to be merely: try harder.

In traditional religion, in the words of Carl Jung: "Every effort is made to teach idealistic beliefs or conduct which people know in their hearts they can never live up to, and such ideals are preached by officials who know that they themselves have never lived up to these high standards and never will. What is more, nobody ever questions the value of this kind of teaching." [4]

The answers of traditional religion have been so disappointing that many people who would formerly have consulted a priest now go instead to see a psychotherapist. How successful has modern psychology been in grappling with the problem of evil?

A recent article about Abraham Maslow, the father of humanistic psychology, states: "In his last years, Maslow was grappling with the nature of human evil. . . . [He] expressed misgivings over the inability of humanistic and transpersonal psychology to assimilate our "dark" side (what Jung termed the shadow) into a comprehensive theory of human nature. Maslow himself found this a troubling issue, and had come to no final conclusions about it by the time of his death." [5]

Those of us who have studied and practiced the Pathwork have discovered, with a sense of relief, that these teachings provide the crucial missing link that has heretofore eluded both religion and psychology.

The vast majority of present-day spiritual transmissions, or channelled material, focuses on the essential goodness of human beings, on our ultimate God-self nature. And this is a valuable message for our time. But what are we to make of our "dark side"? Where does it come from, why is it so intractable, how are we to deal with it?

It is in providing answers to these questions that the message of the Pathwork has its unique value. The transmission that came through Eva Pierrakos teaches us that evil can be found in some form in the heart of every human being, but that it need not be feared and denied. A method is given by which we can see our "dark side" clearly, understand its roots and causes, and, most important, transform it. The result will be peace in the human heart, and only after this is achieved will there be peace on earth.

II. Eva, the Guide, The Pathwork

The material that is gathered here was originally spoken, not written. Eva Pierrakos is not the author of this material, only the channel through which it was delivered. The true author is a discarnate being, who spoke through Eva when she entered a state of altered consciousness. This being tells us nothing about itself—no personality traits, no history, no "glamour". It does not even give itself a name, but it came to be known as "The Guide". The material that was transmitted came to be known as "the Guide lectures", and the process for personal transformation given in the teachings is known as "The Pathwork".

The Guide placed all emphasis on the material delivered, and none on the source. He said, in one of his later transmissions, "do not be concerned with the phenomenon of this comunication as such. The only thing important to understand at the beginning of such a venture is that there are levels of reality which you have not yet explored and experienced and about which you can only theorize at best. Theory is not the same as experience, and letting it go at that for the moment will be so much better than trying to force a definitive conclusion. Do remember that this voice does not express the conscious mind of the human instrument through whom I speak. Furthermore, take into consideration that every human personality has a depth of which he or she may as yet be unaware. At this depth, everybody possesses the means to transcend the narrow confines of his or her own personality, and receive access to other realms and to entities endowed with a wider and deeper knowing." [6]

From 1957 to 1979 the Guide delivered, through Eva, 258 lectures on the nature of psychological and spiritual reality, and on the process of personal spiritual development. A sampler of seventeen of these lectures has been published in an earlier volume entitled *The Pathwork of Self- Transformation.* [7] This present volume will focus on the *method* of self-transformation that the Guide presented. It is not a simple method but it promises, if followed faithfully and courageously, enormously far-reaching results.

"This path demands from an individual that which most people are least willing to give: truthfulness with the self, exposure of what exists now, elimination of masks and pretenses, and the experience of one's naked vulnerability. It is a tall order, and yet it is the only way that leads to genuine peace and wholeness." [8]

During the first ten years of the Guide's transmissions a group of people gathered around Eva, learning the principles that the Guide explained, and attempting to put them into practice. In 1967 Eva met Dr. John Pierrakos, a psychiatrist and co-creator of a school of therapy known as bio-energetics. A few years later they were married, and the merger of his work and hers led to a great expansion of the Pathwork community.

The network of people practicing and teaching the Pathwork now includes two schools that teach the Pathwork (in Phoenicia, New York, and Madison, Virginia), and study groups in many urban areas in the United States, and in Europe.

During Eva's lifetime (she died in 1979) the Pathwork community would gather every month at a location in New York City. Eva would enter a state that she described as a light trance, and the Guide would speak through her for about forty-five minutes. The lectures were recorded, transcribed, and then distributed to the members of the community.

The verbal presentation of the material led to a certain amount of repetition within each lecture. Also, over the course of the twenty-two years of their transmission, many themes were repeated and elaborated upon. In preparing this volume some of the Guide's repetitions have been edited out, but, in keeping with our desire to retain the flavor of the original, some of it remains. At the end of each lecture there was a question and answer period. We have removed most of this material from the present text, but have chosen to leave in several examples of this interchange between the members and the Guide.

III. How to Use This Book

We strongly recommend that you not try to sit down and read this volume straight through. The material was originally presented with the expectation that each lecture would be read and then discussed for a full month, before the next lecture was given. Much of the material is rather dense, and requires re-reading, and thoughtful attempts to apply it to yourself. If you have others that you can share this book with, reading it together and discussing it as you go along, that would be ideal. If not, we recommend that you read a lecture once, wait a few days and then read it again, and then take some time to do your best to apply the principles to yourself and to your own life, before going on to read the next lecture.

The selection of lectures and parts of lectures that appears here is a sampling from the 258 that were delivered. They are presented chronologically, and are best read in that order. However, if you find any one section of the book hard going, we recommend that, rather than put the book aside, you jump ahead to another lecture with a title that interests you.

These lectures elaborate a method of observing yourself, and a theoretical structure which you can use to organize and understand what you observe. The work then requires diligent efforts to remove your masks and defenses, and feel and acknowledge the true feelings that you have repressed and denied. Some of this work can be done alone, but, for most people who have reached this stage of the path, it becomes very difficult to continue the work in solitude. You will need friends and helpers, fellow-travellers, to help you see some aspects of yourself that you prefer to keep in the shadow.

Once you have learned true self-observation—and then have had the courage to bring your shadow, your lower self, into the light—you will be ready and able to begin to practice genuine self-transformation. The work is not quick and not easy, but it will truly change your life.

D.T.

1. C. G. Jung, *Aion.* In *Psyche & Symbol,* edited by V.S. de Laszlo, Doubleday, 1958, ps. 49-50.
2. Pathwork lecture # 184.
3. Susan Thesenga, *The Undefended Self*, Sevenoaks, 1988, p. 19.
4. C. G. Jung, *Memories, Dreams, Reflections,* Pantheon Books, 1973, p. 330.
5. Edward Hoffman, Ph.D., "Abraham Maslow and Transpersonal Psychology", in "The Common Boundary", May/June 1988, p.5.
6. Pathwork Lecture #204
7. Eva Pierrakos, *The Pathwork of Self-Transformation*, Bantam Books, 1990
8. Pathwork Lecture #204

ે

SELF-KNOWLEDGE

A man has many skins in himself, covering the depths of his heart. Man knows so many things; he does not know himself. Why, thirty or forty skins or hides, just like an ox's or a bear's, so thick and hard, cover the soul. Go into your own ground and learn to know yourself there.

Meister Eckhart

It is often tragic to see how blatantly a man bungles his own life and the lives of others yet remains totally incapable of seeing how much the whole tragedy originates in himself, and how he continually feeds it and keeps it going. Not consciously , of course—for consciously he is engaged in bewailing a faithless world that recedes further and further into the distance. Rather, it is an unconscious factor which spins the illusions that veil his world.

C. G. Jung [1]

We begin Part I with an excerpt of one of the Guide's earliest lectures. The lecture concerns happiness, noting that it is something that we all long for, while tending to blame outer circumstances for any feelings of unhappiness that we may have.

The Guide immediately sets forth the doctrine of self-responsibility: "The spiritually immature person thinks that happiness has to be created outside first; that outer circumstances, not necessarily dependent on him, have to fit his wishes—and then inner happiness will follow. The spiritually mature know that it is exactly the other way around." And, "happiness does not depend on outer circumstances or other people, no matter how convinced the spiritually immature person may be of this fallacy. The spiritually mature person knows that he himself is capable of creating a happy life, not only first within himself, but, as an inevitable result of this, also without."

This doctrine is the first foundation stone upon which the Pathwork method of self-transformation is based. The Guide states that it is not required that one believe this in order to begin doing the work. But it is necessary that one at least open one's mind to the possibility that this could be true. Toward this idea, as toward many others that will follow, we are urged to put aside old certainties and open our minds to new possibilities.

This path does not require that we believe any specific dogmas, or subscribe to any creeds. Rather, we are given ideas and methods to try, to work with, to put into practice. If the methods work, we will know it by the results. If the ideas bear fruit, if they help us to understand ourselves better and live more happily and productively, then they will become truly ours; they will be known, not just believed.

The first key to happiness, says the Guide, is self-knowledge. This would seem to be an uncontroversial statement; surely all educated people would agree that self-knowledge is invaluable. But why then is it so difficult to attain? Perhaps because no one likes to hear unpleasant or unflattering truths about oneself, and yet these are the most important ones to know. The lectures that follow in Part I point out how important it is for us to know all those parts of ourselves which we prefer to overlook and forget.

In Jungian psychology the term "shadow" is used to describe that part of ourselves that we prefer not to carry in our conscious mind, that we push into the darkness and hope to forget. In the Pathwork system this complex of character flaws and negativities is termed "the lower self." Hiding the lower self is a mask self, an idealized self-image, a glorified picture of who we think we ought to be, and try to pretend that we are.

The beginning stages of the Pathwork focus primarily on learning how to penetrate the mask self, and then how to become aware of the lower self that hides beneath it; for it is these two layers of the personality that hide the higher self— that spark of inner divinity that is at the core of each of us. The early lectures urge us to fearlessly probe those parts of ourselves that we most wish to hide, and give us practical tools for doing this work. We learn first how to see and evaluate our everyday activities and emotions—material which is fully conscious, and only awaits our turning our full attention to it. Then we learn how to detect our subconscious thoughts, feelings, and attitudes. Amazing things will be found; prepare to be surprised.

D.T.

1. C. G. Jung, *Aion,* As it appears in *Psyche & Symbol*, edited by V.S.de Laszlo, Doubleday, p.8.
2. Pathwork Lecture #204

KNOW YOURSELF

Deep within the heart of each human being is the longing for happiness. Now what is happiness? If you ask different people, you will receive different answers. The spiritually immature, after thinking about it for some time, will say, perhaps, that if they had this or that fulfillment, or a worry eliminated, they would be happy. In other words, happiness means for them that certain wishes are gratified. Yet even if these wishes came true these people would not be happy. They would still feel a certain deep-seated unrest. Why? Because happiness does not depend on outer circumstances or other people, no matter how convinced the spiritually immature person is of this fallacy. Spiritually mature people know this. They know that they themselves are solely responsible for their happiness or unhappiness. They know that they are capable of creating a happy life, first within themselves but then also, inevitably, in their outer life. The spiritually immature think that happiness has to be created first on the outer level because outer circumstances, which are not necessarily brought about by them, have to fit their wishes, and when this is achieved happiness will follow. The spiritually mature know that it is exactly the other way around.

Many people do not want to acknowledge this truth. It is easier to blame fate, the injustice of destiny and higher powers, or circumstances brought about by other people, than it is to be self-responsible. It is easier to feel like a victim. That way one does not have to search, sometimes very deeply and with a maximum of honesty, within oneself. And yet the great truth is: happiness lies in our own hands. It is in your power to find happiness. You may ask, "What must I do?" But let us see first what happiness means in the spiritually mature sense. It means, simply: God.

Many people, in all sincerity, endeavor to find God. However, if they were asked exactly what they meant by it, how they imagined it to take place, it would be difficult for them to give a meaningful answer. Yet, of course, there is such a thing as "finding God." In truth this is a very concrete process. There is nothing hazy, unrealistic, or illusory about it. Finding God really means finding the real self. If you find yourself to some degree, you are in comparative harmony. You perceive and understand the laws of the universe. You are capable of relating, and loving, and experiencing joy. You are truly self-responsible. You have the integrity and courage to be yourself, even at the expense of giving up approval. All of that signifies your having found God— by whatever name this process may be designated. It might also be called *coming home from self-alienation.*

Finding God is the only way happiness can be found. And it can be found right here and right now. "How?" you may then ask. My friends, so often people imagine God is immeasurably distant in the universe, and impossible to reach. This is far from the truth. The whole universe is within each person; therefore God is within each person. Each living creature has a part of God within. The only way to reach this divine part within is on the steep and narrow path of self-development. The goal is perfection. The basis of this is to know yourself!

To know yourself is indeed difficult. For knowing oneself means to face many an unflattering trait. It means a long, continuous, never-ending search: "What am I? What do my reactions—not only my deeds and thoughts—really mean? Are my actions supported by my feelings or do I have motives behind these actions that do not correspond to what I like to believe about myself or what I like other people to believe? Have I been honest with myself so far? What are my mistakes?"

Although some of you may know your weaknesses, most people ignore a good part of them, and this presents a great hurdle, even for those who have reached a certain height on this upward path. You cannot overcome what you do not know. Each fault is nothing more or less than a chain that binds you. By the shedding of each imperfection you break a chain and thus become freer and nearer to happiness. Happiness is meant for each individual, but is impossible to attain without eliminating the causes of your unhappiness, which are your faults—as well as any trend that breaks a spiritual law.

You can find out how advanced you are on this path by viewing your life and your problems. How happy are you? What is lacking in your life? To the extent that unhappiness or discontent exist in your life you have not fulfilled your potential.

For those who really fulfill themselves, there will be a deep and peaceful contentment, security, and a sense of fulfillment. If these are lacking, you are not completely on the right path, or you have not reached the liberation you are bound to experience after the initial difficulties on this path are overcome. Only you will know the answer, where you stand. No one else can or need answer this question for you. If you are on the right path, however, and you have that deep feeling of contentment and fulfillment yet there are still outer problems in your life, that should not discourage you. For the outer form of the inner conflict you may be working on right now cannot be dissolved so quickly.

The more you direct the inner soul currents into the right channels, the more the respective outside forms will change, gradually but surely. Until this process is completely effected the outer problem cannot automatically dissolve. Impatience will only be a hindrance. If you are on the right path, you will live and feel the great reality of God's world in your daily life. It will become just as real, if not more so, than your human surroundings. It will no longer be a theory, mere intellectual knowledge. You will live in this world and feel its effect on you.

I will retire now and say to each one of you: none of you should ever feel alone. The love of God is with all of you. Be in peace, follow this path. It will bring you happiness.

ટ**

HIGHER SELF, LOWER SELF, AND MASK

Blessed is this hour in which I am permitted to speak to you, my friends.

You all know that you have not only a physical body, but also various subtle bodies, each representing something different. Your thoughts have definite spiritual forms, and such forms are created not only by thoughts, but also by feelings, since a feeling is really just an "unthought thought," not yet made conscious. Although thought creates a different form than a feeling docs, nevertheless, both create very definite and substantial forms. Each subtle body, as well as the physical body, has an aura: the vibration and emanation of that body. These forms really do exist in the spirit. All these forms fluctuate and change since everything in spirit is in perpetual motion.

The aura of the physical body shows physical sickness or health, and all other conditions of the physical being. The emotional, intellectual, or spiritual reactions show in the aura of the respective subtle body.

Each living being has a higher self or divine spark. This is the finest and most radiant of the subtle bodies, with the quickest frequency of vibration because the higher the spiritual development, the quicker the vibration. The higher self has surrounded itself slowly and gradually with various layers of denser matter, not quite as dense as the physical body, but infinitely denser than the higher self. Thus did the lower self come into existence.

The aim of spiritual development is to eliminate the lower self so that the higher self becomes free again of all outer layers it has acquired. In your own life, you will be able to sense quite easily, with yourself or others, that certain parts of the higher self are already free, while other parts are still hidden. How much is free or hidden, and how thickly it is hidden, depends on the overall development of the person. The lower self consists not only of the common faults and the individual weaknesses that vary with each person, but also of ignorance and laziness. It hates to change and conquer itself; it has a very strong will that may not always manifest itself outside, and wants its way without paying the price. It is very proud and selfish, and always has a great deal of personal vanity. All these characteristics are generally part of the lower self, regardless of other individual faults.

We can determine very well which thought-forms come from the higher self and which come from the lower self. We can also determine which tendencies, wishes, and endeavors from the higher self may be mixed in with tendencies from the lower self.

When messages from the higher self are tainted with lower-self motives, a disorder is created in the soul that makes its bearer emotionally ill. For example, a person may want something selfish, but because he or she does not want to admit inwardly that this is selfishness, begins to rationalize this selfish desire and fool himself about it. We can see this kind of common self-deception in human beings, because the forms of the higher self have an entirely different character than those of the lower self.

There is another layer that is, unfortunately, not yet recognized sufficiently among human beings for its full significance, and that is what I might term the mask self. The mask self is created in the following way: When you recognize that you may get into conflict with your surroundings by giving in to your lower self, you may nevertheless not be ready to pay the price to eliminate the lower self. This would mean first of all that you would have to face it as it really is, with all its motives and drives, since you can conquer only that which you are fully aware of. This means taking the narrow path, the spiritual path. Many people do not want to think that deeply; instead they react emotionally without thinking about how their lower self may be involved in their reaction. The subconscious mind feels it necessary to present a different picture of the self to the world in order to avoid certain difficulties, unpleasantness, or disadvantages of all sorts. Thus people create another layer of the self which has nothing to do with reality, either with that of the higher self, or with the temporary reality of the lower self. This superimposed mask is what you might call phony; it is unreal.

I will return to the above example. The lower self dictates to the person to be quite ruthless about a selfish desire. It is not difficult for anyone of even the most limited intelligence to realize that by giving in to this desire, he or she will be ostracized, or disliked by others, an outcome no one wants. Instead of overcoming selfishness by the slow process of development, such a person often acts as though she or he were already unselfish. But she actually is selfish, and feels the selfishness. Her giving in to public opinion and her generosity are just a sham, not at all reconciled with her true feelings. In other words, the right act is in this case entirely unsupported by the unpurified inner feelings and therefore the person is at war within. The proper act becomes an act of necessary compulsion, instead of free choice. Such a superimposed goodness does not pay the price in the real sense. While a person may give something, he may hate the idea. Not only is such a person selfish within by inner conviction, but he is also untrue to his nature, violating his reality and living a lie.

I am by no means suggesting that it is advisable to give in to one's lower nature; one must fight for enlightenment and strive for development in order to purify one's feelings and desires. But if this is not accomplished, there should at least be no self-deception. The person should have at least a clear and true picture about the discrepancy between feelings and actions. In this way, no mask self can form.

Ending Self-Deception

However, it is too often the case that such a person tries to believe in his own unselfishness and in that way fools himself about his real feelings and motives by not showing them, and not wanting to look at them. After a while the evil root will sink into the subconscious where it will ferment and create forms that have their effect and cannot be eliminated, because the person is unaware of them. The example of selfishness is merely one instance; there are many other traits and tendencies that go through the same process, my friends.

When people are emotionally sick, it is always a sign that in one way or another a mask self has been created. They do not realize they are living a lie. They have built a layer of unreality that has nothing to do with their real being. Thus they are not being true to their real personality. As I said before, being true to oneself does not mean that you should give in to your lower self, but that you should be aware of it. Do not fool yourself if you still act according to the necessity to protect yourself and not out of enlightened vision and inner conviction. Be aware that your feelings are still unpurified in this or that respect. Then you have a good basis from which to start. It will be easier for you to face yourself in this manner when you realize that underneath the layers of your lower self lives your higher self, your ultimate and absolute reality which you must eventually reach. In order to reach it, you must first face your lower self, your temporary reality, instead of covering it up, because that puts an even greater distance between you and absolute reality, or your own higher self. To face the lower self you must at all costs tear down the mask self. You can bring yourself to do so when you visualize the three selves I am discussing here.

To lie to oneself and not think about one's emotions and true motives at all, but merely to let the emotions react without thinking, may appear at times adequate, but it is not. The person who wants to become happy, healthy, and at peace inwardly, needs, in order to truly fulfill this present life and be in harmony with God and thus with the inner self, to find the answer to these questions once and for all: *What is the actual me? What is my higher self? What is my lower self? Where may there be a mask, a falsehood?*

It is important for all of you to try to train your inner eye to see yourselves and other human beings from this point of view. The more you become spiritually awake, the easier it will be for you to accurately perceive yourselves and others. When you come in contact with the higher self, once your intuition has awakened through your personal spiritual development, you will feel a distinct difference between the mask and the higher self. You will feel the unpleasant manifestations of the mask self, first of all of your own, no matter how pleasant the mask may appear to be.

What then remains to be accomplished is to penetrate the subconscious layers of the personality with these truths as well, so that all inner resistance will be overcome.

If you want to walk this path and be cured of your emotional sicknesses, it is important for you to understand all this. You have to face the lower self which exists in each human being, but also know that this lower self is not the ultimate "I" or true self. The higher self, which is perfection, waiting to grow out of these layers of imperfection, is the true self. Perhaps you have questions on this subject, my dear friends.

QUESTION: How is it possible to undo what your lower self has manifested in the way of physical illness?

ANSWER: In the first place, you should not try to eliminate the consequences first. If your lower self has created an illness, the illness has to be accepted first. You should go about finding the roots or the part of your lower self that has created the illness. The lower self has to be met and completely explored. Your aim must be purification and perfection for its own sake. You do it for the love of God that you have in you, and not in order to avoid putting up with a discomfort. True, it takes a lot of overcoming and inner strength to sufficiently purify the motives first, but that is the necessary foundation. While doing this, you are at the same time learning many other things. Spiritual strength grows as you learn to apply absolute self-honesty. Once your motives are pure, the sickness will not matter half as much as the state of your soul. To the degree that the ego and the comfort of all that goes with it loses importance, you will have followed a very important spiritual law. Your spiritual health will be gradually restored. This law has to do with the giving up of the ego-self which Jesus taught. Only in so doing will you win your life. So begin by meeting your lower self with courage, optimism, humility, and in a spirit of discovery. Once you discover your lower self, and shed all the masks and all the covering layers, you will begin to work on these different aspects of the lower self. You do this by daily self-observation and self-testing, observing again and again how far your inner currents still deviate from what you wish them to be. As you do so, and become master over your lower self, you learn real self-honesty and your motives for development become purer and purer. Your vision will widen, enlightenment will be given to you, and your symptoms and problems will gradually disappear. So you should not even think of your illness first, but of the root of the problem. That will be the only lasting success. If you truly want to purify yourself, not merely rid yourself of unpleasant consequences that are most visible or noticeable to you, help and guidance will come to you so that you can do battle with your lower self, since no one can do it alone.

And with that, my friends, I will leave you. Go your way in peace; know that God is present within you.

ACCOMPLISHING A REAL CHANGE OF FEELINGS

I bring blessings for all of you, my friends. By now you will have understood one thing clearly: the necessity for self-development on this earth plane which exists for that very purpose. No matter how difficult life may be at times, only those who fulfill this purpose can find peace in their souls. I have promised to start this course so that each one of you can find your way by learning how to go about it, where to begin, and what is involved in doing the work. Treat my words as a meditation. You should retain these words and not just read them once, for that will not be enough. You should meditate on these teachings, so that this knowledge may eventually grow from being superficial and intellectual to reaching the deeper regions of your being. Only then will they be really beneficial to you.

Everybody knows that it is important to be a decent person, not to commit so-called sins, to give love, to have faith, and to be kind to others. However, this is not enough. In the first place, knowing all this and actually being able to act on it are two different stories. You may be able by voluntary action to refrain from committing a crime but you cannot possibly force yourself to feel that you do not want to harm anybody, ever. You may act kindly toward another, but you cannot force yourself to feel kindly. Neither can you force yourself to have love in your heart or to have real faith in God. Whatever pertains to emotions is not dependent upon your direct actions or even on your thoughts. Changing your feelings requires the slow process of self-development and self-recognition.

You may realize that you do not have enough faith, but realizing this and trying to force yourself to have it by telling yourself "I must have faith" will not bring you one step closer to it; quite the contrary. Superficially, you may be able to talk yourself into it, but this does not mean your faith or your ability to love is real—and that is what the path is all about: change of feelings.

Now, how to go about changing your innermost feelings— that is the question! That is where we have to begin and where I have to show you the way. In the first place, my friends, you cannot change anything as long as you do not know what is really in you. The greatest difficulty on this path is that people tend to fool themselves about who they really are. Now I am not only talking about the unconscious mind which you all know exists. Between the conscious and the subconscious mind there is another layer which is much closer to the conscious mind. However, you are still unaware of this layer because you want to be unaware of it. You escape from it although its symptoms and signs may be right under your nose. People flee from such awareness because they mistakenly think that what they do not know does not exist. You may not think so in exactly these words, but feelings of this sort go on in you without your quite realizing them. However, even if you turn away from your own inner reality, it does exist. It may be the temporary reality of this present time, but still it is part of the reality of your life and a stage of your development. It is your reality now.

Remember the lecture I gave about the higher self, the lower self, and the mask self. What I have just explained is part of the mask self. All of you know that it is wrong to do or think or feel certain things. If these feelings still exist in your lower self, you turn away from them, thinking you have thereby eliminated what you recognize as wrong. But avoidance or denial is the greatest mistake a human being can make, for it causes infinitely more trouble, more problems, and more inner and outer conflicts than anything you know in your conscious mind.

Facing Life

I have mentioned the various spiritual laws which are constantly being violated by human beings. The process I have just described violates one of these laws: the law of facing life. To face life's reality means to be able to face yourself as you are with all your imperfections. If you do not face life first, you can never develop. No system trying to teach ways to jump over this hurdle can ever be really successful, for seeking such shortcuts also violates a spiritual law.

All of you are unconsciously involved in this harmful process all the time, even though some of you may have already gained a certain amount of self-knowledge. There is not one among you who has not had at least one realization about an inner trend, making this trend really conscious. Nevertheless, in many other areas your conscious mind still flees from facing the inner truth. You may even know your shortcomings, but you certainly do not know all your real motives. You do not understand why you have certain opinions, tastes, or idiosyncrasies; even your good qualities may be partly influenced by an unconscious fault or wrong inner current. The tendencies about which you have hitherto deceived yourself have to be understood with respect to the influences and connections they have.

There is nothing in the human soul that comes entirely from the higher self or the lower self, because everything mixes constantly. Purification means to separate, understand, and rearrange in conscious understanding all these various trends, thus purifying the basic good trends from all masks of self-deception and from influences caused by character weaknesses. The higher self in you says, "I want to be perfect. I know this is the will of God." But it is the ignorance of the lower self that makes you think perfection can be attained by turning away from your imperfections and disregarding them. It is also the lower self that always wants to have everything so very comfortable. The lower self wants to be in a high position too, but for different reasons than the higher self. Your higher self seeks to advance for the love of God by way of recognition and enlightenment, and is aware that only when you are perfect will you be truly capable of loving your fellow creatures. But your lower self wants to be perfect in order to have more ego-gratification and to swell its head, to be admired. All of you, without exception, feel this way. Here is an example where both the higher and the lower self want the same thing, but their motives are entirely different. It is of utmost importance for the purification of your personality and for the sake of a healthy and harmonious soul to separate these motives and to recognize their voices. Do not feel I am blaming you, nor should you blame yourself when you begin to recognize these trends in you. I am stating a fact, and one of the basic requirements for your path is that you accept the fact of many negative trends still existing in yourself. Only from this premise can you go on and change the impurity of your motives.

You must also recognize the reasons why your lower self turns you away from facing yourself. One reason is that to recognize yourself as imperfect is unpleasant. The other is that the lower self is lazy and never wants to work. Yet it requires work to face what is in you, especially when it comes to facing the unpleasant things. So the first step, my friends, in your decision to walk the path of self-development and purification is to become clear about this. If you realize this, you will not be discouraged when you are busy on this first half of the work that is necessary. You can reach perfection only by going through your imperfections, not by going around them.

A Thorough Self-Search Takes Time

Going on this path does not mean a constant and smooth

improvement of yourself and your life conditions. This again would be completely unrealistic. It is necessary for you to face the fact that the path is long and that times of testing will not cease as quickly as you would like. A great deal of harm is being done when people are led to understand that by following certain rules of metaphysical teachings their problems will altogether cease, or that if they appear to cease for a time that will prove a sign of success. To imagine that going on this path of purification will immediately lessen your troubles or problems is immature and childish. Certainly your outer and inner problems will lessen and finally cease, but only after a long time, after you have first thoroughly understood your inner makeup and rearranged your inner currents. In this way you will dissolve inner images that are directly responsible for your conflicts. Once you have attained some victories over yourself you will fully realize this truth, but it will take a long time and years of work. Then very gradually the times of trial will lessen in impact and frequency, as harmony grows in your soul and as you really take charge of yourself and become aware of who you are. When I say "aware of yourself," I mean knowing your lower self utterly and completely, which does not mean that you have already overcome it.

Meditate on the fact that you can expect to find aspects of yourself you may be shocked about. Expect this and meet it halfway instead of hiding and escaping from it. Expect that just as you have had tests before you even started on this direct path, tests will still come your way for quite a time. The only difference is that a person who is on such a path will, after some successful work, understand that each testing and each time of woe means something very particular. A particular lesson to learn about the self is conveyed by each difficult period and every hardship. Only after a considerable time will your mind be trained in this direction so that you will find out faster and faster what the lesson is. The moment you will understand the significance of these periods, such particular testing will cease.

ıu have not understood it, the testing will continue. after a while, but it will come back in the same or ...ıtil you have learned the lesson. Those who have ....ienced what it means to understand the message of a particular hardship, to really understand it to its core, will realize what a blessing it is!

The Price of Spiritual Growth is High

Another thought for meditation: when you go on this path, you must also prepare yourself to abide by another of the spiritual laws, which says that there is a price to be paid for everything. Whoever tries to avoid this will finally pay a much heavier price. Every single person is doing this constantly in one way or another; some do it more obviously, others more subtly and secretively. Many people are not doing it outwardly, but psychologically you are all doing it, particularly when you approach this path with only half-open eyes. Realize that there is a price, but the price is well worth it! When you are about to buy a house and you want a beautiful mansion, you are reconciled to paying an adequate price. You will not expect a palace for the price of a shack. On the material level, you have no quarrel with this truth, but on the emotional, psychological, and spiritual level you constantly wish a palace for the price of a hut—and sometimes not even for any price at all.

The price you pay by going on this path of development is certainly a high one, but there is absolutely no other means on earth or in heaven to gain harmony, love, happiness, and complete inner security. The price is: no self-pity, no self-delusion, utter severance with the little ego, time, effort, patience, perseverance, and courage. What you will receive for this price is indeed a hundred times worth it, but do not expect to see the reward right after you start. By start I mean a period of at least two years of work in this manner, provided you do not work half-heartedly. In other words, and speaking symbolically, your money must first be paid in full!

I know that my words are not what a self-indulgent person likes to hear. There is no easy method and no magic formula by which you can obtain the happiness you all seek. I cannot promise you the precious gifts of heaven on earth if you merely do certain prayer exercises. If I were to tell you such things, you would be well justified in being suspicious and doubtful, even though you might undoubtedly prefer to hear this. What I am offering you is real and true. Each one of you has the chance to find out for yourself by trying and by following my advice. My advice to begin with is: meditate upon the words I have given you here. Consider what the price must be, and what you must expect. Then make your decision. Are you willing to take this path? Oh, you may say, "I am too tired." I can only answer that this is very shortsighted; if you are tired or weak, it is because your inner forces exhaust themselves laboring in the wrong channels, so that your strength cannot organically renew itself as it does in a soul that functions well. If you would only start and not be dismayed by the first struggles, you would finally succeed in setting this inner current right. By doing so, you would set free in yourself a wonderful life force and a spark that will change your life completely.

I cannot promise you that all your problems will cease, for they are a necessary part of your path to begin with, a challenge you can learn from if you meet them maturely. However, I can promise you that after you have fulfilled certain fundamental conditions, you will not be depressed anymore by your life and your difficulties. I can promise you that your tiredness will cease, and that you will have the strength to go through your difficulties and to bear your cross in the right way, knowing why and what it is all about.

The most difficult thing for you and the most weakening aspect of your life is that you cannot see the reason for anything that happens to you. Only on a path into yourself will you find out the reason, and this alone will give you the strength you need. Furthermore, I can promise you that after a certain time on the path you will enjoy life in spite of your difficulties even before they have actually begun to cease. You will come to relish life in a way you have never been able to do before. I can promise that you will be vibrantly alive—first at intervals, and later more consistently. To the extent you understand yourself and begin to put order into your soul, this vibrant life force will fill you. Life will be beautiful to you in all its reality. So I say to you truly, do not postpone this work. No matter how late you think it is, it is never too late. Whatever you accomplish on this earth will have an eternal value. And when I speak of accomplishment, I do mean the conquering of your lower self.

Three Types of Work

Here is another thought, my friends, for this initial decision which you must approach with open eyes: distinguish the three necessary types of work involved in purifying yourself. One is your outer behavior, the recognition of your apparent faults and qualities, as well as every occurrence that is on the surface. The next phase—and these phases often overlap—is tackling that layer of yourself that does not belong directly to your subconscious, but which you are unaware of because you are deliberately escaping it. This layer has to be treated in a different manner, which I will show you. The third and equally important layer is your subconscious mind. Do not believe that what is in the subconscious is so far away that it has no effect on you. You are constantly dominated by your subconscious without knowing it. It is very possible to find out slowly but surely what is in your subconscious, at least to some extent. Distinguish the trends in you which stand in direct relationship to your conscious will and are thus directly controlled through an act of will. You will also discover trends in you which are connected with your emotions and cannot be directly forced to respond to your wishes. The world of emotion can only change by organic growth, not by pressure and voluntary action, except in an indirect way.

Let us assume you find out that deep down you are lacking faith or love. You cannot force yourself to have faith or love, no matter how hard you try directly. But what you can make yourself do is to walk this path, to follow these steps, to overcome perhaps a lack of discipline that makes it so hard for you to work diligently on your path. By doing so, you will not work directly on your lack of love or faith, for instance, but will simply get to know yourself and find out why you lack these attributes. When you gradually understand this without forcing yourself directly to have love or faith, eventually the life force will fill you and will automatically generate these feelings without any direct endeavor on your part. If your emotions begin to change after a few years, you can consider it a wonderful success. The change will happen so naturally that you may not even be fully aware of it at first.

Study these words now; think about them deeply. Believe me, my friends, all this is neither as difficult as it may seem to you now, nor is the path a miracle that will procure happiness for you without demanding from you all you have in honesty, willpower, and effort.

I want to say something else to you about this phase of preparation and decision: expect to have a fight with yourself. It will be the fight between the lower self and the higher self, and your conscious ego-self will determine which side will win. It must be a long fight, which at first will manifest in preventing you from following this path at all. The lower self may send messages such as: "I do not believe in it," or, "It may not be necessary after all," or "I am too tired," or "I have no time." It is necessary for you to recognize these messages for what they are, and understand where they come from. Use them as a starting point to delve deeper into your soul. Try to see clearly what is really speaking within you when you receive these hidden excuses and pretenses. If you anticipate this struggle, you will be able to look and listen and will have a first victory. Also, you will have learned already to some degree the process of uncovering your masks and wrong motives, which will stand you in good stead later on when the lower self will try to obstruct your path by other means. It will simply try to hold on to individual soul-currents. By then you will already know how to deal with it a little better. Do not just put the superficial excuses aside. Test them, deal with them, examine them.

Many of you are frightened of what may come out of your lower self. It is important to learn to interpret and translate such vague feelings into concise thoughts. This fear is an important reason why a person shies away from meeting the self.

It is childish to imagine that whatever you do not cherish in you does not exist if you avoid facing it. The lower self is immature and ignorant—its very nature is faults and distortions. So I say to you: do not shy away from what is in you! All of you know that *the lower self is merely a temporary layer* and does not constitute your entire personality. It is here now to be dealt with, but is not the real you.

Your higher self, which is partly free, already manifests through your good qualities, your generosity, your kindness, or whatever else there is in you that belongs to the higher self. But even where it cannot manifest as yet because it is deeply hidden behind the lower self, your higher self still exists in its shining perfection. How can you reach it unless you penetrate the lower self? So do not be afraid; do not be shocked when you first encounter your lower self where heretofore you had no idea of it. It is a necessary temporary formation, but it never, never represents the ultimate you. As a matter of fact, reaching the stage where you are shocked about some of its facets that you had not suspected before, constitutes a sign of improvement. It strongly implies good progress, for without going through this stage, painful as it may be for a while, you can have no further victory and success. This is part of the path, my friends. If you meditate upon these words and at the same time try to be aware of your fear of your lower self, and your shame of it, and if you learn to live with this truth and knowledge, you will conquer.

Then you will meet your fear realistically, and you will not be hiding from it as you are hiding from a few other things in you.

And now I will retire, my dear friends. God's blessings to all of my dear friends. Peace be with you; be in God.

ﻊ

FINDING ONE'S FAULTS

I bring you blessings, my dear friends.

Last time I talked to you about the difficulty of this path and the dangers of approaching it with the illusion that a few meditations and some miracle-formula will make all your earthly troubles disappear.

Another great misunderstanding is the mistaken idea that to follow the path I am showing you means neglecting your life in other ways. Some of you may believe that devoting a certain amount of time and effort for your spiritual development will take too much time away from your daily struggle for livelihood; you think you may not have enough strength left for your professional efforts and thus fear that your finances may suffer. Others may believe that not enough time would remain for them to enjoy life, and so on. But this way of thinking is so very wrong because spiritual development in general, and this path in particular, is not an extra activity in your life that you simply add on to your other activities, thus diminishing the strength, time, effort, and zest that would otherwise be available to you for all your other duties and pleasures. Actually, it is quite the contrary, my friends.

The truth is that this path of purification represents the foundation of your life. It is the ground you walk on. When you decide to take it, you simply shift the tracks of your life into different channels. After a while, even though your main problems will not disappear from one day to the next, this has the effect of awakening in you a new life spark that furnishes you with a heretofore unfamiliar strength, acumen, vitality, and ability to enjoy life as you have never done before. Thus you will do better work in your profession; you will get more benefit from your times of leisure; you will get more pleasure out of life whatever you may do, whereas now life is still more or less flat for most of you. These are the results I can promise if you work spiritually in the way I am showing you. They won't become apparent at once, but only after a certain time, after some inner victories. Then you will see that this path is well worth taking, even from your selfish point of view, and even though your main conflicts will have not yet disappeared.

This is so because on this path you will eventually find out where in your deeper feelings, reactions, and thoughts, if not in your deeds, you have broken many a spiritual law. This realization will enable you to gradually change inner currents and emotional reactions, and this will automatically free a strength and life force that was previously locked or blocked. So I do not promise you a miracle that will be given to you as a reward from heaven, but show you plainly and logically that this path cannot help but work out because it is based on the law of cause and effect which works quite naturally and impersonally. So I ask you not to consider the decision to take this path as some additional activity in your life, such as taking up some new kind of lessons that might rob you of time and effort you could give to other necessary or desirable things. Consider rather this path as the foundation of your life; it will make it into a well-integrated whole. For if you can solve your inner problems and errors you must eventually also solve your outer problems.

By the same token, you will get so much more out of all the good things in life—happiness, joy, pleasure—if your soul becomes healthy again, if your inner reactions can conform to spiritual law. Only then will you be capable of happiness. For how many people are capable of happiness? Very few, my friends. For only those who embrace life wholeheartedly, without fear, without self-pity, without being afraid of being hurt, follow a very important spiritual law. And only those who can do so are capable of experiencing real happiness.

So everything you do in life will have more flavor, more awareness, and more life spark if you follow the path of self-knowledge. It will not take more time than is reasonable according to your life circumstances. All of you without exception are capable, with a little willpower and determination and proper organization of your everyday life, to spend an average of half an hour a day on your spiritual development. You spend time on your physical body, feed it, rest it, and cleanse it; you certainly do not feel that this takes something away from your other duties or pleasures. You take it for granted that this is a necessary, self-evident part of your life. Yet, when the question arises whether to do the same for your soul, then fears, doubts, and questions bar your way. But they cannot do so if you take the trouble to think reasonably about this matter of spiritual development, my friends. However, you are not thinking reasonably about it because you do not evaluate these doubts as to their proper merit. You have them because you are inspired by your own lower self. As long as you do not recognize how this lower self works, how it manifests, and in what devious ways it hides behind handy excuses, you will not be able to master it.

Not only those traits which are commonly called faults are a hindrance for you, and thus directly or indirectly harm others, but also your fears, which are not generally considered to be faults. You do not realize that your fears cause great harm, not only in your own life but also in the lives of others. Your fears also hide your light of love, understanding, and truth. So, being on this path is not only a matter of overcoming your character weaknesses. Overcoming your own fear is of equal importance, for as long as there is fear in your heart, you harm other people.

I have promised to show you how you should go about actually starting on this path. There are many ways, and each individual reacts to them differently. But I will give you certain basic guidelines to go by as you make your own plan.

You all know that to gain self-knowledge is of imperative importance. Now, how can this be done? The first step will be to think as objectively as you possibly can about your self, about all your good qualities and all your faults. Write down a list, as I have often advised, because writing helps you to concentrate on and condense what you have found out so far. This will prevent your losing your hold on this knowledge. The words in black and white can shed a new light of understanding, and promote a tiny little bit of detachment in your consideration of yourself. Later on, when you have gained further knowledge about yourself and about your subconscious trends, you will be able to connect certain pieces of your first-found knowledge, provided they are clearly and concisely expressed.

The Law of Brotherhood

After you have done this conscientiously, the next step would be to ask someone else, someone who knows you very well, to tell you what he or she honestly thinks about you. I know that it takes a little courage to do that. Consider this your first effort to overcome a little bit of your pride. By doing so, you will have attained some victory that will already free you of one little inner chain.

It is very important not to do this work completely alone. To really open your heart to another person brings a spiritual help that you could not receive by yourself. It is due to the law of brotherhood. For people who are always alone, no matter how hard they work, no matter how intelligently they read or study, no matter how much self-honesty they try to have, become locked in a certain vacuum that bars a complete understanding and evaluation of the self, an understanding which automatically flows into them if they can open themselves to another soul. By remaining all alone, you violate the law of brotherhood in some subtle way.

Not isolating yourself requires a certain amount of humility which does not come easily at the very beginning, but after some time it becomes second nature. Soon you will be able to talk openly about your difficulties, your weaknesses and your problems, and receive criticism. The latter, of course, is equally healthy for the soul. Each one of you who has already tried opening up will confirm that merely discussing a problem you have kept to yourself will cause it to lose its exaggerated proportions, and some of its fearful aspects. Being yourself as you really are with at least one person, with a minimum of masks and defenses, is a very healthy medicine. At the same time you offer an act of love to the other person whom you help more by showing your own human weaknesses than by trying to appear superior. Your partner will do the same for you. So try to organize this with a friend. You will see after a while how helpful and fruitful this will be. It will give you food for thought; you will help each other and you will learn a lot in brotherhood, in humility, and in detached understanding.

I would advise you to ask those who know you really well. No matter what they believe, they will respect you for your sincere endeavor to improve, to learn about your faults, and for listening to them. You can ask in the right way, explaining to them that four eyes often see more than two, and that you want to improve and will not be hurt or angry with them even if they say something that may seem unjust to you.

And when your friends or family do tell you your faults, think about them calmly. Someone may say something that at first will seem entirely unjust and hurtful to you. You may also, for that matter, be even more hurt if a truth is told to you. Even if you have the sincere conviction that the criticism is an injustice, try to evaluate it nonetheless. There may be only one grain of truth in it; the other person may just see you a little differently or see you just on a superficial level. He or she may not have the full understanding of what lies underneath, why you react in this way, and all the complicated mechanisms of the workings of the soul. He or she may not choose the right words. But the one grain of truth in what is said may open a new door of understanding for you. It may not even be something entirely new for you, but it is often necessary to consider the same fault or trait from new angles, under a different light, so as to understand the various effects this same fault may have on your surroundings. If you take all the faults you are beginning to recognize more and more clearly into your daily meditation, and if your wish is truly sincere, you have made the best beginning imaginable.

Train yourself to observe your own inner reactions when you deal with the unpleasant within you. This is of utmost importance. I have begun this lecture by saying that the lower self constantly resists your endeavors. Here you have a wonderful opportunity to observe your undisguised lower self as it works and reacts. Watch it as you would a third person. Be a little less involved in it. Put a little distance between your powers of self-observation and the reaction of your lower self, your ego, your hurt, your vanity that becomes involved when you are dealing with the unpleasant side of your personality. By thus recognizing your own reactions and understanding them, perhaps humoring them a little and not taking yourself so deadly seriously in this respect, you will gain another step up on the ladder. But I admonish you not to expect this awareness to happen from one day to the next. It means constant work, and after some time of regular work each day, even for only half an hour, you will make progress. You will come to the point when you feel quite clearly the distance between the real you and your hurt little ego, and you can humor it a little bit without being so very much in it. Once you have accomplished this, the door will open for further self-understanding.

So, begin by making your own inventory of faults. After you have done your best in this respect, and have also asked someone who knows you really well about your faults, compare their observations with your own findings. These efforts are a wonderful beginning for everyone. They will not be in vain, I promise you. If every day you do some self-observation work, and meditate on some of the pertinent words I am giving here, you will certainly be successful, long before actual results can manifest in your life. A feeling of deep contentment and peace will come to you often.

The Three Main Faults

Now I will mention three main faults in the human character. These three main faults, from which stem directly or indirectly all your various individual shortcomings, are *selfwill*, *pride*, and *fear*. This is very important for you to realize. You may not think fear a fault, but I am telling you that it is; a faultless person would be unafraid. You all know that the opposite of fear is love. But this knowledge in itself will not be sufficient for you to understand why fear is a fault. First you should understand that these three main faults are connected with one another. It would hardly be possible for you to have one or two of these faults without the third. But what may be possible is that out of the three one or two may be unconscious, while the third is quite strongly apparent, even to yourself. Thus, it is very important to write your daily review and to check your reactions to all you have felt during the day in response to often seemingly unimportant incidents. If you try to formulate concisely an unpleasant inner reaction of yours, you will always come to the conclusion that most of the time there is an element of fear involved in it—fear that perhaps other people do not do what you wish or do not react according to your liking. In other words, if there is a strong selfwill, the fear is there automatically that this selfwill will not be gratified, or that your pride may be hurt. If you had no pride, you would not have to fear that it could be hurt. If you had no selfwill, you would not have to fear that it would not be gratified.

If you begin to check your various impressions of the day and your reactions, you can see where the element of fear comes in and whether it is connected with selfwill and pride and to what extent. So begin to observe these inner reactions of yours and analyze them in these terms without trying to change yourself immediately, because feelings cannot be changed by a mere act of will, but they will change if you learn first to observe them.

Daily Review

The practice of the daily review is a powerful tool. You do not have to be far along in self-development in order to accomplish this. Anyone can do it. All you need do is review the day and think of all the events that have caused you disharmony in any manner, shape, or form. Even if at the beginning you cannot understand why, just put down the incident and what you felt. When you have done this for a while, a pattern will evolve. It may still not give you a clue to what is wrong in your inner makeup, but you will at least see some repetition that points to the fact that there must be something in you that is causing the disharmony. If unhappy events or feelings recur constantly, this is a clue to your own soul. These repeated occurrences, along with your reactions to them, may vary in two or three ways; but there must be a basic, underlying problem which you can learn to recognize.

This will not take more than ten or fifteen minutes every day, which should certainly be possible for each one of you. You do not have to write down everything that has disturbed your sense of harmony during the course of a day, just jot down certain key words. By regularly doing this, you will succeed in making the unconscious conscious and you will discover your own inner trends. After doing this for a while, you will most certainly recognize definite patterns in your life which you cannot become aware of otherwise. You will recognize these patterns by certain constant happenings and occurrences in your life and the way in which you react to them. That is all you should do at present. There is no magic trick to it. After you have kept a daily review for a while, read all daily review notes through and recollect the incidents, with your reactions. See whether you can at least sense a pattern. Ask yourself, "Where can I find the point in myself where I deviate from some divine law?" Then begin to think of your various faults, which you have already discovered.

Compare and connect these patterns with your list of faults. Ask yourself questions as to what your feelings are, what your desire currents really want, and whether these feelings and currents are truly in accordance with divine law. This is the way to get right into the middle of this path. Without this help, it would be extremely difficult, perhaps impossible, to gain the self-knowledge which is the essence and the key to this path and without which you cannot reach divinity within yourself. It takes so very little time, and I beg all of you, for your own sake, to do it.

I will retire now with blessings of a special kind that are coming to each one of you, my dear ones. The love of God touches all of you. Be in peace, be in God.

છે.

IMAGES

Blessed is this hour; blessings for all of you, my dear friends. Every personality in the course of a lifetime, usually in earliest childhood, often even in infancy, forms certain impressions due to environmental influences or to sudden unexpected experiences. These impressions are usually based on conclusions formed by the personality. Most of the time they are wrong conclusions. One sees and experiences something unfortunate, an unavoidable hardship of life, and then generalizes these happenings into beliefs. The conclusions formed are not thought out; they are more in the nature of emotional reactions, general attitudes concerning life. They are not completely devoid of a certain kind of logic, but it is of a very limited and erroneous kind. As the years go by, these conclusions and attitudes sink more and more into the unconscious, molding to some extent the life of the person in question.

We call each such conclusion an *image*. You might say that a person could also have a positive, healthy image engraved in the soul. That is true only in some measure, because where no wrong image has been produced, all thoughts and feelings are in motion, fluctuating; they are dynamic and relaxed; they are flexible. Because the whole universe is penetrated by a number of divine forces and energy currents, the thoughts, feelings, and attitudes unconnected with an image *flow* harmoniously with these divine forces and currents, adapting themselves spontaneously to the immediate need, and changing according to the necessity of each moment and situation. But the thought and feeling forms emanating from images are *static* and congested. They do not yield and change in accordance with different circumstances. Thus, they create disorder. The pure currents flowing through a human soul become disturbed and distorted. A short circuit is established. This is the way *we* see it. The way you see and feel it is through unhappiness, anxiety, and puzzlement over many apparently inexplicable events in your life. For instance, you realize that you cannot change what you wish to change or that certain happenings in your life seem to reoccur regularly without an obvious reason. These are just two examples; there are many more.

The wrong conclusions that form an image are drawn in ignorance and half-knowledge and therefore cannot remain in the conscious mind. As the personality grows up, the new intellectual knowledge contradicts the old emotional "knowledge." Therefore the person pushes the emotional knowledge down until it disappears from conscious sight. The more the emotional knowledge is hidden, the more potent it becomes. Often you do not understand what made you retain such an impression from which you formed a wrong conclusion. Your intellect, your mind as a whole, has grown up, has been changed by what you have learned, by your surroundings and by life experience. Yet, while your image is alive, you, on a deeper emotional level, have not changed.

At one time in your childhood, you had a shock. When you think of a shock, you think of a sudden experience with a very strong and unexpected impact, like an accident. But a shock may also happen, particularly to a child, in a more gradual discovery that things are contrary to one's dearest and most cherished expectations. For example, a child lives with the idea that the parents are perfect and omnipotent. When the realization dawns upon the child that this is not so, it comes as a shock, although the realization may often come by a series of events until the new discovery makes its lasting impression. When a child finds out that its heretofore accepted concepts about its parents, or the world as such, are not true, it loses security. It is frightened. It does not like the discovery and will, on the one hand, push this unpleasant knowledge into the subconscious because it feels guilty and, on the other hand, will build defenses against this "threat." Whether it happened suddenly or in a slow realization, this threat is the shock referred to. You all know that shock causes numbness. Your body, as well as your nerves and your mind, become numb, even to the extent that you lose your memory temporarily or have other symptoms. Thus the child will experience a shock because parents, the world, life, are not the way the child thought them to be. Although the impression that created the shock may be objectively correct, still, the deduction the child is capable of making must be wrong. Because children tend to generalize, they project their own experiences onto all other alternatives. A child's parents are its world, its universe, therefore what the child concludes after the shock must be applied to everyone else, to life in general. This general application *is* the wrong conclusion that creates the image.

The image was created when the orderly world and concepts of the child were destroyed. The wrong conclusions derive, first, from the generalization. The reality is that not all people have the same shortcomings as the parents; not all conditions of life are similar to those the child discovered in its own surroundings. Second, the defense mechanism the child chooses with a limited understanding of the world, is wrong *as such*; it is even more so when applied to people and situations other than those in the early surroundings. This, my friends, is the way images are created. But you will not remember offhand your emotions, your reactions, your inner intentions, and your conclusions. You cannot remember them because you felt the need to hide this whole procedure for its lack of rational logic, and also because you were ashamed that your parents were not what you thought they should be.

In your child's mind you assumed that your case was singular. Everyone else had perfect parents, perfect home conditions, and only you alone experienced this shocking uniqueness that had to be hidden from everyone, even from yourself, as well as, of course, from your parents or others close to you. The shame arose from the mistaken idea that your case was unique, and the whole thought and emotional process had to be hidden away because of the shame. When these processes remain hidden, part of your personality cannot grow. If a plant is left hidden in the earth with its roots cut off, it cannot grow. It is the same with every emotional current or tendency. Therefore you should not be surprised when you discover that your image-conclusions conform not at all to your otherwise grown-up intelligence.

An infant or a very young child knows only the most primitive emotions. It knows love and pleasure when its will is done. It knows hatred, resentment, and pain when its will is not done. It is as simple as that. Only much later in life does one learn to evaluate objectively instead of following one's own pain or pleasure. While your image lives, you continue the childish procedure because in that respect your mind remains childish, regardless of how much the rest of your personality has improved and learned. Your developed personality is capable of judging maturely on the intellectual level and, in some instances where no image-currents obstruct your perception, even emotionally. But where this slow or sudden shock impression has affected the soul, one does not assimilate the experience consciously, and therefore one's mind remains childish. It remains in the state it was in when the image-conclusions were formed and put into the unconscious. Consequently, a part of an otherwise mature being remains immature. Actually, this part continues to make the same deductions, emotionally and unconsciously, that the child had made, so long as the image is not lifted into consciousness.

For instance, imagine a baby girl who cries when she wants attention; but the mother believes that to come when the child cries will "spoil" her. The child learns that the mother does not come when she cries, but that the mother does come at other times, seemingly unrelated to the child's cries. Thus the following conclusion is drawn: "In order to have my need fulfilled, I must not show that I have a need." Now, with this particular mother, not showing one's needs may actually be a good strategy. But when the little girl becomes a woman, such a strategy is more often likely to produce the opposite result. Since no one will know that this woman has a specific need, no one will give to her what she needs. However, since she is completely ignorant of her "image," because it has long ago sunk into her unconscious, she will go through life not understanding why she is so unfulfilled. She does not know that she acts in such a way that life will seem to confirm her erroneous belief.

Do I Have an Image?

How can you be sure that such an image exists in you? One indication is that you cannot overcome certain faults, no matter how much you try. Why is it that people love some of their faults? They do this for the simple reason that an image makes certain faults seem like a way of protecting themselves from pain. For example, someone knows that he is lazy. But he may not know that the reluctance to get out of bed and go out into the world is a wrongly conceived protection against being hurt. "If I stay in bed, no one can hurt me," may be the unconscious reasoning. Therefore, an image is at the bottom of such an attitude.

Another sure sign of an image is the repetition of certain incidents in one's life. An image always forms a pattern of behavior or reaction in one way or another; it also attracts a pattern of outer occurrences that seem to come to you without your doing anything to produce them. Consciously the person may fervently wish something that is the very opposite of the image. But the conscious desire is the weaker of the two, since the unconscious is *always* stronger. The unconscious mind does not realize that it prohibits the very wish the person consciously has but cannot fulfill, and that the price for such unconscious pseudo-protection is the frustration of the legitimate desire. This is very important to understand, my friends. It is of equal importance to understand that outer events—certain situations, certain people—can be drawn like a magnet to a person on account of such inner images. This may be difficult to perceive; nevertheless it is so. The only remedy is to find out what the image is, on what basis it is formed, and what were the wrong conclusions.

Often you do not notice the repetition and the pattern in your life, my friends. You just pass over the obvious. You are used to the assumption that certain events are coincidences, or that some fate is testing you arbitrarily, or that other people in your surroundings are responsible for your repeated mishaps. Therefore you pay much more attention to the slight variations of each incident than to its basic character, and fail to note the common denominator of all the happenings due to your image.

Most psychologists have found these patterns and wrong conclusions. What they often do not know is that these images have seldom been started in this lifetime, no matter how early they were formed. Most of the time an image is of old standing, carried over from one lifetime to another. That is why incidents that will not form an image in a child or a person who is free of that particular conflict will help form an image in an entity who has brought that image into this life.

Where images exist from previous lives, the incarnation occurs in an environment that must create provocations to existing images, perhaps by means of similar corresponding images in the parents or others around the growing child. Only in that way will the image emerge again; only if it becomes a problem will the person pay attention to it instead of looking away from it. If the image is ignored, circumstances will be much more difficult in the following life on earth until conflicts become so overwhelming that outside factors cannot be blamed any longer. Then the person begins to turn inward.

The only solution is to make the images conscious. I give you hints on how to begin, but you will not be able to put them into practice completely by yourself. You will need help. But if you are serious in your desire to find and dissolve the images in your soul, further guidance and help will come to you and you will be led to the proper person with whom you can form a cooperative working arrangement. To do this you will need, among other things, humility, essential for your spiritual development. The person who is continually reluctant to work with another must lack humility, even if only in this one respect.

How to Search for Images

Now, how can you find your personal images? You will do it not by working on the symptoms, whatever they may be, but rather by working with the symptoms. Such symptoms are your inability to overcome certain faults and attitudes, your lack of control over certain happenings in your life that come to you regularly and create a pattern, your fears and resistances at specific occasions, to name only a few. The harder you try to eliminate the symptoms without having understood their roots and origin, the more you will exhaust yourself in useless efforts. The symptoms are merely one part of the price you pay for your wrong and ignorant inner conclusions.

Start searching for the images by thinking back in your life to find all the problems. Write them down. Include problems of all sorts. You need to take the trouble to put everything down concisely in black and white. For if you merely think about it, you will not have the overall view necessary for comparison. This written work is essential. It is certainly not too much to ask. You do not have to do it all in one day. Take your time, even if it takes a few months. It is better to do it slowly than not to start at all. Then, when you think of all your big and small troubles, even the most nonsensical, the most insignificant ones, *start to look for the common denominator.* You will find in most instances the existence of one common denominator, sometimes even more than one. I do not say that a difficulty cannot occur only once in your life, independent of any inner image. This is possible. This too is based on cause and effect, as everything in the universe is, but it may not be connected with your image. But be careful, my friends. Do not put an occurrence aside superficially, designating it as being unconnected with your personal image merely because it appears that way at first sight. It is very possible, and even probable, that there are no such happenings in your life. All unpleasant experiences are probably due to your image and connected with it, at least in some remote way.

The common denominator may not be easy to find. Only after you have thoughtfully grasped your images will you be in a position to judge which of your experiences, if any, have something to do with it. Until then you must keep all judgments in reserve, so to speak. In meditation, in serious self-probing, in checking your emotional reactions in the past and present, and with the help of prayer, you will, after a long and arduous search, find what the common denominator is. Do not dismiss it hastily if something appears to be unconnected. Probe and you may experience a surprise. The most apparently unconnected events turn out to have one common denominator. When you have found that, you have made a major step forward in your search, for then you possess a clue to the image. In order to get to the image itself, to all the devious ways in which it was formed, and to the understanding of your reaction when you formed it, you will have to explore your unconscious more thoroughly.

The Benefits of Dissolving Images

Do not let yourself be dissuaded by your own inner resistance. For that resistance is just as erroneous, ignorant and shortsighted as the image itself. The very same force that makes you resist is the one that has created the image in the first place; without your knowing it, it has created and will continue to create misery for you and will counteract your conscious wishes. Indeed, it causes you to lose or never to gain what could be rightfully yours. So have enough wisdom to see through this and to evaluate your own resistance for what it is worth. Do not let yourself be governed by it. How can you be a spiritual person, who is developed and detached in the right sense, if you remain governed by your unconscious forces and by those illogical, erroneous, and ignorant conclusions that have formed such a painful image within you? The image is the one factor in your life that is responsible for every unhappiness. No one else is responsible for it, only you yourself. True, you did not know any better once, but you do now. You are now equipped to eliminate the source of your unhappiness. And please do not say, "How can I be responsible for other people acting in certain ways again and again toward me?" As I said before, it is your image that draws these happenings to you, as inevitably as night must follow day on this earth. It is like a magnet, like a chemical law, like the law of gravity. The components of your reactions forming the image influence the universal currents entering your personal sphere of life in such a way that certain effects must occur, following the cause that you have thus set in motion.

If you do not have the courage to delve into your unconscious, to face your image, to dissolve it and thus to make a really new person out of yourself, you will never be free in this life; you will always be chained and bound. The price for freedom is your courage and humility in facing up to what is within. When you have taken all the necessary steps, the victory of freedom is such joy that no matter what happens outside of yourself, nothing can mar your happiness. Furthermore, you can be quite sure that the images you do not dissolve in this lifetime will have to be dissolved in a future one. This should not be taken as a threat; it is just a logical consequence. And how can anything be a threat that is supposed to liberate you from your own chains? The sooner you find your images of your own accord, the easier your liberation will be. That you may safely believe.

To find, comprehend, and dissolve an image is a long process. Even after you have understood it, the re-education of emotional currents and reactions that have long been conditioned in one direction takes time, effort, and patience. You may revolt against unhappiness; yet when you realize that not God and the fates but you yourself are the cause, your revolt may turn against yourself and you will thus also become impatient with yourself. With such currents you will never, never succeed in finding and dissolving your image; you must be in a relaxed state of mind, and such a state of mind can be yours only if you understand and accept the length of the search.

When you search for the images, do not approach your subconscious with a moralizing attitude. Your subconscious does not like it and will resist. It will fight against you and make it all the harder for your willing consciousness to come to terms with it. Start by thinking about your hurts, conflicts, and problems. Regard your wrong inner attitudes as ignorance and error. Actually, that is what all faults really are! Start by thinking about your idiosyncrasies, your prejudices, your tight emotions in certain domains of life. Think how you react emotionally to certain things and when and how these reactions repeat themselves in a pattern throughout your life. Begin by viewing your disappointments that apparently have nothing to do with your actions or reactions. Afterwards, when you recognize a certain regular pattern you will be able to see the connection with your own inner attitude that may so far have escaped your consciousness.

What I mean by depth prayer or meditation or depth thinking is that you take everything you have found out about these repressed or hidden reactions—whether they concern trends you find repeatedly or whether you come across quite different reactions than your known outer ones—and think about their significance, their meaning, their effect on you and on others. Compare them with spiritual law as you now know it; think about it both from the spiritual and practical point of view. Work with this newly found knowledge by re-feeling and re-experiencing it. Then think about it again as objectively as you know how. Simply shift your thinking to a deeper level and apply it to the knowledge you have found, either the apparently repetitious or the shockingly new and different recognitions. Do not leave the newly found understanding alone, for you may then very well slip back into the same old pattern. You can easily deceive yourself and think that, merely because you have found out an important and significant piece of knowledge about your soul, nothing more is necessary. You can have the theoretical knowledge and still go right on reacting in the same old way. It is not sufficient to find inner understanding about your hidden trends and reactions, and leave it at that. *The work only begins after such recognition.* And that is the meditation in depth, on the deep emotional level you have discovered. If you neglect this meditation, you may retain what you have found, but gradually it will become more remote, a merely theoretical knowledge in your brain, while underneath you go on reacting as before. In that case you have not succeeded in integrating and unifying your erring emotional reactions and wrong conclusions with your intellectual knowledge. Emotions are more habit-bound than outer trends; moreover, they are so elusive that in spite of your efforts, your old patterns may go right on working without your becoming conscious of this fact. You are used to shoving uncomfortable knowledge into your subconscious, and you cannot get out of this habit from one day to the other. It needs a great deal of training, concentration, and effort. New habit patterns have to be established until you recognize the signs of the hidden trends that must be made conscious. You have to develop a special sensitivity for that—and this takes time, of course.

Shame

Everything connected with the wrong inner images causes the person acute shame. The attitude or conclusion in question may not even be shameful, objectively speaking. There might not be any justification for shame if it were out in the open; you would not feel that it deserved this reaction if you encountered it in others. After you have had the courage to bring it out into the open, you will experience for yourself how this feeling of being embarrassed and ashamed completely vanishes. But before it is out, when you are still struggling with it, you will feel the shame very strongly. You may have a fault that is much more embarrassing, but having discovered it a long time ago you have accepted it; you have come to terms with it. Therefore, you do not feel ashamed of it anymore. You may even be able to discuss it openly with others. However, something that is a much lesser fault causes you acute shame, as long as you have not come to terms with it.

Let us say, you find out that you have been very strongly influenced by and dependent on one of your parents. This in itself is nothing to be ashamed of; it is discussed generally every day. But you have been unaware of this trend so far, you ignored how much and in what manner you were influenced, and how much you are still dependent on similar emotions. Yet when you first come across this realization, it causes you a feeling of acute embarrassment. This is a typical image reaction, my friends. And if you anticipate this, you will again make things easier for yourself. You will not be under the emotional, subjective impression that you stand alone in this world or that you alone have such feelings. For that is what your emotions believe and why you feel so ashamed. This belief is a sign of the separateness you have built for yourself with all your wrong defenses and from which you suffer at such moments. But if you realize that everybody is going through this reaction, that it is a symptom to be expected, you will be able to counteract your subjective and fallacious emotional impression by not heeding it, instead of continuing to let yourself be governed by it. Only by doing so will you free yourself of the separating wall that encloses you in darkness, loneliness and fear, in guilt and false shame. Only in this way can you evolve as a free person, with your head up high, instead of being governed and suppressed by your wrong impressions and false shame. It only takes a moment of courage to go through that which seems so shameful, and to face yourself as you are. You will then discover that you have lived in a phantom world of fears and shames that have absolutely no reality whatsoever.

Very often the shame is not because all of a sudden you have discovered something very wicked or hideous. No! You may be much more ashamed of something that is merely silly. If you understand that when you formed the image the reasoning that now makes you ashamed was then in accord with your capacity to reason and think. Only relatively is it silly. And you, intelligent human being that you are, cannot reconcile the fact that such a "silly" reaction still lives in you. You are now at the point when you actually recognize that this has been your deduction, your conclusion for years up to the present, and you are now quite embarrassed to see that this was a part of your mind, your "undermind" but still your mind, your reaction. It will make it easier for you to accept this if you consider that in this respect you remained a child because you left the whole reasoning process in the darkness of your subconscious mind. It will also help if you realize that there is no one you can name among all those you know who does not have his own images, and therefore similar incongruities. If you conversed with a child of, let us say, four to ten, you would not be surprised at such reasoning. Realize that and you will overcome your embarrassment.

Before you can change anything, you must understand what it is in you that brings all the suffering. Only then, slowly, gradually, will you be able to re-educate your emotions, dissolve your images, and create new, productive forms in your soul that correspond to divine law.

I will retire now with blessings of a special kind that are coming to each one of you, my dear ones. It is the blessing of courage that you all so badly need. Be in peace; be in God.

THE VICIOUS CIRCLE
OF IMMATURE LOVE

Greetings, my dearest friends. God bless this gathering, God bless all of you.

I shall now discuss one of the vicious circles that is very common among human beings. To some degree it operates in every human soul. Most of the time it lives in the subconscious, although some parts of the circle may be conscious. It is important in this work that you follow this circle until you uncover it in its entirety, for otherwise you cannot dissolve it. My words are not addressed so much to your conscious mind, to your intellect, but to the level of your feelings where this vicious circle exists.

Even if you are aware of some parts of this vicious circle, use these words to search for all the other parts you are still unaware of. Perhaps there are a few among you who are utterly unaware of any part of this circle. In that case, my words will guide you to make at least one part conscious. This will not be so difficult because many of your symptoms will easily show you that, though unconscious, such a circle very much lives within you. Still, do not interpret these words to mean that you consciously think and react according to this vicious circle; realize that it is hidden. It will be up to you to make this chain reaction conscious in your work on this path of self-finding and self-development. Becoming conscious of these hidden currents will give you freedom and victory.

Most of my friends realize that an illogical way of thinking, feeling, and reacting exists in every personality, even though consciously you may know a better logic. Everything in the unconscious is primitive, ignorant, and very often illogical, although it does follow a certain limited logic of its own.

The vicious circle that is my subject tonight begins in childhood, where all images are formed. The child is helpless; it needs to be taken care of; it cannot stand on its own two feet; it cannot make mature decisions; it cannot be free of weak and selfish motives. Hence the child is incapable of unselfish love. The mature adult grows into such love provided the whole personality matures harmoniously and provided that none of the childish reactions remain hidden in the unconscious. If they do, only part of the personality will grow, while another part—and a very important one at that—will remain immature. There are very few adults who are as mature emotionally as they are intellectually.

The Child Wants Exclusive Love

The child comes in contact with more or less imperfect surroundings that bring its inner problems to the fore. The child in its ignorance craves an exclusive love that is not humanly possible. The love it wants is selfish; it does not want to share love with others, with brothers or sisters or even with the other parent. The child is often unconsciously jealous of both parents. Yet if the parents do not love each other, the child suffers even more. So the first conflict arises from two opposite desires. On the one hand the child wants the love of each parent exclusively; on the other, it suffers if the parents do not love each other. Since the love-capacity of any parent is imperfect, the child misunderstands that despite this imperfection most parents are still fully capable of loving more than one person. The child feels excluded and rejected if the parent also loves others, however. In short, the exclusive love the child craves can never be gratified. Furthermore, whenever the child is prohibited from having its way, this is taken as an additional "proof" that the child is not sufficiently loved.

This frustration causes the child to feel rejected, which, in turn, causes hatred, resentment, hostility, and aggression. This is the second part of the vicious circle. The need for love that cannot be gratified causes hatred and hostility toward the very people one loves most. Generally speaking, this is the second conflict of the growing human being. If the child hated someone it did not love at the same time, if it loved in its own way and did not desire love in return, this conflict could not arise. The very fact that hatred exists for the very person one loves dearly creates an important conflict in the human psyche. It is self-evident that the child feels ashamed of these negative emotions, and therefore it puts this conflict into the subconscious where it festers. This hatred causes guilt because the child is taught early that it is bad, wrong, and sinful to hate, particularly one's parents whom one is supposed to love and honor. It is this guilt, living on and on in the subconscious, which in the adult personality causes all sorts of inner and outer conflicts. Moreover, people are unaware of the roots of these conflicts until they decide to find out what is hidden in their subconscious.

Fear of Punishment, Fear of Happiness

This guilt has a further, and again inevitable, reaction. Feeling guilty, the child's unconscious says, "I deserve to be punished." Thus a fear of punishment arises in the soul, which again is almost always completely unconscious. However, the manifestations can be found in various symptoms, which, if followed through, will finally lead to the chain reactions I will describe next.

With this fear of punishment a further reaction sets in, that whenever you are happy and enjoy pleasure, in spite of this being a natural longing, you feel you do not deserve it. The guilt of hating those it loves most convinces the child that it is undeserving of anything good, joyful, or pleasurable. The child feels that if it were ever to become happy, the punishment, which seems inevitable, would be that much greater. Therefore the child unconsciously avoids happiness, thinking to atone in this way and thus to avoid even greater punishment. This avoidance creates situations and patterns that always seem to destroy everything most dearly wished for in life.

It is this fear of happiness that leads a person to all sorts of unhealthy reactions, symptoms, endeavors, manipulations of emotions, and even to actions which indirectly create patterns that appear as if they would happen involuntarily, without the personality being responsible for them at all. Thus a further conflict comes into existence. On the one hand, the personality is yearning for happiness and fulfillment, on the other, a fear of happiness prohibits the fulfillment. Although the desire for happiness can never be eradicated, yet, due to this deeply hidden guilt feeling, the stronger one desires happiness, the guiltier one feels.

Now, the fear of being punished and the fear of not deserving happiness creates a further and more complicated reaction. The unconscious mind thinks, "I am afraid to be punished by others, although I know I deserve it. It is much worse to be punished by others, for then I am really at the mercy of others, be it people, be it the fates, be it God, be it life itself. But perhaps if I punished myself I could at least avoid the humiliation, the helplessness, and the degradation of being punished by forces outside myself." These basic conflicts of love and hatred, of guilt and fear of punishment exist in every human personality. The compulsive desire for self-punishment due to wrong and ignorant conclusions exists in every human being to some degree.

Thus the personality inflicts punishment on itself. This may happen in various ways, either by physical disease that the psyche produces, or by various mishaps, difficulties, failures, or conflicts in any area of life. In each case the area affected depends on the personal image the child has formed and carried around during this lifetime until it is found and eventually dissolved. Thus, if an image exists regarding profession and career, for instance, it will be fortified by the inherent desire for self-punishment; difficulties in this respect will constantly arise in the person's life. Or, if an image connected to love and marital life exists, the same pattern will hold true there.

Hence, if and when you do not succeed in a conscious and legitimate desire, and looking at your life you find the pattern that the fulfillment of this conscious desire was constantly frustrated, as though you had nothing to do with it (as though an unkind fate had befallen you) you can be sure that not only does an image and a wrong conclusion exist within you, but that, in addition, the need for self-punishment is also present.

A further chain reaction in this vicious circle is the personality's split in its desire currents. The original split between love and hate, which started the vicious circle, causes further splits, as you can see quite clearly by now. One of these conflicting feelings is the need for self-punishment, yet, on the other hand, the desire not to be punished coexists with it. Thus a hidden part of the psyche argues, "Perhaps I can get around it. Perhaps I can atone in another way for my great guilt of hating." This imaginary atonement amounts to a kind of bargaining. One does so by setting such a high standard for oneself that it is impossible to live up to it in reality. The little inner voice argues, "If I am so perfect, if I have no fault and no weakness, if I am the best in everything I undertake, then I can make good for my past hatred and resentment." And since this little voice was at one point repressed into the unconscious, it did not die; it is still alive in the present.

Two Consciences

You get over something only if you can air it out. That is why the same old hatred still lingers on in you. That is also why you constantly feel guilty. If it were really a matter of the past, you would not feel this acute guilt all the time, even though the guilt is not conscious. You think that by being so perfect you can avoid punishment. In this way a second conscience is being created. In reality only one conscience exists: it is the higher self, which is eternal and indestructible; it is each human being's divine spark. Do not confuse this conscience with the second conscience that has been artificially created out of compulsion to atone for a supposed sin, or even for a real failing. Neither imaginary sins nor real failings can be atoned for by this artificial and over-demanding conscience; in reality no one needs to be punished. As you all know by now, the way to eliminate real failings is very different and much more constructive. If and when you finally differentiate between these two kinds of conscience, you will have taken a great step forward.

The compulsive second conscience makes demands that are impossible to fulfill. What happens when you cannot attain these goals? Inevitably, the result must be a feeling of inadequacy and inferiority. Since you do not know that the standards of your compulsive conscience are irrational, unreal, and impossible to realize, and since you believe, behind your wall of separation, that others can succeed while you alone do not, you feel completely isolated and ashamed, with your guilty secret of not only hating, but also of being unable to be good and pure.

The second conscience is motivated by weakness and fear. It is too proud to realize that you simply cannot be so perfect yet. It is also too proud to let you accept yourself as you are now. You must therefore feel inferior because you are not able to live up to these high standards. All inferiority feelings in human nature can be reduced to this common denominator. As long as this fact is not felt and experienced, you cannot shed inferiority feelings. You have to uncover this whole vicious circle and see its lack of reason; you have to live through the emotions that led you to create it. Only then will you dissolve the chain reaction point by point and create new concepts within your emotional self.

Whatever rationalizations you use to explain your inferiority feelings, they are never the real cause. Others may indeed be more successful in one way or another, but this by itself could never make you feel inferior. Without your artificially high standards, you would not feel the need to be better than or at least as good as others in every realm of your life. You could accept with equanimity that others are better or do better in some areas of life while you have advantages that others may lack. You would not have to be as intelligent, as successful, as beautiful as other people are. This never is the real reason for your feelings of inadequacy and inferiority! This truth is borne out by the fact that you see the most brilliant, most successful, most beautiful people often having worse inferiority feelings than others who are less brilliant, less successful, or less beautiful.

Perpetuation of Inadequacy and Inferiority

This inadequacy and inferiority serve to further close this vicious circle. Again, your unconscious little voice argues, "I have failed. I know I am inferior, but perhaps, if I could just receive a great amount of love and respect and admiration from others, this would feel like the same gratification which I originally yearned for and which was withheld from me back then, thereby forcing me into the position of hating and creating this entire circle. Admiration and respect from others would also be the proof that I was justified, for it is possible to receive now what my parents have denied me. It will also show that I am not as worthless as I suspect when I fail to live up to the standards of my compulsive conscience."

Naturally, these thoughts are never reasoned out consciously; yet this is the way emotions argue below the surface. So the circle closes where it started, and the need to be loved becomes much more compulsive than it originally was. All the various points of the chain reactions make the need much stronger. Besides, there always exists a suspicion that the hate was unjustified—which it was, but in a different sense. The personality feels in the unconscious that if such love does exist at all, then the child was right, and your parents, or whoever else it was who did not give it to you, were wrong. Thus the craving for love becomes more and more strained and tense. Since this need can never be fulfilled—and the more this becomes apparent, the greater the guilt becomes—all ensuing points in the vicious circle become worse and worse as life goes on, always creating more problems and conflicts. Only when you desire love in a healthy and mature way and *only when you are willing to love to the same degree as you desire to be loved, will love be forthcoming.*

Remember that the personality in which this vicious circle is strong can never take that risk as long as it continues to desire immature childish love. As long as it cannot risk anything for love, it does not know how to love maturely. The child is not supposed to take that risk; yet the adult is. The inner child has only the immature desire and craving for love, and wants to be loved and cherished, cared for and admired even by people he or she has no intention to love in return. And with those people who may have the intention to love in return, to some degree, the proportion between their willingness to give and their compulsive need to receive is very uneven. Because of this basic unfairness, such a scheme cannot work. For divine law is always just and fair. You never receive more than you invest. When you invest freely you may not get the love back immediately from the same source you invested it in, yet eventually it must flow back to you, this time in a benign circle. What you give out will flow back, provided you do not give in weakness, with a motive of proving something. If the motives for the limited love you give are unconsciously based on this vicious circle, you can never receive love in return. The love you crave in the mistaken idea that this will set you right is not the answer. In other words, you look for a remedy that is no remedy for your sickness, so your hunger for love will remain, never to be stilled. It is like a bottomless well. Thus the circle closes.

Dissolving the Circle

It is your work on this path to find this circle within yourself, to experience it, particularly as to where, how, and in respect to whom it lives within you. All this has to become a personal experience before you can really dissolve it. If you let this circle be only an intellectual knowing, without emotionally reliving it, the knowledge will not help you. To repeat: if you cannot identify the various points of this vicious circle in your emotions, the existence of this chain reaction will just be another piece of theoretical knowledge you have absorbed, entirely separated from your emotions. Once you find this circle in your personal work, you can break it, but only after realizing where the wrong premises are. You will have to see that as a child you were justified in having certain feelings, attitudes, needs and incapacities which are now obsolete. You also have to learn to be tolerant with your negative emotions. You have to understand them. You have to discover where you deviate in your emotional tendencies, requirements, and desires from your conscious knowledge. You may know perfectly well, and even preach, that you have to give love and not be so concerned with receiving. But all of you, in your emotions, still deviate from such intellectual knowledge. The discrepancy has to be made fully conscious before you can hope to break the circle. Only after you have realized and fully absorbed all that, and after you have thought about the irrationality of certain hitherto hidden emotions, will they begin to change, slowly, gradually. Do not expect them to change the very moment you understand their lack of reason. When you face these emotions—their ignorance, selfishness, and immaturity—without being ashamed, and apply your conscious knowledge to them, catching yourself whenever you fall back into old, bad emotional habits, your subconscious will gradually reveal more and more wrong conclusions. Each act of recognition will help you further to break your personal vicious circle. Thus you will become free and independent.

The human soul contains all the wisdom, all the truth it needs. But all these wrong conclusions cover it up. By making them conscious and then working them through point by point, you will finally reach the goal of unfolding your inner voice of wisdom that guides you according to the divine conscience, according to your personal plan. When the divine laws are violated in your inner and outer reactions, your divine conscience leads you inexorably in such a way as to restore order and balance in your life. Situations will occur that seem like punishment, while they are actually the remedy to set you on the right track. Wherever and whenever you deviate, the balance must be reestablished, so that through your difficulties you will finally get to the point where you change your inner direction. You will change, not necessarily in your outer and conscious actions, but in your unconscious childish requirements and aims.

So, my dear friends, work through this vicious circle and experience how it is active in your personal life.

Are there any questions?

QUESTION: What happens to a child whose hatred and hostility breaks out in the open? Would such a child still have a guilt feeling?

ANSWER: Such outer manifestations often occur in children. Whenever a child has a so-called temper tantrum, these emotions do break out into the open. But invariably the child is scolded and learns how "bad" this is. That fortifies the need to keep the true meaning of such tantrums hidden. And even if hatred is at times entirely conscious, later it is often suppressed. Then the same tantrums may continue inwardly in the adult with no age limit, and cease only when this vicious circle is made conscious. Some people may develop a sickness which will be a form of childish temper tantrum, or they may simply make life difficult for those around them. By their unhappiness such people constantly inflict hardship on others with the aim of forcing their will and their compulsive childish need to receive the child's utopia of perfect love and care. This may happen to various degrees. Sometimes it is very obvious, at other times it is much more subtle and hidden. What people say when they indulge in such behavior is, "I am unhappy, you see. You have to take care of me. You have to love me." That is a temper tantrum without the outer manifestation of the child. The mere fact that this hostility may at times break out in the open during childhood does not necessarily mean that it might not be suppressed later.

Be blessed every one of you, all my friends who read these words. Take these blessings with you, let them strengthen your courage, your willpower on the path of self-finding. This is the only liberation possible, liberation from your compulsive high standards which make you feel guilty and undeserving of what God wants you to have: happiness, light, love. Be in peace my dear friends. Be in God.

CHAPTER 7

ॐ

COMPULSION TO RECREATE AND OVERCOME CHILDHOOD HURTS

Greetings, my dearest friends. God bless all of you. May the divine blessings extended to every one of you help you assimilate the words I speak.

We have in the past discussed the fear of loving. You will remember that I mentioned how the child desires to be loved exclusively and without limits. In other words, the child's desire to be loved is unrealistic.

The Lack of Mature Love

Since children so seldom receive sufficient mature love and warmth, they continue to hunger for it throughout life unless this lack and hurt is recognized and properly dealt with. If not, as adults they will go through life unconsciously crying out for what they missed in childhood. This will make them incapable of loving maturely. You can see how this condition continues from generation to generation.

The remedy cannot be found by wishing that things were different and that people would learn to practice mature love. The remedy lies solely in you. True, if you had received such love from your parents, you would be without this problem of which you are not really and fully aware. But this lack of receiving mature love need trouble neither you nor your life if you become aware of it, see it, and rearrange your former unconscious wishes, regrets, thoughts and concepts by aligning them to the reality of each situation. As a consequence, you will not only become a happier person, but you will also be able to extend mature love to others—to your children, if you have any, or to other people in your environment—so that a benign chain reaction can start. Such a realistic self-correction is very contrary to your present inner behavior which we shall now consider.

All people, including even those few who have started to explore their own unconscious mind and emotions, habitually overlook the strong link between the child's longing and unfulfillment and the adult's present difficulties and problems, because only very few people experience personally—and not just recognize in theory—how strong this link is. Full awareness of it is essential.

There may be isolated, exceptional cases where one parent offers a sufficient degree of mature love. Even if one parent has it to some degree, very likely the other does not. Since mature love on this earth is only present to a degree, the child will suffer from the shortcomings of even a loving parent.

More often, however, both parents are emotionally immature and cannot give the love the child craves, or give it only in insufficient measure. During childhood, this need is rarely conscious. Children have no way of putting their needs into thoughts. They cannot compare what they have with what others have. They do not know that something else might exist. They believe this is the way it should be. Or, in extreme cases, they feel especially isolated, believing their lot is like no one else's. Both attitudes deviate from the truth. In both cases the real emotion is not conscious and therefore cannot be properly evaluated and come to terms with. Thus, children grow up never quite understanding why they are unhappy, nor even that they are unhappy. Many of you look back on childhood convinced that you had all the love you wanted just because you actually did have some love, but rarely all that you wanted.

There are a number of parents who give great demonstrations of love. They may spoil or pamper their children. This very act of spoiling and pampering may be an overcompensation and a sort of apology for a deeply suspected inability to love maturely. Children feel the truth very acutely. They may not think it, or consciously observe it, but inwardly children keenly feel the difference between mature, genuine love and the immature, over-demonstrative variety offered instead.

Proper guidance and security are the parents' responsibility and call for authority on their part. There are parents who never dare to punish or exert a healthy authority. This failing is due to guilt because real, giving, warming, comforting love is absent in their own immature personalities. Other parents may be too severe, too strict. They thereby exert a domineering authority by bullying the child, and not allowing its individuality to unfold. Both kinds fall short as parents, and their wrong attitudes, absorbed by the child, will cause hurt and unfulfillment.

In the children of strict parents, the resentment and rebellion will be open, and therefore more easily traced. In the other case, the rebellion is just as strong, but hidden, and therefore infinitely harder to trace. If you had a parent who smothered you with affection or pseudo-affection, yet lacked in genuine warmth, or if you had a parent who conscientiously did everything right but was also lacking in real warmth, unconsciously you knew it as a child and you resented it. Consciously you may not have been aware of it at all, because, when a child, you really could not put your finger on what was lacking. You were outwardly given everything you wanted and needed. How could you draw the subtle, fine borderline distinction between real affection and pseudo-affection with your child's intellect? The fact that something bothered you without your being able to explain it rationally made you feel guilty and uncomfortable. You therefore pushed it out of sight as far as possible.

Attempts to Remedy the Childhood Hurt in Adulthood

As long as the hurt, disappointment, and unfulfilled need of your early years remain unconscious, you cannot come to terms with them. No matter how much you may love your parents, an unconscious resentment exists in you, which prevents you from forgiving them for the hurt. You can only forgive and let go if you recognize your deeply hidden hurt and resentment. As an adult human being you will see that your parents, too, are just human beings. They were not as faultless and perfect as the child thought and hoped, yet they are not to be rejected now, because they had their own conflicts and immaturities. The light of conscious reasoning has to be applied to these very emotions you never allowed yourself to be aware of fully.

As long as you are unaware of this conflict between your longing for a perfect love from your parents and your resentment against them, you are bound to try remedying the situation in your later years. This striving may manifest in various aspects of your life. You run constantly into problems and repeated patterns which have their origin in your attempt to reproduce the childhood situation so as to correct it. This unconscious compulsion is a very strong factor, but is so deeply hidden from your conscious understanding!

The most frequent way of attempting to remedy the situation is in your choice of love partners. Unconsciously you will know how to choose in the partner aspects of the parent who has particularly fallen short in affection and love that is real and genuine. But you also seek in your partner aspects of the other parent who has come closer to meeting your demands. Important as it is to find both parents represented in your partners, it is even more important and more difficult to find those aspects which represent the parent who has particularly disappointed and hurt you. So you seek the parents again—in a subtle way that is not always easy to detect—in your marital partners, in your friendships, or in other human relationships. In your subconscious, the following reactions take place: since the child in you cannot let go of the past, cannot come to terms with it, cannot forgive, cannot understand and accept, this very child in you always creates similar conditions, trying to win out in the end in order to finally master the situation instead of succumbing to it.

The Fallacy of This Strategy

This entire procedure is utterly destructive. In the first place, it is an illusion that you were defeated. Therefore, it is an illusion that you can now be victorious. Moreover, it is an illusion that the lack of love, sad as that may have been when you were a child, is indeed the tragedy that your subconscious still feels it to be. The only tragedy lies in the fact that you obstruct your future happiness by continuing to reproduce the old situation and then attempting to master it. My friends, this process is a deeply unconscious one. Of course, nothing is further from your mind as you focus on your conscious aims and wishes. It will take a great deal of digging to uncover the emotions that lead you again and again into situations where your secret aim is to remedy childhood woes.

In trying to reproduce the childhood situation, you unconsciously choose a partner with aspects similar to those of the parent. Yet it is these very aspects which will make it as impossible to receive the mature love you rightfully long for now as it was then. Blindly, you believe that by willing it more strongly and more forcefully, the parent-partner will now yield, whereas in reality love cannot come that way. Only when you are free of this ever continuing repetition, will you no longer cry to be loved by the parent. Instead, you will look for a partner or for other human relationships with the aim of finding the maturity you really need and want. In not demanding to be loved as a child, you will be equally willing to love. However, the child in you finds this impossible, no matter how much you may otherwise be capable of it through development and progress. This hidden conflict eclipses your otherwise growing soul.

If you already have a partner, the uncovering of this conflict may show you how he or she is similar to your parents in certain immature aspects. But since you now know that there is hardly a really mature person, these immaturities in your partner will no longer be the tragedy they were while you constantly sought to find your parent or parents again, which of course could never come to pass. With your existing immaturity and incapacity, you may nevertheless build a more mature relationship, free of the childish compulsion to recreate and correct the past.

You have no idea how preoccupied your subconscious is with the process of reenacting the play, so to speak, only hoping that "this time it will be different." And it never is! As time goes on, each disappointment weighs heavier and your soul becomes more and more discouraged.

For those of my friends who have not yet reached certain depths of their unexplored subconscious, this may sound quite preposterous and contrived. However, those of you who have come to see the power of your hidden trends, compulsions, and images will not only readily believe it, but will soon experience the truth of these words in their own personal lives. You already know from other findings how potent are the workings of your subconscious mind, how shrewdly it goes about its destructive and illogical waysIf you learn to look at your problems and unfulfillment from this point of view and follow the usual process of allowing your emotions to come to the fore, you will gain much further insight. But it will be necessary, my friends, to reexperience the longing and the hurt of the crying child you were once, even though you were also a happy one. Your happiness may have been valid and without self-deception at all. For it is possible to be both happy and unhappy. You may now be perfectly aware of the happy aspects of your childhood, but that which hurt deeply and that certain something you greatly longed for—you did not even quite know what—you were not aware of. You took the situation for granted. You did not know what was missing or even that there was anything missing. This basic unhappiness has to come to awareness now, if you really want to proceed in inner growth. You have to reexperience the acute pain you once suffered but you pushed out of sight. Now you have to look at this pain conscious of the understanding you have gained. Only by doing this will you grasp the reality value of your current problems and see them in their true light.

Reexperiencing the Childhood Hurt

Now, how can you manage to reexperience the hurts of so long ago? There is only one way, my friends. Take a current problem. Strip it of all the superimposed layers of your reactions. The first and most handy layer is that of rationalization, that of "proving" that others, or situations, are at fault; not your innermost conflicts which make you adopt the wrong attitude to the actual problem that confronts you. The next layer might be anger, resentment, anxiety, frustration. Behind all these reactions you will find the hurt of not being loved. When you experience the hurt of not being loved in your current dilemma, it will serve to reawaken the childhood hurt. While you face the present hurt, think back and try to reconsider the situation with your parents: what they gave you, how you really felt about them. You will become aware that in many ways you lacked a certain something you never clearly saw before—you did not want to see it. You will find that this must have hurt you when you were a child, but you may have forgotten this hurt on a conscious level. Yet it is not forgotten at all. The hurt of your current problem is the very same hurt. Now, reevaluate your present hurt, comparing it with the childhood hurt. At last you will clearly see how it is one and the same. No matter how true and understandable your present pain is, it is nevertheless the same childhood pain. A little later you will come to see how you contributed to bringing about the present pain because of your desire to correct the childhood hurt. But at first you only have to feel the similarity of the pain. However, this requires considerable effort, for there are many overlaying emotions that cover the present pain as well as the past one. Before you have succeeded in crystallizing the pain you are experiencing, you cannot understand anything further in this respect.

Once you can synchronize these two pains and realize that they are one and the same, the next step is much easier. Then, by looking over the repetitious pattern in your various difficulties you will learn to recognize the similarities between your parents and the people who have caused you hurt or are causing you pain now. Experiencing these similarities emotionally will carry you further on the particular road toward dissolving this basic conflict. Mere intellectual evaluation will not yield any benefit. When you feel the similarities, while at the same time experiencing the pain of now and the pain of then, you will slowly come to understand how you thought you had to choose the current situation because deep inside you could not possibly admit "defeat."

It goes without saying that many people are not even aware of any pain, past or present. They busily push it out of sight. Their problems do not appear as "pain." For them, the very first step is to become aware that this pain is present and that it hurts infinitely more as long as they have not become aware of it. Many people are afraid of this pain and like to believe that by ignoring it they can make it disappear. They chose such a means of relief only because their conflicts have become too great for them. How much more wonderful it is for a person to choose this path with the wisdom and conviction that a hidden conflict, in the long run, does as much damage as a manifest one. They will not fear to uncover the real emotion and will feel, even in the temporary experience of acute pain, that in that moment it turns into a healthy growing pain, free of bitterness, tension, anxiety, and frustration.

There are also those who tolerate the pain, but in a negative way, always expecting it to be remedied from the outside. Such people are in a way nearer to the solution because for them it will be quite easy to see how the childish process still operates. The outside is the offending parent, or both parents, projected onto other human beings. They have only to redirect the approach to their pains. They do not have to find it.

How to Stop Recreating

Only after experiencing all these emotions, and synchronizing the "now" and the "then," will you become aware of how you tried to correct the situation. You will further see the folly of the unconscious desire to recreate the childhood hurt, the frustrating uselessness of it. You will survey all your actions and reactions with this new understanding and insight, whereupon you will release your parents. You will leave your childhood truly behind and start a new inner behavior pattern that will be infinitely more constructive and rewarding for you and for others. You will no longer seek to master the situation you could not master as a child. You will go on from where you are, forgetting and forgiving truly inside of you, without even thinking that you have done so. You will no longer need to be loved as you needed to be loved when you were a child. First you become aware that this is what you still wish, and then you no longer seek this kind of love. Since you are no longer a child, you will seek love in a different way, by giving it instead of expecting it. It must always be emphasized, however, that many people are not aware that they do expect it. Since the childish, unconscious expectation was so often disappointed, they made themselves give up all expectations and all desire for love. Needless to say, this is neither genuine nor healthy, for it is a wrong extreme.

To be fruitful and bring real results, this knowledge must go beyond mere intellectual understanding. You have to allow yourself to feel the pain of certain unfulfillments now and also the pain of the unfulfillment of your childhood. Then compare the two until, like two separate photographic slides, they gradually fade into each other, move into focus and become one. The insight that you gain, once you feel this experience exactly as I describe it here, will enable you to take the further steps you need to take.

To work on this inner conflict is of great importance for all of you, so that you gain a new outlook and further clarification in your self-search. At first these words may give you perhaps only an occasional glimpse, a temporary flickering emotion in you, but they should be of help and open a door toward knowing yourself better, toward evaluating your life with a more realistic and more mature outlook.

Now, are there any questions in connection with this lecture?

QUESTION: It is very difficult for me to understand that one continually chooses a love object who has exactly the same negative trends that one or the other parent had. Is it reality that this particular person has these trends? Or is it a projection and response?

ANSWER: It can be both and it can be either. In fact, most of the time it is a combination. Certain aspects are unconsciously looked for and found and they are actually similar. But the existing similarities are enhanced by the person who is doing the recreation. They are not only projected qualities, "seen" while they are not really there, but are latent in some degree without being manifested. These are encouraged and strongly brought to the fore by the attitude of the person with the unrecognized inner problem. He or she fosters something in the other person by provoking the reaction that is similar to the parent's. The provocation, which of course is entirely unconscious, is a very strong factor here.

The sum total of a human personality consists of many traits. Out of these, a few may be actually similar to some traits in the recreator's parent. The most outstanding would be a similar kind of immaturity and incapacity to love. That alone is sufficient and potent enough in essence to reproduce the same situation.

The same person would not react to others as he or she reacts to you because it is you who constantly do the provoking, thereby reproducing conditions similar to your childhood for you to correct. Your fear, your self-punishment, your frustration, your anger, your hostility, your withdrawal from giving out love and affection, all these trends of the child in you constantly provoke the other person and enhance a response coming from that part which is weak and immature. However, a more mature person will affect others differently and will bring out that in them which is mature and whole, for there is no person who does not have some mature aspects.

QUESTION: How can I make the distinction as to whether the other person provoked me or I the other person?

ANSWER: It is not necessary to find who started it, for this is a chain reaction, a vicious circle. It is useful to start by finding your own provocation, perhaps in response to an open or hidden provocation of the other person. Thus you will realize that because you were provoked, you provoke the other person. And because you do so, the other again responds in kind. But as you examine your real reason, not the superficial one, the reason why you were hurt in the first place and therefore provoked, according to tonight's lecture you will no longer regard this hurt as disastrous. You will have a different reaction to the hurt, and, as a consequence, the hurt will diminish automatically. Therefore, you will no longer feel the need to provoke the other person. Also, as the need to reproduce the childhood situation decreases, you will become less withdrawn and you will hurt others less and less so that they will not have to provoke you. If they do, you will now also understand that they reacted out of the same childish blind needs as you did. Now you can see how you ascribe different motivations to the other person's provocation than to your own, even if and when you actually realize that you initiated the provocation. As you gain a different view on your own hurt, understanding its real origin, you will gain the same detachment from the reaction of the other person. You will find exactly the same reactions in yourself and in the other. As long as the child's conflict remains unresolved in you, the difference seems enormous, but when you perceive reality, you begin to break the repetitive vicious circle.

As you truly perceive such a mutual interplay, it will relieve the feeling of isolation and guilt you all are burdened with. You are constantly fluctuating between your guilt and your accusation of injustice you direct at those around you. The child in you feels itself entirely different from others, in a world of its own. It lives in such a damaging illusion. As you solve this conflict, your awareness of other people will increase. As yet, you are so unaware of the reality of other people. On the one hand you accuse them and are inordinately hurt by them because you do not understand yourself and therefore do not understand the other person. On the other hand, and at the same time, you refuse to become aware when you are hurt. This seems paradoxical yet is not. As you experience for yourself the interactions set forth tonight, you will find this to be true. While sometimes you may exaggerate a hurt, at other times you do not allow yourself to know that it happened at all, because it may not fit the picture you have of the situation. It may spoil your self-constructed idea, or it may not correspond to your desire at the time. If the situation seems otherwise favorable and fits into your preconceived idea, you leave out all that jars you, allowing it to fester underneath and create unconscious hostility. This entire reaction inhibits your intuitive faculties, at least in this particular respect.

The constant provocation that goes on among human beings, while it is hidden from your awareness now, is a reality you will come to perceive very clearly. This will have a very liberating effect on you and your surroundings. But you cannot perceive it unless you understand the patterns in yourself which I discussed tonight.

That will be all the questions for now. Go your way, my dearest ones, and may the blessings we bring to all of you envelop and penetrate your body, your soul, and your spirit, so that you open up your soul and become the real self, your own real self. Be blessed, my friends, be in peace, be in God.

੨♠

THE IDEALIZED SELF-IMAGE

Greetings. God bless all of you, my dearest friends.

It is about the mask self, or idealized self-image, that I want to speak to you now.

Pain is part of the human experience, beginning with birth, which is a painful experience for the infant. Though pleasurable experiences are bound to occur as well, the knowledge and fear of pain are always present. And the fear of pain creates a basic problem. The most significant countermeasure to which people resort in the false belief that it will circumvent unhappiness, pain, and even death, is the creation of the idealized self-image.

The idealized self-image is supposed to be a means of avoiding unhappiness. Since unhappiness automatically robs the child of security, self-confidence is diminished in proportion to unhappiness, though this unhappiness cannot be measured objectively. What one person may be able to cope with quite well and does not experience as drastic unhappiness, another temperament and character feels to be dismal woe.

At any rate, unhappiness and lack of belief in oneself are interconnected. By pretending to be what one is not, that is, by creating the idealized self-image, one hopes to reestablish happiness, security, and self-confidence.

In truth and reality, healthy and genuine self-confidence is peace of mind. It is security and healthy independence, and allows one to achieve a maximum of happiness through developing one's inherent talents, leading a constructive life, and entering into fruitful human relationships. But since the self-confidence established through the idealized self is artificial, the result cannot possibly be what was expected. Actually, the consequence is quite the contrary and frustrating because cause and effect are not obvious to you. .

You need to grasp the significance, the effects, the damages that follow in the wake of the idealized self-image and to fully recognize its existence, in the particular way it manifests in your individual case. This requires a great deal of work for which all the preceding work was necessary. The dissolution of the idealized self is the only possible way to find your true self, to find serenity and self-respect, and to live your life fully.

I have occasionally used the term mask self in the past. The mask self and the idealized self-image are really one and the same. The idealized self masks the real self. It pretends to be something you are not.

Fear of Pain and Punishment

As a child, regardless of what your particular circumstances were, you were indoctrinated with admonitions on the importance of being good, holy, perfect. When you were not, you were often punished in one way or another. Perhaps the worst punishment was that your parents withdrew their affection from you; they were angry, and you had the impression you were no longer loved. No wonder "badness" associated itself with punishment and unhappiness, "goodness" with reward and happiness. Hence to be "good" and "perfect" became an absolute must; it became a question of life or death for you. Still you knew perfectly well that you were not as good and as perfect as the world seemed to expect you to be. This had to be hidden; it became a guilty secret, and you started to build a false self. This, you thought, your protection and your means of attaining what you desperately wanted—life, happiness, security, self-confidence. The awareness of this false front began to vanish, but you were and are permanently permeated with the guilt of pretending to be something you are not. You strain harder and harder to become this false self, this idealized self. You were, and unconsciously still are, convinced that if you strain hard enough, one day you will be that self. But this artificial squeezing-into-something-you-are-not process can never attain genuine self-improvement, self-purification and growth, because you started building an unreal self on a false foundation and leave your real self out. In fact, you are desperately hiding it.

The Moral Mask of the Idealized Self

The idealized self-image may assume many forms. It does not always dictate standards of recognized perfection. Oh yes, much of the idealized self-image dictates high moral standards, making it all the more difficult to question its validity. "But isn't it right to want to be always decent, loving, understanding, never angry, and to have no faults, but try to attain perfection? Isn't this what we are supposed to do?" Such considerations will make it difficult for you to discover the compulsive attitude that denies present imperfection, the pride and lack of humility that prevents you from accepting yourself as you are now, and above all, the pretense with its resulting shame, fear of exposure, secretiveness, tension, strain, guilt, anxiety. It will take some progress in this work before you begin to experience the difference in feeling between the genuine desire to gradually work toward growth, and the ungenuine pretense imposed upon you by the dictates of your idealized self. You will discover the deeply hidden fear that says your world will come to an end if you do not live up to its standards. You will sense and know many other aspects and differences between the genuine and the ungenuine self. And you will also discover what your particular idealized self demands.

There are also facets of the idealized self, depending on

personality, life conditions and early influences, which are not and cannot be considered good, ethical, or moral. Aggressive, hostile, proud, overambitious trends are glorified or idealized. It is true that these negative tendencies exist behind all idealized self-images. But they are hidden, and since they crassly contradict the morally high standards of your particular idealized self, they cause additional anxiety that the idealized self will be exposed for the fraud it is. The person who glorifies such negative tendencies, believing them to prove strength and independence, superiority and aloofness, would be deeply ashamed of the kind of goodness another person's idealized self uses as a front, and would consider it weakness, vulnerability, and dependency in an unhealthy sense. Such a person entirely overlooks the fact that nothing makes a person as vulnerable as pride; nothing causes so much fear.

In most cases there is a combination of these two tendencies: overexacting moral standards impossible to live up to and pride in being invulnerable, aloof, and superior. The co-existence of these mutually exclusive ways presents a particular hardship for the psyche. Needless to say, the conscious awareness of this contradiction is missing until this particular work is well in progress.

Let us now consider some of the general effects of the existence of the idealized self and some of the implications. Since the standards and dictates of the idealized self are impossible to realize, and yet you never give up the attempt to uphold them, you cultivate within yourself an inner tyranny of the worst order. You do not realize the impossibility of being as perfect as your idealized self demands, and never give up whipping yourself, castigating yourself, and feeling a complete failure whenever it is proven that you cannot live up to its demands. A sense of abject worthlessness comes over you whenever you fall short of these fantastic demands and engulfs you in misery. This misery may at times be conscious but most of the time it is not. Even if it is, you do not realize the entire significance, the impossibility of what you expect from yourself. When you try to hide your reactions to your own "failure," you use special means to avoid seeing it. One of the most common devices is to project the blame for "failure" into the outer world, onto others, onto life. The more you try to identify with your idealized self-image, the harder the disillusionment whenever life brings you into a position where this masquerade can no longer be maintained. Many a personal crisis is based on this dilemma, rather than on outer difficulties. These difficulties then become an added menace beyond their objective hardship. The existence of the difficulties is a proof to you that you are not your idealized self, and this robs you of the false self-confidence you falsely tried to establish with the creation of the idealized self.

There are other personality types who know perfectly well that they cannot identify with their idealized self. But they do not know this in a healthy way. They despair. They believe they ought to be able to live up to it. Their whole life is permeated with a sense of failure, while the former type experiences it only on more conscious levels when outer and inner conditions culminate in showing up the phantom of the idealized self for what it really is—an illusion, a pretense, a dishonesty. It amounts to saying: "I know I am imperfect, but I make believe I am perfect." Not to recognize this dishonesty is comparatively easy when rationalized by conscientiousness, honorable standards and goals, and a desire to be good.

Self-Acceptance

The genuine desire to better oneself leads one to accept the personality as it is now. If this basic premise is the main governing force of your motivation for perfection, any discovery of where you fall short of your ideals will not throw you into depression, anxiety, and guilt, but will rather strengthen you. You will not need to exaggerate the "badness" of the behavior in question, nor will you defend yourself against it with the excuse that it is the fault of others, of life, of fate. You will gain an objective view of yourself in this respect, and this view will liberate you. You will fully assume responsibility for the faulty attitude, being willing to take the consequences upon yourself. When you act out your idealized self, you dread nothing more than that, for taking the responsibility of your shortcomings upon yourself is tantamount to saying, "I am not my idealized self."

The Inner Tyrant

A sense of failure, frustration, and compulsion, as well as guilt and shame, are the most outstanding indications that your idealized self is at work. These are the consciously felt emotions out of all those that lie hidden underneath.

The idealized self has been called into existence in order to attain self-confidence and therefore, finally, happiness, pleasure supreme. The stronger its presence, the more genuine self-confidence fades away. Since you cannot live up to its standards, you think even less of yourself than you originally did. It is therefore obvious that genuine self-confidence can be established only when you remove the superstructure which is this merciless tyrant, your idealized self.

Yes, you could have self-confidence if the idealized self were really you; and if you could live up to these standards. Since this is impossible and since, deep down, you know perfectly well you are not anything like what you think you are supposed to be—with this "super self" you build up additional insecurity, and further vicious circles come into existence. The original insecurity which was supposedly whisked away by the establishment of the idealized self, steadily increases. It snowballs, and becomes worse and worse. The more insecure you feel, the more stringent the demands of the superstructure or idealized self, the less you are able to live up to it, and the more insecure you feel. It is very important to see how this vicious circle works. But this cannot be done until and unless you become fully aware of the devious, subtle, unconscious ways in which this idealized self-image exists in your particular case. Ask yourself in what particular areas it manifests. What causes and effects are connected with it?

Estrangement from the Real Self

A further and drastic result of this problem is the constantly increasing estrangement from the real self. The idealized self is a falsity. It is a rigid, artificially constructed imitation of a live human being. You may invest it with many aspects of your real being; nevertheless, it remains an artificial construction. The more you invest your energies, your personality, your thought processes, concepts, ideas, and ideals into it, the more strength you take from the center of your being, which alone is amenable to growth. This center of your being is the only part of you, the real you, that can live, grow, and be. It is the only part that can properly guide you. It alone functions with all your capacities. It is flexible and intuitive. Its feelings alone are true and valid even if, for the moment, they are not yet fully in truth and reality, in perfection and purity. But the feelings of the real self function in perfection relative to what you are now, not being able to be more, in any given situation of your life. The more you take out of that live center in order to invest into the robot you have created, the more estranged you become from the real self and the more you weaken and impoverish it.

In the course of this work, you have sometimes come upon the puzzling and often frightening question: "Who am I really?" This is the result of the discrepancy and struggle between the real and the false self. Only upon solving this most vital and profound question will your live center respond and function to its full capacity, will your intuition begin to function to its full capacity, will you become spontaneous, free of all compulsions, will you trust in your feelings because they will have an opportunity to mature and grow. Feelings will become every bit as reliable to you as your reasoning power and your intellect.

All this is the final finding of self. Before this can be done, a great many hurdles have to be overcome. It seems to you that this is a life or death struggle. You still believe you need the idealized self in order to live and be happy. Once you understand that this is not so, you will be able to give up the pseudo-defense that makes the maintenance and cultivation of the idealized self seem necessary. Once you understand that the idealized self was supposed to solve the particular problems in your life above and beyond your need for happiness, pleasure, and security, you will come to see the wrong conclusion of this theory. Once you go a step still further and recognize the damage the idealized self has brought into your life, you will shed it as the burden it is. No conviction, theory, or words you hear will make you give it up, but the recognition of what specifically it was supposed to solve and what damage it has done and is continuing to do will enable you to dissolve this image of all images.

Needless to say, you also have to recognize most particularly and in detail what your specific demands and standards are, and, further, you have to see their unreasonableness, their impossibility. When you have a feeling of acute anxiety and depression, consider the fact that your idealized self may feel questioned and threatened, either by your own limitations, by others, or by life. Recognize the self-contempt that underlies the anxiety or depression. When you are compulsively angry at others, consider the possibility that this is but an externalization of your anger at yourself for not living up to the standards of your false self. Do not let it get away with using the excuse of outer problems to account for acute depression or fear. Look into the question from this new angle. Your private and personal work will help you in this direction, but it is almost impossible to do it alone. Only after you have made some substantial progress will you recognize that so many of these outer problems are directly or indirectly the result of the discrepancy between your capacities and the standards of your idealized self and how you deal with this conflict.

So, as you proceed in this particular phase of the work, you will come to understand the exact nature of your idealized self: its demands, its requirements of self and others in order to maintain the illusion. Once you fully see that what you regarded as commendable is really pride and pretense, you will have gained a most substantial insight that enables you to weaken the impact of the idealized self. Then, and then only, will you realize the tremendous self-punishment you inflict upon yourself. For whenever you fall short, as you are bound to, you feel so impatient, so irritated, that your feelings can snowball into fury and wrath at yourself. This fury and wrath is often projected on others because it is too unbearable to be aware of self-hate, unless one unrolls this whole process and sees it entire, in the light. Nevertheless, even if this hate is unloaded upon others, the effect on the self is still there and it can cause disease, accident, loss, and outer failure in many ways.

Giving Up the Idealized Self

When you make the very first steps toward giving up the idealized self, you will feel a sense of liberation as never before. Then you will be truly born again; your real self will emerge. Then you will rest within your real self, centered within. Then you will truly grow, not only on the outer fringes that may have been free of the idealized self's dictatorship, but in every part of your being. This will change many things. First will come changes in your reactions to life, to incidents, to yourself and others. This changed reaction will be astounding enough, but little by little, outer things are also bound to change. Your different attitude will have new effects. The overcoming of your idealized self means overcoming an important aspect of the duality between life and death.

At present you are not even aware of the pressure of your idealized self, of the shame, humiliation, exposure you fear and sometimes feel, of the tension, strain, and compulsion. If you have an occasional glimpse of such emotions, you do not as yet connect them with the fantastic demands of your idealized self. Only after fully seeing these fantastic expectations and their often contradictory imperatives will you relinquish them. The initial inner freedom gained in this way will allow you to deal with life and to stand in life. You will no longer have to hold on frantically to the idealized self. The mere inner activity of holding on so frantically generates a pervasive climate of holding on in general. This is sometimes lived out in external attitudes, but most often it is an inner quality or attitude. As you proceed in this new phase of your work, you will sense and feel this inner tightness and gradually you will recognize the basic damage it causes. It makes the letting go of many an attitude impossible. It makes it unduly difficult to go through any change that would allow life to bring forth joy and a spirit of vigor. You keep yourself contained within yourself and thereby you go against life in one of its most fundamental aspects.

The words are insufficient; you have to sense rather what I mean. You will know exactly when you have weakened your idealized self by fully understanding its function, its causes and effects. Then you will gain the great freedom of giving yourself to life because you no longer have to hide something from yourself and others. You will be able to squander yourself into life, not in an unhealthy, unreasonable way, but healthily as nature squanders herself. Then, and then only will you know the beauty of living.

You cannot approach this most important part of your inner work with a general concept. As usual, your most insignificant daily reactions, considered from this viewpoint, will yield the necessary results. So continue your self-search out of these new considerations and do not be impatient if it takes time and relaxed effort.

Coming Home
One more word: The difference between the real and the

85

idealized self is often not a question of quantity, but rather of quality. That is, the original motivation is different in these two selves. This will not be easy to see, but as you recognize the demands, the contradictions, the cause-and-effect sequences, the difference in motivation will gradually become clear to you.

Another important consideration is the time element. The idealized self wants to be perfect, according to its specific demands, right now. The real self knows this cannot be and does not suffer from this fact.

Of course you are not perfect. Your present self is a complex of everything you are at the moment. Of course you have your basic egocentricity, but if you own up to it, you can cope with it. You can learn to understand it and therefore diminish it with each new insight. Then you will truly experience the truth that the more egocentric you are, the less self-confident you can be. The idealized self believes just the opposite. Its claims for perfection are motivated by purely egocentric reasons, and this very egocentricity makes self-confidence impossible.

The great freedom of coming home, my friends, is finding your way back to the real you. The expression "coming home" has often been used in spiritual literature and teachings, but it has been much misunderstood. It is often interpreted to mean the return into the spirit world after physical death. Much more is meant by coming home. You may die many deaths, one earth life after another, but if you have not found your real self, you cannot come home. You may be lost and remain lost until you do find the way into the center of your being. On the other hand, you can find your way home right here and right now while you are still in the body. When you muster the courage of becoming your real self, even though it would seem much less than the idealized self, you will find out that it is much more. Then you will have the peace of being at home within yourself. Then you will find security. Then you will function as a whole human being. Then you will have broken the iron whip of a taskmaster whom it is impossible to obey. Then you will know what peace and security really mean. You will cease once and for all to seek them by false means.

Now my dearest ones, each one of you, receive our love, our strength, and our blessings. Be in peace, be in God.

CHAPTER 9

ॐ

LOVE, POWER, AND SERENITY

Greetings, my dearest friends. God bless each one of you. Blessed be this hour.

I would like to discuss three major divine attributes: love, power, and serenity, and how they manifest in their distorted forms. In the healthy person these three principles work side by side, in perfect harmony, alternating according to the specific situation. They complement and strengthen one another. Flexibility is maintained between them so that none of these three attributes can ever contradict or interfere with another.

However, in the distorted personality they mutually exclude one another. One contradicts the other, so that they create conflict. This happens because one of these attributes is unconsciously chosen by the person to use for the solution of life's problems.

The attitudes of submissiveness, aggressiveness, and withdrawal are the distortions of love, power, and serenity. I would now like to speak in detail about how they work in the psyche, how they form a supposed solution, and how the dominant attitude creates dogmatic, rigid standards that are then incorporated in the idealized self-image.

As a child, the human being encounters disappointment, helplessness, and rejection—both real and imagined. These feelings create insecurity and lack of self-confidence, which the person seeks to overcome, unfortunately often in the wrong way. In order to master the difficulties created, not only in childhood but also later in life as a consequence of resorting to wrong solutions, people involve themselves more and more in a vicious circle. Unaware that the very "solution" they undertake brings problems and disappointments, they try even more strenuously to follow through with that which they regard as the solution. The less they are able to do so, the more they doubt themselves. And the more they doubt themselves, the more they stray into the wrong solution.

Love/Submissiveness

One of these pseudo-solutions is love. The feeling is, "If only I would be loved, everything would be all right." In other words, love is supposed to solve all problems. Needless to say, this is not so, especially when one considers the way this love is supposed to be given. In reality, a disturbed person who adopts such a solution is hardly able to experience love. In order to receive love, such a person develops several typical personality trends and patterns of inner and outer behavior and reaction which tend to make one weaker and more helpless than one actually is. Taking on more and more self-effacing characteristics in order to gain love and protection, which alone seem to promise safety from annihilation, the person complies with the real or imagined demands of others, cringing and crawling to the point of selling his soul to receive approval, sympathy, help, and love. Unconsciously such people believe that self-assertion and standing up for their wishes and needs amounts to forfeiting the only value in life: that of being cared for as a child—not necessarily in financial matters but emotionally. Such people claim an imperfection, a helplessness, a submissiveness which are not genuine. They use these fake weaknesses as a weapon and a means to finally win and master life.

To avoid uncovering this falsity, these trends become incorporated into the idealized self-image. Thus people succeed in believing that all these trends are signs of their goodness, holiness, unselfishness. When they "sacrifice" in order to finally possess a strong and loving protector, they are proud of their capacity to sacrifice unselfishly. Proud of their "modesty," they never claim knowledge, accomplishment, strength. Thereby they hope to force others to feel loving and protecting toward them. There are many, many aspects to this pseudo-solution. They have to be found painstakingly in the work you are doing. It is not easy to detect them since these attitudes are deeply ingrained and seem to have become a part of the "loving" person's nature. Moreover, they can often be rationalized away by seemingly real needs. Last, they are always thwarted by the opposite trends of other pseudo-solutions which are also always present in the soul, though not as predominant. In the same way, the other types who use pseudo-solutions will find aspects of submissiveness in their psyche. The extent to which this pseudo-solution is predominant varies with each individual. So does the extent it is counteracted by the other "solutions."

The person with the predominantly submissive attitude will have a somewhat harder time discovering the pride that prevails in all these attitudes. The pride in the other types is quite on the surface. The other types may be proud of their pride, they may be proud of their aggressiveness and cynicism; but once they have seen it, it can no longer be covered up by "love," "modesty," or any other "holy" attitude. The submissive type will have to look with very discerning eyes at these trends in order to find out how he or she idealized them. There may be a reaction of aloof criticism and contempt for all people who assert themselves, be it only healthy assertiveness and not an aggressiveness which arises out of the distortion of power. The submissive type may simultaneously also admire and envy the still despised aggression of others, in spite of feeling superior in "spiritual development" or "ethical standards," and may wistfully think or say, "If only I could be like that, I would get much further in life." In doing so, however, such a person stresses the "goodness" which prevents him or her from having what "less good" people attain. The pride of self-sacrificing martyrdom makes it difficult to discover what is beneath the surface. Only very truthful insight into the real nature of these motives will reveal the fundamental selfishness and egocentricity prevailing in this attitude, just as much as they do in the other attitudes linked to pseudo-solutions. Pride, hypocrisy, and pretense are present in all of them when incorporated in the idealized self-image. The submissive type will have a harder time finding the pride, while the aggressive type will have a harder time finding the pretense. For the second pretends an "honesty" in being ruthless, cynical, and out for his own advantage.

The need for protective love has a certain validity for the child, but if it is maintained into adulthood, this need is no longer valid. In this search to be loved there is the element of, "I must be loved, so that I can believe in my own worth. Then I may be willing to love in return." It is ultimately a self-centered, one-sided desire. The effects of this entire attitude are grave.

The need for such love and dependency actually makes you helpless. You do not cultivate in yourself the faculty of standing on your own feet. Instead, you use your entire psychic strength to live up to this ideal of yourself so as to force others to comply with your needs. In other words, you comply in order to have others comply with you; you submit in order to dominate, although such domination must always manifest in soft, weak helplessness.

It is no wonder that a person engulfed in this attitude becomes estranged from the real self. The real self has to be denied, for its assertion seems brash and aggressive. This has to be avoided at all costs. But the indignity inflicted on the individual by such self-denial has its effect in self-contempt and self-dislike. Since this is painful, aside from being contradictory to the idealized self-image which recommends self-effacement as supreme virtue, it has to be projected onto others. Such emotions of contempt and resentment for others in turn contradict the standards of the idealized self. Consequently, they, too, have to be hidden. This double hiding causes inversion and has serious repercussions on the personality, also manifesting in physical symptoms of all sorts.

Anger, fury, shame, frustration, self-contempt, and self-hate exist for two reasons. They exist, first, as a result of denying one's true self, and for the indignity of being prevented from being who one truly is. One then believes that the world prevents self-realization and abuses and takes advantage of one's "goodness." This is sheer projection. Secondly, they exist because one is incapable of living up to the dictates of one's particular "loving" idealized self, which are that one must never resent, despise, dislike, blame, find fault with others, and so on. As a result, one is not as "good" as one ought to be.

In a very brief outline, this is the picture of a person who has chosen "love," with all its subdivisions of compassion, understanding, forgiveness, union, communication, brotherhood, sacrifice, as a rigid, one-sided solution. This is a distortion of the divine attribute of love. The idealized self-image of this type will have corresponding standards and dictates. One must always be in the background, never assert oneself, always give in, never find fault with others, love everybody, never recognize one's own true values and accomplishments, and so on. On the surface this looks, indeed, like a very holy picture, but, my friends, it is but a caricature of true love, understanding, forgiveness, or compassion. The poison of the underlying motive distorts and destroys that which could really be genuine.

Power/Aggressiveness

In the second category is the seeker for power. This person thinks that power and independence from others will solve all problems. This type, just as the other, can present many variations and subdivisions. It can be predominant or subordinated to one or both of the other two attitudes. Here the growing child believes that the only way it can be safe is by becoming so strong and invulnerable, so independent and emotionless, that nothing and no one can touch it. The next step is to cut off all human emotions. When, nevertheless, they come to the fore, the child feels deeply ashamed of any emotion and considers it as weakness, whether it be an actual weakness or an imagined one. Love and goodness would also be considered as weakness and hypocrisy, not only in their distorted forms as in the submissive type, but also in their real and healthy form. Warmth, affection, communication, unselfishness: all that is despicable, and whenever an impulse of this sort is suspected, the aggressive type feels as deeply ashamed as the submissive type is ashamed of the resentment and self-assertive qualities that smolder underneath.

Power drive and aggressiveness can manifest in many ways and areas of life and of the personality. It may be directed mainly at accomplishments, when the person with a power drive will compete and try to be better than everyone else. Any competition will be felt as an injury to the exalted special position one needs for this private solution. Or, it may be a more general and less defined attitude in all of one's human relationships. Artificially cultivating a toughness that is no more real than the helpless softness of the submissive person, the power type is just as dishonest and hypocritical, because such a person, too, needs human warmth and affection, and without these suffers from isolation. In not admitting the suffering this type is as dishonest as the other types. This particular idealized self-image dictates standards of godlike perfection regarding independence and power. Believing in complete self-sufficiency, such a person does not feel the need for anyone, contrary to mere human beings who do. Neither are love, friendship, or help acknowledged as important. The pride in this image is very obvious, but the dishonesty will be less easy to detect, because such a type hides under the rationalization of how hypocritical the "goody-goody" type is.

Since this idealized self-image demands such power and independence from feelings and human emotions as no human being can possibly have, it is constantly proven that the person cannot live up to this ideal self. Such "failure" throws the person into fits of depression and self-contempt which, again, have to be projected onto others, in order to remain unaware of the pain of such self-castigation. The inability of being the idealized self-image always has this effect. When closely analyzing the demands of any idealized self-image, omnipotence is always contained in it. However, these emotional reactions are so subtle and elusive, and so covered up by rational knowledge, that it takes a very painstaking look at certain feelings, at certain occasions, to gain an awareness of all this. Only the work you are doing can bring out how any of these attitudes exist in you. They are, of course, much easier to find when one type is very dominant. In most cases, however, the attitudes are more hidden and are in conflict with attitudes of the other types.

A further symptom of the aggressive type, who thinks that power is the solution, is the artificially cultivated view of, "How bad the world and people really are." A person who looks for proof of this negative view receives plenty of confirmation, and takes pride in being "objective" and the opposite of gullible— which serve as the reasons for not liking anyone. The idealized image in this case dictates that love is forbidden. Loving, or at times showing one's true nature, is a crass violation of the idealized self-image and brings on deep shame. Conversely, the submissive type is proud of loving everybody and of considering all other human beings good. This outlook is needed for maintaining and following through with the submissive attitude. In reality, the person of this type does not really care whether others are good or bad as long as they love, appreciate, approve, and protect him. All evaluation of others hinges on that, no matter how well it can be "explained." Since everyone possesses both virtues and faults, either can be singled out depending on the prevailing attitude of the other person to the submitter.

The seeker for power must never fail in anything. Contrary to the submissive type who glorifies failure, because it proves one's helplessness and forces others to give her love and protection, the seeker for power takes pride in never failing in anything. In certain combinations of the pseudo-solutions failure may be permitted because in some specific area the prevailing attitude may be submissiveness. Likewise, the submissive type may in certain cases resort to the power solution. Both are equally rigid, unrealistic and unrealizable. Either of these "solutions" is a constant source of pain and disillusionment regarding the self, and therefore brings on an ever greater lack of self-respect.

I indicated before that there is always a mixture of all three "solutions" in a person, although one may be predominant. Hence, the person cannot do justice even to the chosen solution's dictates. Even if it were possible never to fail, or to love everyone, or to be entirely independent of others, this becomes more and more impossible when the dictates of a person's idealized self-image simultaneously demand one to love and be loved by everyone and to conquer them. For such a goal one needs to be aggressive and often ruthless. An idealized self-image may therefore simultaneously demand of a person on the one hand to be always unselfish, so as to gain love, and, on the other, to be always selfish so as to gain power. In addition one also has to be completely indifferent and aloof from all human emotions so as not to be disturbed. Can you picture what a conflict this is in the soul? How torn a soul must be! Whatever it does is wrong and induces guilt, shame, inadequacy, and therefore frustration and self-contempt.

Serenity/Withdrawal

Let us now consider the third divine attribute, serenity, chosen as a solution and being thereby distorted. Originally, a person may have been so torn between the first two aspects that a way out had to be found by resorting to a withdrawal from inner problems, and thereby from life as such. Underneath the withdrawal, or false serenity, that soul is still torn in half, but no longer aware of it. Such a strong facade of false serenity has been built that, as long as life's circumstances permit, this person is convinced of having attained true serenity. But let life's storms touch him, let the effects of the raging, underlying conflict finally emerge, and it will show how false the serenity was. It will be borne out that it was indeed built on sand.

The withdrawn type and the seeker for power seem to have something in common: aloofness from their emotions, non-attachment to others, and a strong urge for independence. However much the underlying emotional motivations may be similar—fear of getting hurt and disappointed, fear of being dependent on others and thereby feeling insecure—the dictates of the idealized self-image of these two types are very different. While the seeker for power glories in hostility and aggressive fighting spirit, the withdrawn type is entirely unaware of such feelings, and whenever they come to the fore is shocked by them because they violate the dictates of the withdrawal solution. These dictates are, "You must look benignly and detachedly at all human beings, knowing their weaknesses and good qualities, but without being bothered or affected by either." This, if true, would indeed be serenity. But no human being is ever quite so serene. Hence such dictates are unrealistic and unrealizable. They, too, include pride and hypocrisy: pride, because this detachment seems so godlike in its justice and objectivity. In reality, one's view may be just as colored by what another thinks, as is the case with the submissive type. But being too proud to admit that an exalted one can be touched by such human weaknesses, such a person tries to rise above all that. This is not possible. Since this type, too, is as much dependent on others as the other two types, the dishonesty is just the same. And since the serene independence of this type is not true and cannot ever be true as long as we talk of a human being, such a person must fall short of the standards and dictates of the particular idealized self-image which makes him or her just as self-contemptuous, guilty, and frustrated as the other two types when they fall short of their respective standards.

These three major types are outlined here very briefly, in a very general way. Needless to say, many variations exist. According to the strength, intensity, and distribution of these "solutions" will the tyranny of the idealized self-image manifest. All this has to be found in the individual work. It must never be forgotten that such attitudes born of the idealized self can hardly ever be total in a person. The attitude may be present to a stronger degree in certain areas of life and of the personality, and to a lesser degree in others; in still other facets of life it does not appear at all. The most important part of this work is to feel the emotions, to truly experience them. It is impossible to get rid of the life-prohibiting idealized self-image if you merely look on and observe in a detached way, with your intellect, what is in you. You have to become acutely aware of all these often contradictory trends, and this will be painful.

The Necessity of Emotional Growth

The pain that was always in you but was hidden, against which you "protected" yourself by unloading it on others, on life, and on fate, will become a conscious experience which you absolutely need. At first sight this will appear as a relapse. You will believe you are even worse off than before you started with this work. But this is not so. It is your very progress that made it possible for all these hitherto hidden emotions to become conscious, so that you can really use them for analysis. Otherwise you could not possibly dissolve the superstructure of your tyrant, your idealized self-image with all the unnecessary harm it does you. You are so conditioned by the emotional reactions you have become accustomed to, you are so involved in them, that you cannot see what is right before your eyes. While you watch for new and hidden recognitions, you look past the seemingly unimportant emotional reactions to certain situations simply because they have become a part of you. But it is these actual emotional reactions that will furnish the clue, once your attention is focused on them. This would be impossible if you were not disturbed. Therefore, the disturbance is bound to come into the open and this is the moment when you can come to terms with it.

So, my friends, begin to see your emotions in this light. You will then find what impossible demands your idealized self-image makes on you. You will see that it is your idealized self-image, and not God, not life, not other people, who demand all that. You will also begin to see that, because of these demands of the self, you need other people to help you to cope with them. This makes you unconsciously demand of others what they are incapable of giving. You are then much more dependent than you need be, in spite of all your striving toward a distorted independence of either the aggressive or the withdrawn type.

You also have to find the cause and effect of these conditions. You will see your life, and your past and present difficulties, with a new outlook. You will understand that you have created many, if not all, of these difficulties, just because of your "solution."

It does not suffice to comprehend intellectually that the more you are involved in your pseudo-solutions, the less of your real self can manifest. You also need to experience this. Such experience must happen if you allow your emotions to come to the fore and work with them. Then, and then only, will you begin to sense the intrinsic value of your real self. Only then will it become possible to let go of the false values of your idealized self. It is a mutual process: by allowing yourself to see the false values, however painful this process may be, your real values will gradually emerge so that you no longer need the false ones.

Since the idealized self alienates you from your real self, you are utterly unaware of your real values. Throughout your life you concentrate unconsciously on the false values: either on values you lack, but think you should have while you pretend to yourself and others that you do have them, or you concentrate on values which are potentially there, but have not yet been developed to the extent that they can be rightfully called yours. Since your idealized self does not admit that these values still need development, you do not develop them and yet you claim them as though they were already fully ripe. Because you use all your efforts in concentrating on these false or unripe values, you do not see the real values. Because you cannot see them, you are frightened to let go of the false ones fearing that then you will have nothing. Thus your real values do not count. You do not feel they exist, either because they contradict the demands of your idealized self, or because everything that comes naturally and without effort does not appear real. You are so conditioned to strain for the impossible that it does not occur to you that there is nothing to strain for, because what is actually valuable is already there. But when you do not utilize these values, they often lie fallow. This is a great pity, my friends, because after all, you established the idealized self-image because you did not believe in your real worth. Because you build the idealized self and try to be it, you cannot see what in you is actually worth accepting and appreciating.

To unroll this entire process is painful at first, because the emotions of anxiety, frustration, guilt, shame, and so on, have to be acutely experienced. But as you courageously proceed, you will gain a very different outlook on everything. Last, you will begin to see your real self for the very first time. You will see its limitations. At the beginning it will be a shock to have to accept these limitations which are such a far cry from the idealized self. But as you learn to do so, you will begin to see values you have never truly seen or been aware of. Then a feeling of strength and self-confidence in a very different way will make you see both life and yourself. Gradually the process of growing into the real self will take place in you. It will strengthen your true independence, not the false kind, so that being appreciated by others will no longer be the yardstick for your own sense of value. Validation by others assumes such great importance only because you do not evaluate yourself honestly. Thus validation by others becomes a substitute. As you begin to trust and like your own self, what other people think about you will not matter half as much. You will rest secure within, and you will no longer need to build false values with pride and pretense. You will no longer rely on an idealized self, which cannot really be trusted and therefore weakens you. The freedom of shedding this burden cannot be described in words.

But, my friends, this is a slow process. It does not come overnight. It comes from steady self-search and analysis of your problems, your attitudes, and your emotions. As you proceed in this way, the real you with its real values and capacities will evolve through a process of inner and natural growth. Your individuality will then become stronger and stronger. Your intuitive nature will manifest without inhibition, with a natural and reliable spontaneity. This is how you will make the best of your life. Not faultlessly, not by being free of all failure, not excluding the possibility of making mistakes. Yet failures and mistakes will be made in a very different way than before. More and more you will combine the divine attitudes of love, power, and serenity in a healthy way, as opposed to a distorted way.

Love will not be a means to an end. It will not be a need that saves you from annihilation. It will, therefore, cease being self-centered. Your own capacity to love will combine power and serenity. Or, to put it differently, you will communicate in love and understanding while being truly independent. Love, power, and serenity will not be used to furnish you with your missing self-respect. Genuine, not self-centered, love will then no longer interfere with healthy power, which is not the power of pride and defiance, neither power to triumph over others, but the power to master yourself and your difficulties without proving anything to anyone. When you seek mastery by distorting the attribute of power, you do so for the sake of proving your superiority. When you gain mastery by healthy power you do so for the sake of growing. Not to have the mastery occasionally will not present a threat as it did while you were in distortion. It will not diminish your worth in your own eyes. Thus you will truly grow with each life experience. You will learn, and accomplish, and gain real power, not the false kind. There will not be any distorted ambitiousness, compulsion, and haste.

Serenity in the healthy way will not cause you to hide from emotions, experience, life, and your own conflicts; love and power in their original divine forms will give you a healthy detachment when looking at yourself so that you will truly become more objective. True serenity is not avoiding experience and emotions which may be painful at the moment but might yield an important key when the courage is there to go through them and find what is behind them.

Love, power, and serenity can go hand in hand. In fact, when each is healthy, they complement one another. But they can cause the greatest war within yourself if distorted.

May these words again give you food, not only for further thought, but for insight and understanding. May you thus gain a further step toward light and freedom. Proceed on your path of happiness. Gain more and more strength, and let our blessings and love help and invigorate you. Be blessed, my dear ones. Be in peace. Be in God.

MEETING THE PAIN
OF DESTRUCTIVE PATTERNS

Greetings, my dearest friends. God bless each one of you. Blessed is this hour. Most of my friends who work on this path approach a certain area of their soul problems where they encounter pain. To understand the meaning of this pain, I should like to give you an overall view of the process for dissolving it.

First, let us recapitulate. The child suffers from certain imperfections of the parents' love and affection. It also suffers from not being fully accepted in its own individuality. By this I mean the common practice of treating a child as a child, rather than as a particular individual. You suffer from this, although you may never be aware of it in these terms or in exact thoughts. This may leave as much of a scar as the lack of love or attention. It causes as much frustration as does the lack of love, or even cruelty.

The general climate in which you grow up affects you like a constant minor shock that often leaves more of a mark than one traumatic shocking experience. That is why the latter is so often easier to cure than the former. The constant climate of non-acceptance of your individuality, as well as the lack of love and understanding, cause what is called a neurosis. You accept this climate as a matter of course. You take it for granted. You believe that it has to be so. Nevertheless, you suffer from it.

The combination of suffering it and believing it to be unalterable fact, conditions you to develop destructive defenses.

The original pain and frustration the child could not deal with is repressed. It is put out of awareness, but it smolders in the unconscious mind. It is then that the destructive images and defense mechanisms begin to form. The images that you create are defense mechanisms. Through their wrong conclusions you seek a way of fighting against the unwelcome influences that have created the original pain. The pseudo-solutions are a way of battling the world, the pain, and all that you wish to avoid.

The Pain of the Pseudo-solutions

When your pseudo-solution is a withdrawal from feeling, from loving, and from living, it is a defense against being hurt. Only after considerable insight into yourself will you see what an unrealistic, shortsighted "remedy" this is. You will want to change and would rather welcome the pain than the self-alienation of feeling nothing, or very little. Continuing the work and courageously going through the temporary periods of discouragement and resistance, you will come to the point when this hard shell breaks down and you are no longer dead inside. But the first reaction will not be pleasant. It cannot be. All the repressed negative emotions, as well as the repressed pain, will at first come into awareness, and it will then seem to you that your withdrawal was right. Only after plowing ahead will you have the reward of good, constructive feelings.

If your pseudo-solution is submissiveness, weakness, helplessness, and dependency as a means of having someone care for you—not necessarily materially, but emotionally—that is equally shortsighted and unsatisfactory as a solution. The constant dependency on others creates fear and helplessness. It further diminishes your already existing lack of belief in yourself. As the withdrawal-solution makes you dead in feeling and robs you of the meaningfulness of life, so does the submissive-solution rob you of independence and strength and creates no less isolation than the withdrawal, although it does so through a different inner road. Originally you wished to avoid the pain by providing yourself with a strong person to care for you. In reality you inflict upon yourself more pain because you can never find such a person. That person must be yourself.

By making yourself deliberately weak, you exert the strongest tyranny over others. There is no stronger tyranny than that which a weak person exerts over the stronger, or upon his or her entire environment. It is as though that person was constantly saying: "I am so weak. You have to help me. I am so helpless. You are responsible for me. The mistakes I commit do not count because I do not know any better. I cannot help it. You must constantly indulge me and allow me to get away with everything. I cannot be expected to take full responsibility for my actions or the lack of them, for my thoughts and feelings or for the lack of them. I may fail because I am weak. You are strong, therefore you must understand everything. You cannot fail because your failure would affect me." The self-indulgent, lazy self-pity of the weak exerts stringent demands on their fellow-creatures. This becomes evident if the unspoken expectancy, the meaning of emotional reactions, are investigated and then interpreted into concise thought.

It is fallacious to think that the weak person is harmless and hurts others less than the domineering and aggressive person. All pseudo-solutions bring untold pain to the self, as well as to others. By withdrawing, you reject others and withhold from them the love you want to give them and that they want to receive from you. By submitting, you do not love, but merely expect to be loved. You do not see that others, too, have their vulnerabilities and weaknesses and needs. You reject all of that part of their human nature, and thus hurt them. By the aggressive solution, you push people away and openly hurt them with false superiority. In all instances, you hurt others and thus inflict further hurt upon yourself. The hurt you inflict cannot help but bring consequences, and thus the pseudo-solutions, intended to eliminate the original pain, only bring you more pain.

All pseudo-solutions are incorporated into your idealized self-image. Since the nature of the idealized self-image is self-aggrandizement, it separates you from others. Since its nature is separateness, it isolates you and makes you, and those you deal with, lonely. Since its nature is falsity and pretense, it alienates you from yourself, from life, and from others. All of that is bound to bring you pain, hurt, frustration, unfulfillment. You chose a way out of pain and frustration, but this way has proven not only inadequate, it actually brings you much more of that which you wished to avoid. However, to clearly recognize this fact and to put the links together requires the active work of sincere self-search.

The perfectionism that is so deeply ingrained in you and in your idealized self-image makes it impossible for you to accept yourself and others, to accept life in its reality, and you are therefore incapable of coping with it and resolving its problems and your own problems as well. It causes you to forego the experience of living in the true sense.

If you have become, at least to some extent, aware of some of your images, pseudo-solutions, and the nature of your particular idealized self-image, you may have by now an inkling as to the way in which you are self-alienated and perfectionistic. You have therefore realized the extent of the damage you have inflicted upon yourself and others. You may be near the threshold opening the way to a new inner life of being emotionally willing to let go of all the defenses. If you are not there yet, you will approach this phase quite soon, provided you continue in your work with inner willingness.

The mere exercise of constantly observing your unrealistic and immature emotions and reactions weakens their impact and begins a process of dissolving them, so to say, automatically. When a certain dissolution has taken place, the psyche is ready to cross the threshold. But the act of crossing it is a painful one in the beginning.

The Painfulness of Change

You would expect, when crossing this important threshold, that the new, constructive patterns can immediately replace the old destructive ones. Such an expectation is unrealistic and not according to truth. Constructive patterns cannot have a solid foundation before you experience and go through the original pain and frustration, and all that which you ran away from. That which you turned away from has to be faced, felt, experienced, understood, coped with, come to terms with, and assimilated before what is unhealthy and unrealistic is dissolved, the immature matured, and the healthy but repressed forces brought into their proper channels so as to work constructively for you. The longer you delay this painful process, the more difficult and lasting is it bound to be when you are finally ready to pass from childhood into adulthood. The pain is a healthy growing pain, and the light is in sight if and when you overcome your resistance to the process. The strength, the self-reliance, and the capacity to live fully with all your constructive patterns beginning to work, is ample compensation for all the years of destructive and unproductive living, as well as for the pain of crossing the threshold into emotional adulthood.

Can you imagine being spared experiencing the pain against which you instituted the destructive patterns? You used them to run away from something that occurred in your life, whether actual or imaginary makes little difference. It is the wishful-thinking process of running away and looking away from something that is or was, thus not facing and coping with your reality, that caused your soul's sickness. Hence it is this area that has to be tackled now. This is why those of you who have made your first tentative steps over the threshold are puzzled by the pain you experience. Often you do not quite understand why this is so. You may have some vague idea and some partial answers, but this lecture will help you to derive a more profound understanding of the reason.

Intellectually, you all know that this path is not a fairy tale in which you find your deviations and misconceptions and evasions, and, after having done so, nothing but bliss follows. In the last analysis it is true, of course, that being freed of your shackles of error and deviation is bound to bring you happiness. But until you reach that stage, many areas of your soul have to be experienced until your psyche is truly equipped to make the best of life. Even after the acute pain has been properly dealt with and is no longer present, the unrealistic, although often unconscious expectation exists that now life will always grant you what you wish. No, my friends. However, the reality is much better. In reality you will learn to cope with the mishaps and difficulties, rather than becoming broken by them. You will not fortify your destructive defenses. This, in turn, will equip you with the tools to make the best out of each opportunity, and to derive the maximum benefit and happiness out of every experience of life.

Needless to say, this is never accomplished with your destructive defense mechanisms and various images. Let me repeat here what I have often said: First the outer negative events will continue to come your way, as a result of your past ingrained patterns, but you will encounter them in a different way. As you learn to do so, you will become aware of many opportunities for happiness that you ignored in the past. In this way, you begin to change the patterns, until very, very gradually the unhappy outer events cease more and more. But when you find yourself at the beginning of this stage, do not expect immediate fulfillment and happiness in every respect. First you need to see your possibilities and opportunities and independent ability to choose, instead of being utterly helpless and waiting for fate to bring you happiness.

By now you must understand how in many respects you have caused your own unhappiness through your own destructive and unrealistic evasions and defenses. You will now realize, with a new sense of strength, that you can bring about your own fulfillment and happiness. Again, this cannot be done by intellectual understanding. It is an inner process that grows organically. As you now deeply understand that no unkind fate or cruel god has punished or neglected you, so you will deeply understand and know that it is you who can create all the fulfillment your soul craves for with a craving you were not even conscious of when you first began this path.

This consciousness may emerge only after a fuller understanding of all your pseudo-solutions and misconceptions, whose depths will make you aware of your needs. The primary result on this path is the understanding of your own causes and effects and of the sense of strength, independence, self-reliance, and justice that this understanding gives to an individual. How much time it takes to reach the first tentative beginnings of this new strength and later to increase it, depends on your efforts, your inner will, and your overcoming the ever-present resistance which wears off only after you gain sufficient recognition of its devious ways.

The Pain of Unfulfillment

Now, my friends, when you come across this pain, is it really merely the pain you once experienced as a child? Is it really the frustration the child suffered from the parents, and nothing more? No, this is not entirely correct. It is true that this original pain and frustration has afflicted the resiliency of your psyche and thus made you incapable of properly dealing with it. It caused you to turn away from it and look for unsatisfactory "solutions." But the pain you now experience is much more the present pain of unfulfillment, caused by your unproductive patterns. Consciously you cannot distinguish this. You may not even be aware of the original childhood pain. It may take time and self-observation to distinguish the pain at all. After you do so, you will see that the more acute pain is your despair with yourself and with life now, not in the past. The past is important only because it caused you to institute the unproductive ways responsible for your present pain.

If you do not shy away from the pain but go through it, becoming aware of its significance, you will realize that your present unfulfilled needs cause the pain. Your frustration will be with your inability, at this time, to bring about fulfillment. You cannot as yet see what you can do about it. You feel caught in your own trap, not seeing how to get out of it, thus being dependent on outer intervention over which you have no control. Only after courageously becoming aware of all these impressions and reactions will you gradually see a way out, and thereby decrease your helplessness and increase your independent strength and resourcefulness.

In a previous lecture we discussed the human needs. Before you uncover your various "protective layers," you cannot even be fully aware of your real needs. You may know some of your unreal, superimposed needs, but only after a fuller understanding of yourself do you gradually become aware of the basic, naked needs that you have held in check. When you experience the pain, before crossing the threshold into emotional maturity and productive patterns, you have the possibility, if you so choose, to become precisely aware of these needs. This is inevitable if you wish to come out of your present state of unproductive living.

As you go through the process of becoming aware of your needs and of the frustration of their unfulfillment, you will find first the stringent need to be loved just as the child needs to receive love and affection. However, it cannot be said that the need to be loved is childish and immature. It is only so when the adult person has locked his soul and refused to grow in his own capacity to give love, so that the need to receive remains isolated, as well as covered. Through your destructive patterns, you pushed your painful need to receive love into the unconscious. Due to this unawareness and to your defense mechanisms of various sorts, your ability to give could never grow within your psyche.

However, during all the work you have done, you have not

only become aware of so much that was hidden away, but, as I said before, you have begun to dissolve certain destructive levels. This has, as it were inadvertently, caused your ability to give love to surface, even though you may not yet be fully aware of it. As you encounter the pain, you actually experience the tremendous pressure of your needs. On the one hand, you face the need to receive which remains ungratified so long as the destructive patterns prevail. It requires some time to gain the necessary strength and resourcefulness to bring about fulfillment of *the need to receive*. On the other hand, *the need to give* cannot find an outlet until this stage is reached. Thus a double frustration is caused—and this generates tremendous pressure. It is this pressure that is so painful. It seems to tear you apart.

The Shift from Evasion to Reality

However, do not believe, my friends, that this pressure, this entire frustration, did not exist before you became aware of it. It did exist, but it created other outlets, perhaps in physical sickness, or in other symptoms. As you become aware of the central core, the pressure and pain may feel more acute, but such must be the healing process. You thus draw your awareness to the central cause where the problem really lies. You focus your attention upon the root. You shift your emphasis from evasion to reality. The real pain has to be experienced in all its shades and varieties. You have to become aware that your needs are exactly both to give and to receive. You need to feel and observe the frustration of not finding an outlet, the accumulated pressure, the momentary feeling of helplessness about finding relief; the temptation to evade yet again. As you battle through this phase and grow stronger, you will no longer run away from yourself and from the apparent risk of living. Opportunities will come your way. You will see them and make use of them. They will teach you to further your growth and strength until your needs can find partial fulfillment, and then little by little increase it as you grow and change your patterns.

You must understand that at this period you find yourself in an interim stage. You have become aware of your need to receive, which is in itself healthy. But this need has become exaggeratedly strong and therefore immature, because of your repression of it and the consequent frustration of the healthy fulfillment of receiving. If you do not receive enough, your demand grows out of proportion, especially when you are unconscious of this stringent demand.

Due to your progress and to the growth that has taken place within you, the mature need to give has also grown. You could not find an outlet for this because the destructive patterns were still in effect; perhaps only partly so, perhaps in a modified form. You may even have begun attempts to compromise between the old and the new, desired, way. However, do not forget that effective results can come only when the new patterns become an integral and almost automatic reaction in you. Your old patterns have been in existence for years, decades, and often for longer. Now, as you learn to do so and have begun to change inwardly, outer change does not come at once. In this period, the pressure inside may become most stringent. However, if you realize all this and have the courage to go through it, you are bound to come out a stronger, happier person, better equipped to live in the true sense of the word. Beware of turning back into evasion all over again. Do not believe that this temporary period in which you encounter all the accumulated inner pressure, with the accompanying helplessness, inadequacy, and confusion, is the final result. It is the tunnel through which you must pass, my friends.

After you do so, your sense of strength, adequacy, and your own resourcefulness will grow steadily—with occasional relapses, of course—but if you make each relapse serve as a further stepping stone, further lesson, the new patterns will eventually establish themselves in your inner being and will make you see the possibilities you have overlooked for so long.

You will then have the courage to take these possibilities, instead of rejecting them in fear. Thus, and thus only, will the fulfillment come.

It is so important for you to understand this and deeply absorb it, my friends. If you do, it must help you.

My dearest friends, be blessed, each one of you. May these words be a further key and a help for your continued growth and liberation. May they help you to become yourself, to be in full possession of the individual you are, with all the resources, the strength, the ingenuity, the creativity and love force that is inherent in you, waiting to be allowed to function freely. Be in peace. Be in God.

ₐ

ATTACHMENT TO NEGATIVITY

*The individual who wishes to have an answer to
the problem of evil, as it is posed today, has need,
first and foremost, of self-knowledge; that is, the
utmost possible knowledge of his own wholeness.
He must know relentlessly how much good he can
do, and what crimes he is capable of, and must
beware of regarding the one as real and the other
as illusion. Both are elements within his nature,
and both are bound to come to light in him,
should he wish—as he ought—to live without self-
deception or self-delusion.*

C. G. Jung [1]

*There is no doubt that healthy-mindedness is
inadequate as a philosophical doctrine, because
the evil facts which it positively refuses to account
for are a genuine portion of reality; and they may
after all be the best key to life's significance, and
possibly the only openers of our eyes to the deepest
levels of truth.*

William James [2]

Part I of this book has set the stage—teaching us how to observe ourselves more closely, recognize the irrational and unhappy child that lives within each one of us, and see the masks, self-deceptions and pseudo-solutions that we have adopted in our attempts to get one-up on life.

Part II now zeroes in more closely on our personal evil as the source of all our unhappiness.

It is not easy to look at our own evil. To do so requires great courage, and also great compassion toward ourselves. You may be tempted, somewhere in the middle of this book, to put it down and not return to it. It took me a very long time to truly enter upon this path, and I remember the many times I threw down a lecture in dismay, creating for myself a reason not to believe it. I found that to look at my own flaws and shortcomings, in depth and at length, was not one of life's greatest pleasures.

It was hard for me to move from the theoretical to the personal and practical. I believed in the importance of loving all humankind; I even sometimes preached it; and yet I found in practice that I often was indifferent to the sufferings of others, was spiteful toward my friends, and at times was cruel even to my wife and to my children. What is more, I often overlooked this dissonance, and failed to see the contradiction between my stated beliefs and my actual behavior.

One of the reasons that I was tempted to remain in blindness is that I was seeking to avoid pain, emotional as well as physical, as we all do. How distressing then to discover that I had to be willing, if I truly sought the truth, to feel pains that I had successfully repressed for years!

And the reward for this work? First, discovering the joy that comes from living in truth, without a mask, without pretense. Second, discovering that through the gateway of feeling my pain comes a life of true pleasure, and of no longer holding back from life due to fear of feeling pain. And there are many further rewards beyond these; here is one of the Guide's descriptions:

"There is a state in which you can live without painful, tortured confusions, where you can function on a level of inner resilience, contentment and security; where you are capable of deep feelings and of blissful pleasure; where you are capable of meeting life as it is, without fear, and therefore capable of finding life, even its problems, to be a joyful challenge." [3]

Many spiritual paths teach that the way to deal with the large and small negativities that we all have is to rise above them, to transcend them. The idea seems to be that if we turn our attention always to the true, the good, and the beautiful, the lower self will wither away. The Pathwork states that the "rising above" method does not work; that it represents wishful thinking and denial, and leads to repression and subsequent unacknowledged acting-out. The Pathwork teaches that the lower self must be transformed, rather than transcended.

The lectures in Part II approach this issue from several different points of view. The Guide stresses the importance of finding the unconscious "no-current" that sabotages our conscious desires; describes the imbalances between the ego and the real self and how these need to be corrected; points out how numbing oneself to pain is a major cause of personal negativity; and how our having learned to attach the pleasure principle to negative occurrences perpetuates the lower self. None of these lectures, taken alone, adequately describes the functioning of the lower self; but all of them together should provide you with a powerful understanding of its nature, and with an impetus to transform it.

D. T.

1. C. G. Jung, *Memories, Dreams, Reflections*. Pantheon Books, 1973. p.330
2. William James, *The Varieties of Religious Experience*. Mentor, 1958. pp.137-138.
3. Pathwork lecture #204.

ॐ

FINDING THE UNCONSCIOUS "NO"

Greetings, my dearest friends. Blessings for every one of you. Blessed be this hour. May this lecture help you again discover more of yourself, to widen and raise your consciousness, to strengthen your grasp on reality.

The universe, up to a certain degree of development or awareness, consists of two primary currents: a yes-current and a no-current. The yes-current includes every constructive energy because it accords with truthful insight, which cannot help but breed love and unity. The no-current is destructive because it inadvertently deviates from truthfulness, thereby breeding hate and disunity. This general explanation applies to your individual daily life as well as to great concepts in the history of creation.

It is easy and absolutely feasible to detect the yes- and no-currents within yourself, in your daily lives, if you learn to understand and to interpret the language of your personal unconscious. To do so requires a certain technique, the same as in learning any new language.

The yes-current is often the more noticeable of the two because it is mostly conscious. Whenever you find yourself disturbed because of a persistent unfulfillment, you can be sure that both currents must be strongly at work, thus putting the brakes on. Consciously the yes-current is stronger and blots out the unconscious no-current. The more the latter is squelched with the erroneous idea that this eliminates it, the more it is driven underground, where it continues to do its work. And the more this happens, the more urgent and frantic the yes-current becomes. These currents pull the personality in two opposite directions, creating stronger and stronger tension and pressure. The way to eliminate this short circuit is to uncover the no-current, understand its faulty premises, and thereby gradually shed the belief in the necessity for its existence.

In those areas of your life where things go easily, where you appear to be lucky, where most of the time you are fulfilled without any problematic and confusing crises, you can be sure that there is very little no-current and the yes-current predominates without a contradictory hidden undercurrent. To put it differently: not only is yes current the surface attitude, but it is also the attitude of your entire being, undivided and in accord with reality. You are not split in motivation and in desire.

Change Through Detection of the No-Current

But in areas where you are repeatedly "unlucky," the no-current must be at work in one form or another. Of course, the reasons may vary with each individual, but the underlying causes have to be clearly defined in order to inactivate them. Most of you have begun to detect them at least in part.

Any goal you consciously desire and yet do not attain is proof that an undetected no-current is at work. It is not sufficient to have gained understanding of your images and misconceptions, nor how and why they came into existence in the particular circumstances of your childhood. Important work as that is, it is only one step. The only way change can come about is through detection of how the no-current continues to work, even prohibiting the very change so ardently striven for by the yes-current.

Let us assume you wish for a certain fulfillment in your life, a fulfillment you have lacked until now. You may have been aware of a strong desire for this fulfillment and in your pathwork you have discovered certain unconscious misconceptions, false guilts, and destructive attitudes that prohibit this fulfillment. You may even have discovered a fear of the very fulfillment you wish and consequently a subtle attitude of rejecting it. The fear may be based on an entirely illusory premise and therefore be unnecessary. It may be due to the childish desire of not wanting to pay the necessary price connected with the fulfillment. It may be a feeling of not deserving this happiness. It may be any number of further reasons, or a combination of all of them. Whatever they are, you have in essence discovered what stands in your way. You may experience this discovery as a one-time nucleus, as it were, like a package of disturbance. But it rarely occurs to my friends that this package continues to send forth its expressions in spite of having been detected. And this is the important part of the work, without which real liberation cannot be achieved.

In view of all this, it is necessary to renew your efforts in daily detection of the no-current at work. Its manifestations may be ever so subtle, diffuse, and almost too elusive to catch. But, if you set out to do so, what was once so hazy as to be almost impossible to formulate will become obvious. It will stand out in clear contour. You will discover how you slightly cringe at the thought of the fulfillment whenever it approaches reality. You may detect a vague feeling of familiar uneasiness which you used to push aside, when you thought about the fulfillment. Is it a feeling of fear or false guilt that you do not deserve it? Whatever it is, try to take these vague, hazy emotional impressions and question them in the daylight of consciousness. Examine the faraway fantasy when, apparently, only the yes-current is at work. In this fantasy do you wish for the impossible in that you do not take into consideration the human imperfections in all concerned? Or, do you subtly feel that life should furnish you with the ideal fulfillment without necessitating change, adjustment, and relinquishing on your part? This prevalent attitude may be extremely subtle and require all your discernment to discover it. When you do, you will have found a reason for the existence of the no-current.

When you become aware of the constantly working no-current, even before fully understanding its presence, you will find relief from hopelessness and the way out will be in sight. You will understand why your life has not changed in spite of extensive recognitions of images and childhood lessons. You will now detect the destructive feelings in the service of the no-current: fear, guilt, anger, frustration, hostility, etc. These feelings continue to smolder, but they may be artfully camouflaged, explained away by apparently real provocations, and "successfully" projected onto others. Discovering all these mechanisms is learning the language of the unconscious.

Let us now be more specific about the detection of a no-current. You may be sure it exists if frustration remains in your life in spite of having found relevant images. You may also be sure about its existence if you are desperate in your yes-current; if you fear that the fulfillment will never come; if you believe your life is dismal without it. After having thus determined that the no-current must exist, it is now a question of experiencing it—not just once, but whenever it is at work.

To become more acutely aware of its existence, the practice of the daily review, as you have learned, is immensely helpful and has to be applied in this direction. Observation and questioning of your emotional reactions must extend in width and depth on the path, instead of diminishing. If you progress in the right direction, you will now observe more, rather than less—contrary to the mistaken idea that there is less to see because of your improvement. Close scrutiny of your emotions is a number one prerequisite.

To observe productively what the unconscious expresses, it is important to separate the healthy part of yourself from the unhealthy, confused, involved part. This detached observation of something obscure and strange is the most healing procedure on the path of liberation. When your yes-current observes the no-current without frantic self-accusations, it becomes possible to translate the latter into concise human language. This concise formulation of previously vague feelings is invaluable, and I have often emphasized it in the early stages of this path.

Observing the Half-Conscious Thoughts

You are erroneously convinced that to understand what occurs in your unconscious means merely finding hitherto unknown elements. You do not have to wait for something faraway and completely hidden. First, observe those layers that are easily accessible when you focus your attention on them. These are the half-conscious thoughts, the vague and diffuse attitudes and expressions that are almost second nature and so easily overlooked because they have become a part of you. But none of the half-conscious feelings, reactions, and concepts are clearly formulated into concise thoughts. If you watch these half-conscious reactions in the problem areas of your life, you will learn all you need to know about yourself. This is a vital part of learning the language of your unconscious.

The half-conscious material comprises your immediate emotional reactions as well as your fantasy life. Comparison of both often demonstrates your discrepancies and contradictions, as well as your immature expectations.

The more clearly you see how you push away, or withdraw from, the very fulfillment you crave—as you see it again and again in action—the closer you come to eliminating the no-current. You weaken it merely by observing it.

It is essential that you pay more attention to the no-current in its exact form. A certain type of meditation can help. Become very quiet and relaxed and begin by observing your thinking process, and even your initial inability to do so. This eventually leads to keeping thoughts out for a short while and making yourself utterly empty. In the emptiness it is possible for hitherto checked and repressed material to surface, if you express this purpose and desire it strongly enough without shying away from the effort to reach the goal. Though difficult at the beginning, this effort will after a while establish a channel to a part of you that you could not previously tap. At first, you see the destructive elements floating up, and then you will be able to tap the constructive elements, hidden deeply within.

Your unconscious speaks steadily, my friends. It speaks without your hearing it, so you do not communicate with it and therefore miss a very important part of your work. So often you go on searching for an intellectual understanding of misconceptions, thereby overlooking the steady flow of the no-current, and how it works. This should become a task for you, with the main emphasis on your self-observations. If every day you devote a little time to this all-important issue, the results will be most wonderful.

(1) Ask yourself: What is my goal now? Where am I dissatisfied? What would I want to be different?

(2) How much do I want it?

(3) To what extent is there something in me that does not want it? Or fears it? Or, for one reason or another, says no to it?

(4) How can I detect the various forms and manifestations of the no-current in my daily life?

If you clearly formulate these four questions and begin truthfully to answer them, your work on the path will be most dynamic and your progress will astound and delight you.

Be blessed, all of you, in body, in soul, and in spirit. Be in peace, my dearest friends. Be in God.

ॐ

TRANSITION FROM THE NO-CURRENT TO THE YES-CURRENT

Greetings, my dearest friends. God bless every one of you. Blessed be this hour.

Many people believe that a positive attitude toward life means ignoring the negative in oneself, but nothing could be further from the truth. This is a misunderstanding of the processes of growth and development. It is impossible to adopt a truthful concept and to replace the old untruthful one unless one clearly understands why the old concept is untruthful. The real impetus to transform oneself can never come unless one sees the destructive nature of a false image and evaluates its effects on self and others. This alone will make you summon all your resources to bring about a change. Vague knowledge of the general principles of this process cannot suffice when you deal with a deeply imprinted no-current.

It is You Who Says No

When you discover specifically how you say No to a special desire or a cherished fulfillment, you reach a major transition in your entire development, in your outlook toward life. After such a discovery, you can never be the same. For the first time, you comprehend the fact that you do not have to depend on circumstances outside your control, that you are not a persecuted victim of an unfair and unkind fate, that you do not live in a chaotic world, where the law of the jungle seems the most appropriate. Such discoveries must lead away from the false concept of a punishing or rewarding deity up in the sky, and from the equally false idea that there is no order, no superior intelligence in the universe. When you discover that you say No to the very thing you desire most, you can no longer be insecure and frightened and hanging on to the misconception that you are unlucky and inferior. Suddenly the truth of divine order will come so near that you can grasp it—and this, indeed, is a wonderful experience, even if at first you may not be able to hold on to it. It means the extension of your grasp, the deepening of your understanding. You are becoming more acutely aware of the fact that all your unhappiness and unfulfillment is not a remote effect of a remote cause, even remote in yourself, but a very direct effect of a cause that is right in front of your eyes, if you choose to look at it. Of course it requires the training of becoming aware of hidden emotional reactions, of subtle, elusive, vaguely felt emotional movements. But once your mind is accustomed to observing these reactions, such awareness is not far away. The No that you, and you alone, can recognize is as distinct as any object in your outer environment you wish to grasp, touch and see.

Finding such a No must not be a superficial, glib acknowledgement. Allow yourself to feel the full impact and significance of it by first acknowledging that it exists at all, and then ascertaining why it exists, and on what specific misconceptions it is based. When this is perceived for the first time, hopelessness, defeatism will make room for genuine—not superimposed—hope, and a positive attitude toward life.

Before you gain a clear vision of the specific area of its operation, the no-current will act against the very endeavor of discovery and change. Some of my friends have already found that the moment they successfully fought and overcame their resistance against the work at a particular phase, they found a corresponding No toward a general life situation. While on a conscious level an urgent, frantic, hopeless Yes clamors, cries and trembles, the underlying No defeats all efforts and makes the entire process seem truly hopeless. The temptation to blind oneself to the true issue, to project and displace, increases. This often blurs one's memory of past victory; of the proper procedure of prayer, meditation, and daily review; of formulating confusions, unanswered questions, vague uneasy feelings in a concise way and tackling them as they barricade the way; of asking for help; of cultivating one's inner will to overcome all barriers toward seeing the truth about oneself and having the willingness to change; of registering the inner No during these endeavors; of tackling these No's in the only productive way, namely with the intent of wanting to see and understand the truth about the matter.

Opening oneself to the truth is a decisive step toward bringing the personality into the yes-current. Change, such as transformation of character structure, as well as of false imprints or images, is hardly possible as long as one does not understand why such a change is truly desirable. Therefore, the path can roughly be divided into two major phases: first, enlisting divine help for recognition of truth; second, enlisting this same agency for the strength, stamina, and ability to change. These two fundamental desires, being part of the great yes-current, must be cultivated in the details of daily living, reactions, thoughts, and feelings.

Some time ago, when we discussed the images, I also mentioned the soul substance which is the material that registers an individual's outlook on and attitudes to life. When these attitudes derive from a truthful impression and a constructive attitude prevails, the soul substance is molded in such a way that the person's life is meaningful, fulfilling and happy. When the impressions are based on wrong conclusions, the molds in the soul substance create unfavorable, destructive situations. In short, a man's and woman's fate is nothing more or less than the sum total of their personalities, what they express and emanate, which, in turn, determines how the soul substance is molded in terms of reality or unreality. Human consciousness is the sculptor, the soul substance the material which it molds. It is the entire personality, including all levels, which determines the fate. If a person has a healthy, constructive, realistic, truthful concept in some levels of the personality while other levels express the opposite, such a contradiction affects the soul substance negatively, even if the positive attitude is stronger and conscious, while the negative one remains hidden. It is therefore essential that the hidden areas of the soul substance be uncovered in order to understand, from seeing the imprints, why the desired fulfillment is still missing in life.

Only recently, and for the first time, have a number of my friends on the path discovered that in those hidden areas there existed a No which they never could have felt before. On the contrary, they were convinced that they wanted with all their being what remained unfulfilled, or that they certainly did not want an undesirable experience. The mere suggestion that there might be an unconscious contrary striving would have seemed preposterous to them.

Such No's are directly connected with the original image, with the false concept which molded the image into the soul substance. It is this basic misconception which makes one reject what one wants most, subtly acting in such a way that the image inevitably appears to be confirmed. For example, if you are under the basic misconception that you are inadequate and cannot succeed, this conviction will make you behave in such a way that you will indeed act inadequately. What is more, you will fear success, because your conviction of not being able to live up to it will make it frightening. Once you find this particular No, as well as your resultant behavior, your both obvious and subtle expressions in this area, you come to understand that you lack success not because you are inadequate, but you are inadequate because you think you are and fear any event that might put it to the test.

Changing from a deeply engraved no-current to a yes-current can occur only when this entire process is profoundly understood; when the subtle shrinking away from a desirable goal is observed and finally changed into, "I want this goal with all my heart. I have nothing to fear from it." Meditation on why there is nothing to fear, why the old fear was false, and why the new accepting attitude to the life experience is entirely safe, is the final step in moving from a no-current to a yes-current. This should be done as daily meditation work, creating a new mold in the soul substance—this time a flexible, light, truthful one which finally erases the old, rigid, heavy, untruthful one.

Compare the Positive to the Negative

On this path, you have learned to review your life in the light of progress already made, and to determine not only in what respect you have outgrown old obstructions, but also what remains to be accomplished. When you examine still unfulfilled areas of your life, looking for the underlying no-current, it is also helpful to compare these areas with the aspects of your life in which you are fulfilled. Then consider the underlying yes-current: the subtle but distinct expression of certainty that this good thing is yours, will always easily be yours, that it does not present a difficulty and does not induce fear that you may lose it. It might be wise to also investigate the areas in which you feel deserving, where you are willing to pay the price, to give, and then realize that, actually, your attitudes in those healthy areas vastly differ from your feelings and expectations in the unfulfilled areas. Making such a comparison is a useful endeavor which will yield much understanding. Feel distinctly the difference between your approach, emotions, and subtle expressions in your healthy, fulfilled, happy life situations and those in which you consistently find a frustrating, unhappy pattern.

You cannot possibly come out of the no-current as long as you cling to the conviction that you have nothing to do with your problem, that you are helpless to change your predicament. But when you realize that the final decisive factor is you—your will and your determination—then the end of your suffering is near. Say, "I want to come out of it. In order to do so, I want to know specifically what obstructs the way at this moment. I know that the constructive universal forces help and guide me the moment I decide to do something about it. I will be ready to see what comes up." Continue your activities in this direction, and what had seemed impossible will suddenly become feasible. Relaxed meditation, concentration, and a minimum of daily self-observation cannot possibly be dispensed with. They are the tools; learning to use them in the appropriate way is part of your growing process.

I have often mentioned that nothing in itself is right or wrong, healthy or unhealthy, constructive or destructive. It is the same with feeling, experiencing, and expressing the attitude of "I want to," regarding a particular fulfillment. The mere fact of its existence is no guarantee that your wanting it is a yes-current. Apart from the opposite desire on an unconscious level, such a "yes" may come out of greed and fear, of too much wanting, and greed and fear are products of the no-current. If there was no hidden no-current, there would be no doubt that you could have it, therefore there would be no fear that you could not have it. You need not be greedy, for if you are in truth and in harmony with the cosmic forces, the yes-current will function as a natural and easy and calm flow within you. You can issue the "I want" into the yes-current with a fullness and wholeness which is devoid of anxiety, doubt, and greed.

Yes or no, "I want to" or "I do not want to," can only be determined as expressions of the yes- or no-current if these wishes are closely observed, if one listens to any harsh or disturbing emotion contained in them.

I have often mentioned that *contact with the divine spark, or your real self, is an outcome of this pathwork.* Some of my friends are beginning to experience this indescribable event. The safety, security, conviction of truth, the harmony and rightness of it are worth all the effort of overcoming resistance. It alone can truly guide you. But the ego-mind so often stands in the way. It believes that it alone exists and determines. But now it must decide to let the greater mind determine your life. Let the innermost self, the greater intelligence within you, answer your confusions and guide you to the truth you need to know about yourself. Let it strengthen you to change your false images, and help you to swing from the no-current into the yes-current, with its promise which will be inevitably fulfilled.

Talking Out the Problem

An additional source of help is the method of talking things out. This has proven to be true before in other phases of the work and it is of equal importance in this phase. Talking out what you want, what your obstruction is, the extent of it, and the reason for the no-current observed has a therapeutic value beyond your present comprehension. As you talk to another person, things will take shape and gain a clarity that you missed as long as you merely thought about them, or even wrote them down. Also, the insight an uninvolved outsider may gain and point out to you is often impossible to attain by yourself alone because you are too deeply involved. In talking out the problem, a pressure is relieved which sets valuable energy free, and a new perspective is gained. Something begins to change inside before you even know it. Something is set in motion when you a) deliberately tap your divine self for answers and guidance, and b) when you "talk out" the pressure area. The effect of these two important activities will be experienced by anyone who follows this advice.

For the yes-current to express itself in any area of your life and personality, your entire being must be of one piece, a wholeness. Your consciousness cannot be divided, with different levels expressing different goals, opinions, concepts, and emotions. The yes-current cannot manifest by talking yourself into it. Many systems and approaches try to forcibly superimpose the yes-current on the consciousness. People are then misled into a temporary hopefulness, into temporary success, which cannot be real and permanent unless all levels of your being are filled with one expression and there is no area left that nurtures doubts and fears, and that fails to know and express the truth. Nor can this happen unless some parts of the character structure are truly transformed—"reborn," as Jesus said.

When you reach this state of oneness with yourself, with your innermost divine self, in the flow and harmony of the yes-current, you have nothing to fear. You stand on firm ground.

Nothing stands in the way of a full, fulfilled, rich life. These are not empty promises. All the tools you need are given to you, but you and you alone must use them. Those of you who steadfastly make progress, fighting against the No within, doing the work day in and day out, register the growing conviction that you are slowly stepping out of confinement and darkness into the freedom and light of truth. Anyone who claims that he has done his best but has not succeeded is not in truth. He is suffering from self-delusion. He or she may make good efforts in areas of lesser importance, but refuses to see the truth where it hurts most, where the person still misses liberation.

Are there any questions, now?

QUESTION: I feel that I have the no-current inward and outward; everything is No. Can you help me understand why?

ANSWER: Yes, and I can also help you to come out of it. This is the reason: You fear that if you do not say No, a specific inadequacy and shame would have to be tackled. It is, of course, no real inadequacy or real shame, but you unconsciously think so. The No seems to eliminate the necessity of looking closer. You may not be able to feel this yet, but you will if you proceed with your pathwork. Once you do, it will become easier to tackle the inner enemy—the No.

As for immediate advice on how to proceed: Take any of the

many little No's coming up in your work in your daily life and enter into your private meditation, all alone, peaceful and relaxed. Such meditation might be somewhat like this, but use your own words: "Why do I say No? I have the power not to say No. And I now say Yes to really and truly wanting to find out my particular No's." Take one at a time. "With all my heart I say Yes to wanting to understand the No." First you will feel a strong negative pull against it, but, expecting it, you are prepared and do not allow it to dissuade you. You go on saying, "The truth cannot harm me, although something ignorant in me rebels against it. In spite of it, I say Yes. It has no power over the way I direct my will and my endeavors. This very same No has brought me much destructiveness and misery, and I do not allow it to rule over me any longer. I take the reins in my hands." Do this daily for a while and open yourself up to what comes.

If you meditate in such a way, enlisting the divine forces inside your being, you will indeed experience a great transformation. The first time will be difficult, but if you persevere it will become easier and yield more and more results. And, I beg of you, choose to remember the many times on this path you were in a fierce and fearful No, but after you overcame it, the relief and release, the renewed energy, the increased understanding and health, and also the knowledge and certainty that what you had feared before was entirely groundless, all that was in proportion to the fear and resistance that you harbored. Make use of the considerable progress already made, rather than letting yourself slide into inertia again. Then you will yet experience the greatest victory and liberation so far! When you follow this advice, you will truly make the transformation from a downward curve, from the no-current, to a building up, to the upward life- giving stream, to the yes-current.

My dearest friends, you are all blessed. May these words be more than words, may they remain not theory, but may they become the tools they are meant to be. Thus you will finally allow yourself to be happy, you will no longer cringe from fulfillment. Be in peace. Be in God!

ठ▲

THE FUNCTION OF THE EGO
IN RELATION TO
THE REAL SELF

Greetings, my dearest friends. Blessings and guidance are extended so that each and every one of you finds your path easier and reaches the goal with less struggle and resistance.

What is the goal? The goal, as far as you are concerned, can be only one thing: becoming your real self.

First I wish to discuss how the inner self differs from the outer self, or the real self from the ego. What is their relationship to each other? There are many confusing theories about the function of the ego. According to some the ego is essentially negative and undesirable and the spiritual goal is to get rid of it. Other theories, particularly those that characterize psychoanalytic thinking, say that the ego is important, that where there is no ego there can be no mental health. These are two entirely opposing views. Which one is correct? Which one is false?

Let us briefly recapitulate the essence of the real self. Your inner self is an integral part of nature, bound to the laws of nature. Therefore to distrust this innermost self is unreasonable, for nature can be wholly trusted. If nature seems like an enemy to you, it is only because you do not understand its laws. The inner self, or the real self, is nature; it is life; it is creation. It is more accurate to define the real self this way than to say it is "a part" of nature. The real self and nature are one and the same.

Whenever you function from your real self you are in truth, you are joyful. The most creative and constructive contributions to life come from your inner self. Everything that is great and generous, everything that is life-expanding, beautiful, and wise comes from the inner or real self.

The Need for a Strong Ego

If this is so, what then is the function of the ego, meaning by this word the outer level of personality? The ego level is more accessible to you and you are more acutely and more directly aware of it. The ego is the part that thinks, acts, discriminates, and decides. The person whose ego has not sufficiently grown, whose ego is weak, is incapable of mastering or coping with life. And the person whose ego is overgrown and overemphasized cannot come to the real self. In other words, both extremes of the ego's weakness and its inflation must hinder the reaching of the real self.

Only when the ego is sufficiently developed can it be adequately dispensed with. Now, this may sound like a contradiction, my friends, but it is not. For if the ego is underdeveloped, your efforts to compensate create a weakness and evasion that can produce only more weakness. As long as the ego is not strong enough, you lack the faculties characteristic of your outer self, which are to think, discriminate, decide, and act appropriately in any situation you encounter in the outer world.

Anyone who strives to reach the real self by rejecting the development of a healthy ego, does so out of poverty. Such people do not yet own their outer self. This may be due to laziness since ego development is so difficult, and they hope that this vital step can simply be avoided. But this error, like all errors, is costly. It actually delays reaching the goal. Only when you are fully possessed of your outer self, your ego, can you dispense with it and reach your real self.

Only when the ego is healthy and strong can you know that it is not the final answer, the final realm of being. Only when you possess a strong and healthy ego that is not overgrown and overemphasized, can you use this ego to transcend itself and reach a further state of consciousness.

In your work on this path you learn through your meditations to use all the faculties of your ego to reach beyond it. What you absorb from outside must first pass your ego faculties. In practical terms: you first reach out with your ego faculties and use them to grasp truths that you later experience on a deeper level of consciousness.

Reaching Beyond the Ego

There are many human beings who do not realize that there is anything beyond the ego. Their final goal is to cultivate a strong ego, whether or not they think about it in these terms. This striving may lead them to the distortion of an over-developed ego. It is a dead-end street: instead of transcending the stage of the powerful ego, one's energies are used to further aggrandize it.

The law that *you have to reach a certain state and fully be there before you can abandon it for a higher state* is extremely important to understand, my friends. Humans often overlook it and, even more often, totally ignore it. The importance of this law has not been clear enough to humanity, in spite of the discovery of many spiritual and psychological truths.

In a variant form, the essence of this very law can be seen in the topic under discussion: the function of the ego in relation to the real self. The real self knows that the universe has no limitations; that in truth absolute perfection does exist, attainable for each individual; that unlimited expansion of faculties and forces, in the universe as well as in the individual, makes this perfection possible.

The little child at birth does not yet possess an ego. Without the ego, it is possible to perceive this message from the real self quite clearly. But without the ego, the meaning of the message must be distorted. Perhaps you have found and experienced within yourself the childish striving for perfection, for omnipotence, for pleasure supreme, the ultimate bliss that knows no lack, no unfulfillment or frustration.

When there is no ego, these strivings are unrealistic, even destructive. Some of you have experienced in your pathwork that you first have to shed these desires or strivings before you can come to them anew and realize them.

In other words, every one of you who is on this path has to accept your limitations as a human being before you can realize that you have an unlimited fount of power at your disposal. You all have to accept your own imperfections, as well as this life's imperfections, before you can experience that absolute perfection that you will ultimately realize is your destiny. But you can comprehend this only after you have shed the childish distortion of this knowledge. Only when your ego deals adequately with the realm in which your personality and your body now live can you then deeply comprehend your real faculties, possibilities, and potential.

When I speak of the ultimate aim of perfection, of limitless power, of pleasure supreme, I do not mean that this realization will occur in a distant future when you no longer possess a body. I do not speak of this state in terms of time, but in terms of quality; it could happen at any moment, at the moment when you awaken to truth. Awakening to truth is possible only when you have first found and then let go of the childish distortions of utter perfection, utter power, and utter pleasure. In the underdeveloped ego, these desires are not only illusory but selfish and destructive. They have to be abandoned before they can be attained.

My dearest friends, this lecture is of very great importance to all of you. It may not only dispel the confusion about apparent contradictions in philosophical ideas about life, but, even more important, it may provide an essential key to your own development. It may facilitate a letting go that can happen only when you trust your innermost self as an integral part of nature and creation.

When you feel and experience your real self, you will not overemphasize your ego faculties. Nor will you leave important underdeveloped ego faculties to slumber untended.

All blessings are extended to every one of you. These blessings are a reality that envelop you. They are the universal love, responding to your valiant efforts of self-expansion. Be in peace, be in God.

CHAPTER 14

WHAT IS EVIL?

Greetings, my dearest friends. May this lecture prove helpful, and thus a blessing. May these words shed light and clarification into your search for liberation.

Most Western religions take a dualistic approach to the great question of evil; they say that evil is a separate force from good. According to this idea, people have to cope with making the decision between good and evil. The religious point of view recognizes the danger of evil, its life-defeating power, and the unhappiness and suffering it brings. On the other hand, there are also philosophies which state that evil does not exist, that it is an illusion. Both of these opposing teachings express great truths, but the exclusiveness with which they state them ultimately renders their truth untrue. In fact, to deny the existence of evil is exactly as untrue as it is to believe that two separate forces of good and evil exist. You must struggle between these two alternatives to find the true answer. This lecture will help you in this endeavor.

Evil as Numbness

Evil is, or results from, numbness in the soul. Why is evil numbness? When you think of the defense mechanisms operating in the human psyche, the connection between numbness and evil becomes quite clear. Children who feel hurt, rejected, and helplessly exposed to pain and deprivation often find that numbing their feelings is their only protection against suffering. This is often a useful and quite realistic protective device.

Likewise, when children are confused because they perceive contradiction and conflict around them, equally contradictory emotions arise in their own psyche. Children cannot cope with either. Numbness is also a protection against their own contradictory responses, impulses, and reactions. Under such circumstances, it might even be a salvation. But when such numbness has become second nature and is maintained long after the painful circumstances have changed and when the person is no longer a helpless child, this, in the smallest measure, is the beginning of evil.

Numbness and insensitivity toward one's own pain in turn means equal numbness and insensitivity toward others. When examining one's reactions closely, one might often observe that the first spontaneous reaction to others is a feeling for and with them, a compassion or empathy, a participation of the soul. But the second reaction restricts this emotional flow. Something clicks inside and seems to say no, which means that a protective layer of unfeelingness has formed. In that moment one stands separate—apparently safe but separate. Later the separateness may be overcompensated for by a false sentimentality, dramatization, and insincere exaggerated sympathy. But these are only substitutes for the numbness. The numbness, instituted for oneself, inevitably spreads to others, just as every attitude adopted toward the self is bound to expand toward others.

We might differentiate between three stages of numbness. First, *numbness toward the self*, as a protective mechanism. Second is the *numbness toward others*. In this stage, it is a passive attitude of indifference that enables one to watch others suffer without feeling discomfort oneself. Much of the world's evil is caused by this state of soul. Just because it is less crass, in the long run it is more harmful, for active cruelty induces quicker counter-reactions. Passive indifference, however, born out of numbing the feelings, can go unnoticed because it can so easily be camouflaged. It permits the person to follow the most selfish impulses without open detection. Indifference may not be as actively evil as cruelty acted out, but it is just as harmful in the long run.

Cruelty

The third stage of numbness is *actively inflicted cruelty*. This stage arises from fear of others who seem to expect such acts, or from an inability to cope with pent-up rages, or from a subtle process of strengthening the protective device of numbness. At first, this may appear incomprehensible. But when you think about it deeply, you will find that people may occasionally, almost consciously, find themselves on the brink of a decision: "Either I allow my feelings to reach out in empathy with the other, or, in order to deflect this strong influx of warm feelings, I have to behave in the exact opposite way." The next moment such reasoning is gone, the conscious decision forgotten, and what remains is a compelling force toward cruel acts.

In all these instances, it can be seen, again and again, how all harm, all destructiveness, all evil, results from the denial of the spontaneous real self, and the substitution of secondary reactions which, in one way or another, are always connected with fear.

The borderline between passive numbness and active cruelty is often very thin and precarious, very much dependent upon apparently outer circumstances. If people understand these processes not only intellectually but within themselves, they are adequately equipped to cope with the world's cruelty, which so often gives rise to despair, doubt, and confusion.

Active cruelty numbs the person who perpetrates it to an even greater extent; it not only prohibits the influx of spontaneous positive feelings but also wards off fear and guilt.

The act of inflicting pain on others simultaneously kills off one's own ability to feel. Hence, it is a stronger device used to attain numbness.

You must always distinguish between the *active deeds* of either indifference or cruelty, and *emotional tendencies*. The indifference or numbness may not be actively executed; it is possible to experience this nonparticipation and numbness but not act upon it. You may do all you can to help another, perhaps sometimes even overdo it, just because you do not wish, on the conscious level, to be so indifferent. The desire to hurt others may exist merely as an emotion, without ever being acted upon. However, when you feel guilt, you do not differentiate between these vital manifestations, so it makes no difference whether you feel or act in destructive, harmful ways. Hence, the entire trouble area is denied, pushed out of consciousness, where it can no longer be corrected. Admitting, acknowledging, facing an emotion, no matter how undesirable, can never harm the self or others and is eventually bound to dissolve the negative feeling. Confusing the impulse with the deed and therefore denying both, results in extreme disturbance for the self, indirectly affecting others, with no hope of change as long as the process remains unconscious.

Seen in this light, it will be clear that numbness in its extreme becomes active cruelty. The difference between these two is only in degree. It is exceedingly important for you to understand this, my friends. For those who are most shocked, afraid of, and unable to cope with the existing cruelty in the world, and suffer most by the mere knowledge that it exists, have inevitably made themselves numb in some way and consequently suffer from guilt. Therefore a correlation must exist between one's numbness and one's approach or attitude toward the evil aspects of life. Some may be overly burdened, some may be overly sentimental, still others may be overly tough and indifferent to the existence of evil. Any such overreaction must be connected with the numbness that, in some respect, has been instituted in the psyche. At one time this numbness seemed like the only available protection; later it was unwittingly maintained.

Attachment of the Life Force to Negative Situations

The question is often asked why destructiveness, illness, war and cruelty exist. The answers that have been given are often not sufficiently understood, but even when they are somewhat understood, something is missing. I think most of my friends are now ready to understand this on a deeper level. I have often said that misconceptions create strife, and this is perfectly true. But there exists an additional element without which no misconception, regardless of how off the mark, could have power. It is this: Mere negativity, as in a destructive attitude, has a much less destructive effect than *destructiveness attached to and combined with the positive life principle*. This is what makes manifestations on this earth plane particularly serious or severe. In other words, when a positive force mingles with a negativity or a destructive attitude, the combination creates evil. Real destructiveness is, therefore, not only a distortion of truth and of the constructive universal powers, but a distortion that must be permeated with the powerful life principle and its constructive power. If the positive life principle were not involved and inadvertently used, then evil, or destructiveness, would be of very short duration.

The best way that you can apply what I say here and derive more from this lecture than a vague, abstract principle, is by looking at yourself from the following point of view: All of you who are on this path have found certain hurts and pains you endured as a child. Some of you have begun to grasp, if ever so slightly, that at the moment when you were hurt a specific process took place. The erotic, or pleasure, principle, was put in the service of your hurt, your suffering, your pain. All the emotions arising from this original hurt, according to character and temperament, also combine with the pleasure principle.

This attachment creates all the personal difficulties, all the unwelcome circumstances.

All the many souls inhabiting this earth, added together, create the general strife of humankind. When you realize how many people, regardless of their outer action, can experience the pleasure principle only in fantasies of cruelty, you will understand that this is the actual nucleus of war—of cruelty as a whole. This should not make you feel guilty. It should rather enlighten you and free you, to allow your inner processes to transform. For it is a misapplied and misunderstood hurt that has created this condition. Cruelty without the pleasure principle could never have real power. Lack of awareness of this combination of cruelty and pleasure by no means alleviates the effect it has on the overall climate of humanity's emanation.

The Persistence of Evil: Pleasure Connected to Cruelty

If you have experienced cruelty, your pleasure principle is attached to cruelty and functions somewhat in connection with cruelty. Often the guilt and shame of this are so strong that the entire fantasy life is denied, but sometimes it is conscious. Awareness of this must be established and understood from an overall point of view, for if it is truly understood, both guilt and shame will be removed. As understanding grows, the pleasure principle will gradually respond to positive events.

The combination of the pleasure principle and cruelty can exist either actively or passively. That is, pleasure is experienced either in inflicting cruelty or in enduring it—or both. Attaching the pleasure principle to a condition where it functions most strongly in conjunction with cruelty, creates a holding back from love, limits it, and makes the actual experience of love impossible. Love exists only as a vague yearning that cannot be maintained or followed through. Under these circumstances love is not the tempting, pleasurable experience it may be to another part of the personality. The yearning for the pleasure of love and the ignorance about the fact that one rejects its actual experience because one fears the attachment of the pleasure principle to negativity often creates a deep hopelessness. The hopelessness can be understood and instantly relieved only when this particular fact is profoundly comprehended.

In less obvious cases, when the child experiences not so much outright cruelty, but vague rejection or nonacceptance, the pleasure principle will attach itself to a similar situation, so that in spite of the conscious desire for acceptance, the pleasure current will only be activated in conjunction with rejection. There are many degrees and variations of this. There are, for example, situations where a child experiences partial acceptance and partial rejection. Then the pleasure principle is attached to an exactly similar ambivalence. This, then, creates a conflict in actual relationships.

The first instance, of attaching cruelty to the pleasure principle, will make a relationship so hazardous that it is often avoided altogether. Or you find it so frightening that you are puzzled. You then feel incapable of following through with it. Or, you are inhibited because the shame of the desire for either inflicting or enduring cruelty may prohibit all spontaneity and make you withdraw from and numb all feelings.

My dearest friends, this is a tremendously important principle to understand. It applies to humanity as a whole as well as to the individual. Generally, it has not been sufficiently understood because psychology and spiritual science have not merged sufficiently. Vague attempts have been made by psychology to grasp this factor, and it has been understood in some measure, but the vast significance in terms of civilization and its fate, or its evolution, is not understood. The world is now ready to understand this fact of life.

Evolution means that each individual, through the process of personal self-confrontation and self-realization, gradually changes the inner orientation of the pleasure principle. In their spontaneous reaction, more and more individuals will respond to positive events, situations, conditions.

You all know that such inner change cannot be willed directly. The direct expression of your outer will can and must go in the direction of maintaining and sustaining a pathwork such as this, which increases the ability to understand and cultivate the will and the courage to look at the self to find and overcome resistance. And as you do this, as you use your will and your ego faculties in this constructive manner, the real change happens, as some of you begin to experience, almost as though it had nothing to do with these efforts, as if it were a byproduct, an unconnected unfoldment. That is the real thing! This is the way progress and growth must happen.

Gradually, through this process of growth, one individual after another reorients the soul movements, the soul forces. The expression of the cosmic movement within the psyche will then attach itself to purely positive conditions and circumstances. Positive or pleasurable feelings will no longer be derived from negative circumstances. You are now used to the latter, hence you repress the combination of pleasurable feelings and negative events.

Instead of repressing it, denying it, looking away from it, you must face it. As you face it and understand it, without guilt or shame, you must learn in the course of growing that all imperfection must be accepted and understood before it can be changed. So, to the extent that you succeed in facing and understanding your conflict, the pleasure principle will run in different channels. As this happens, mobility will exist without tension and anxiety, and relaxation will exist without stagnation.

All of you, my friends, try to find your specific inner "marriage" between the pleasure current and a negative condition. As you find this marriage within your own soul forces, in specific terms, you will know and perfectly understand certain outer manifestations of your problems. The relief of thorough understanding can come about only when you have the courage to face this marriage. As you become capable of clearly and concisely formulating how the positive and negative forces are combined in your specific case, you will clearly see the exact image of your unfulfillment. You will see why you keep yourself hidden from yourself and from life; why you withdraw from your own feelings; why you repress and why you stand guard over the most spontaneous and creative forces within yourself. You will see why you block out feelings, sometimes with a great amount of pain, then try to rationalize and explain them away.

Make attempts to find the two factors I have discussed:

First, discover how you have numbed yourself; find the areas in which you have developed an insensitivity to your own pain. Stay alert when interacting with others, and look for times when you will have an immediate, momentary feeling of compassion or empathy, and then quickly shut this off and become separate and unfeeling.

Second, discover in what respect the life and pleasure principle is attached to a negative condition. To what extent does this manifest—perhaps only in your fantasies—and how does this hold you back from self-expression, from union, from experience, from a fearless state of self-realization with a kindred spirit?

Now, are there any questions in connection with this topic?

QUESTION: I would like to understand a little more concretely about this marriage between the forces of love and cruelty. For instance, in the case of children who feel rejected by their mother, does this marriage mean that the person cannot experience pleasure without also experiencing revenge—some kind of sadistic wish toward the mother? This happens perhaps only in fantasy, never in reality, and then the person is usually unaware that the partner represents the mother?

ANSWER: Yes, it might be exactly that. Or it might also be that pleasure can be experienced only in connection with being rejected again, or a little rejected, or being fearful that rejection may occur.

QUESTION: But they didn't experience pleasure when they were rejected.

ANSWER: Of course not. But the child uses the pleasure principle to make the negative event, the suffering, more bearable. This happens unconsciously, unintentionally, and almost automatically. Inadvertently, as it were, the pleasure principle combines with the negative condition. The only way this can be determined is by investigation of one's fantasy life. It is that way that the marriage is established. The automatic reflexes are then geared to a situation that combines the inherent pleasure current with the painful event.

QUESTION: And the child wishes to reproduce this rejection?

ANSWER: Not consciously, of course. No one really wants to be rejected. The trouble is that people consciously wish to be accepted and loved, but unconsciously, they cannot respond to a completely accepting and favorable situation. In such cases the pleasure principle has already been led into the negative channel and can be rechanneled only through awareness and understanding. The very nature of this conflict is that the pleasure principle functions the way people consciously want least of all. It cannot be said that a person unconsciously desires rejection, but the reflex was already established at a time when this way of functioning made life more bearable for the child. Do you understand that?

QUESTION: I don't quite understand how pleasure can be experienced at all when someone is rejected, except in the form of revenge. That I can understand.

ANSWER: Perhaps you can imagine also—one sees this over and over again—that when people feel too secure in being accepted and loved, they lose the spark of interest. This, too, is rationalized by claiming it to be an inevitable law, happening through habit, or other circumstances. But it would not have to be that way if it were not for the factors discussed in this lecture. The spark, the interest, the dynamic flow exists only when there is an unsure or an unhappy situation. You see this frequently. Sometimes the negative condition manifests only in fantasies. These fantasies are, when closely examined, in one way or another, attached to suffering, humiliation, or hostility. This is then called masochism or sadism. Do you understand now?

QUESTION: Yes, I think I do.

ANSWER: There is no doubt, my dearest ones, that everyone of you, who truly wishes, will find more and more the beauty, the peace, dynamic life, inner security, that exist in the self-realization you have begun to cultivate. Hence you experience moments of living in the eternal now of yourself, instead of striving away from it. Each now must bring you answers. If you recall this simple fact in your meditations, in your approach to yourself, your meditations will become more fruitful as you go on. What you have to look forward to in the time to come will be even more liberating than what you have already begun to experience.

Be blessed, be in peace, be in God.

&

THE CONFLICT OF POSITIVE AND NEGATIVE PLEASURE AS THE ORIGIN OF PAIN

Greetings, my dearest friends. Blessings, again, for each and every one of you, for every step, for every effort you undertake on your road to liberation.

As a preface to this lecture, I should like to discuss the meaning of pain and its real cause. Pain is the result of conflict. It occurs when two opposite directions co-exist in a personality. The direction of the universal creative forces is toward light, life, growth, unfoldment, affirmation, beauty, love, inclusion, union, pleasure supreme. Whenever this direction is counteracted by another, a disturbance is created. It is not the disturbance itself that creates the pain, but the imbalance and a special sort of tension caused by the opposite direction. This is what causes the suffering.

Life and Anti-Life

The principle I explain here holds true on all levels. It is indeed ascertainable on the physical level. The physical system, like all other systems or planes, also strives toward wholeness and health. When a disturbing force pulls in an opposite direction, the pull of the two directions creates the pain.

When the disturbance is fought against ineffectively, and the personality wants health, it negates that it also wants non-health. Since the striving for non-health is repressed and ignored, the struggle toward health becomes all the more tense. That is the origin of pain. If the personality were conscious of wanting non-health as well as health, the struggle would cease instantly, for the former wish cannot be maintained; only the latter can. It is the unconsciousness that creates a gap between cause and effect. The cause is the negative wish; the effect is the disturbance in the system. The two pulls continue, and pain comes into being.

But when this process is fully understood, and the temporary, still unavoidable consequences of the negative wish are accepted, one can let oneself go into this now existing pain, and the pain must cease. This is not a destructive way of embracing pain, or a masochistic, self-punishing element that in itself harbors and perpetuates a negative wish. It is a full acceptance of what is—and with that, pain ceases. It is the principle, for instance, of painless birth. It is the principle of non-struggle. It is the principle that Jesus Christ explained when he said, "resist not evil."

On the mental and emotional planes, something similar exists. When the struggle is fully understood and accepted as a temporary manifestation, as an effect—accepted as such without finality, and yet with awareness of the rightness of these consequences—the mental or emotional pain ceases. This does not happen when the negative is wanted, for as we have seen, this wanting merely creates the new direction, contrary to the original, positive one. Nor does this happen by forfeiting the affirmative principle, but by understanding the now. Then mental and emotional pain cease, just as physical pain ceases when the opposite pull is abandoned. All this is verifiable and has been verified the world over. All of you who are on a path of self-realization have, at least occasionally, experienced this.

On the spiritual plane, my friends, it is different. For the spiritual plane is the cause, while all other planes or spheres of consciousness are effects. The spiritual plane is the origin of the positive direction. It does not, and cannot, contain a negative direction. The negative direction creates, and is created by, various attitudes incompatible with the origin of all life. The spiritual plane is unity itself, therefore conflict, opposing directions and, consequently, pain are unthinkable and illogical there.

It is very important to understand, my friends, that the negative can be desired only by one part of the personality, never by the whole of it. There will always be another part of the psyche that violently objects to the negative desire, so that pain must result. On the physical as well as the emotional and mental levels, it is possible temporarily to accept the negative as a passing stage, in the understanding that it is the effect of an inadvertent cause and a mere momentary disturbance. In this understanding and acceptance one ceases the struggle. One accepts the negative without finality and with an objective, non-indulgent attitude.

Pain and suffering are always the result of the pull on the personality by two tendencies which are the life and the anti-life directions. They can also be called the love/hate and the positive and negative directions. The outer layers of personality must suffer as long as unity is not achieved. Unity exists exclusively in the full reality of the cosmic creative principle. It is exceedingly important, my friends, to understand what I am saying here, for this understanding must open new doors.

Desire for the Negative

It makes all the difference to be or not to be aware of one's negative desires. There are, of course, degrees of awareness. It is possible to be aware of them casually and fleetingly, or to have gained one important insight into their existence but to dilute this awareness. The more you are aware of a deliberate desire for the negative, the more you will be in control of yourself, of life, and the less you will feel victimized, helpless, and weak.

When an entity is not aware of its deliberate desire for the negative, the suffering must be infinitely greater than any suffering or pain that can ensue when one is aware of having wanted it oneself. Lack of such awareness must create a psychic climate in which the individual feels singled out as a victim. Separation between cause and effect in one's consciousness must create confusion, doubt, and hopelessness. The moment awareness of the negative desire has been attained, you at least know, what causes your outer difficulties and unwelcome situations. Even before you are capable of giving up the negative desires, because you do not yet understand the reason for their existence, merely knowing that you have created the undesirable manifestations in your life will render you a freer person.

Those of you who have made these initial inroads to awareness of your negative desires must be careful to extend this awareness and to link it with the unwelcome manifestations in your life. This essential step must not be overlooked. For it is indeed possible to be aware, to some extent at least, of a negative desire and nevertheless ignore that the negative desire is the immediate cause of any number of manifestations in your life that you strenuously struggle against. And that is exactly your pain. You struggle against something that you have yourself induced, and continue to induce, while, at the same time, there must always be the pull toward the light, toward wholeness, toward loving, inclusion and constructiveness, toward beauty and unfoldment. Your denial of the direction toward wholeness and your oblivion of this denial—not knowing that you want two opposing things at the same time—confuses and pains you.

Those of you who have recognized your negative desires have gained new strength and new hope. For then you see, at first as a principle and as a possibility, how your life can be when you no longer have the negative desires, even though you do not yet know why you harbor them in the first place. But merely knowing that you have them and, subsequently, connecting them with the unwelcome results must give you new hope and a new outlook.

Those friends who have not yet gained this awareness should try their very best to find their negative desires. On the surface, the majority of people cannot imagine how they might harbor destructive desires. Meditate and truly want to find what is in you. To do this is even more difficult when a person busily denies those aspects in life that leave something to be desired, and does not want to face missing something, suffering from something. This kind of denial of what you really feel and miss makes it impossible ever to bring real fulfillment into your life.

So ask yourself, "Do I experience everything to the maximum of my potential? What disturbs me possibly more than I admit?" That would be the first pertinent question for those whose tendency is to escape from their unfulfillments, to deny them, to gloss over them, and falsify their situation. And then, of course, there are those who are only too keenly aware of their suffering and of what they miss, but they are disconnected from the inner mechanism that wishes the negative result.

The work on this path continues with becoming aware of deliberate negative desires, or of the avoidance of positive results, which amounts to the same thing. It is, as you can see, an essential milestone on your whole road of evolution. It constitutes the difference between feeling like a helpless straw in the wind, and feeling one's self to be self-governing, autonomous. The principle of cycles or circles—whether benign or vicious—is always the principle of self-perpetuation. Autonomy is positively self-perpetuating, set in motion by reality consciousness.

Self-Perpetuating Cycles

When you come to a certain degree of insight into your psyche, you see how both the positive and negative attitudes are self-perpetuating. Take, for example, any healthy attitude. When you are outgoing, constructive, open, inclusive, all things go easily. You do not have to work hard at them. They perpetuate themselves. You do not even have to spend energy on any deliberate kind of meditation. By themselves, your positive thoughts, attitudes, and feelings create more positive thoughts, attitudes, and feelings. These, in turn, create fulfillment, productiveness, peace, and dynamism. The principle is exactly the same in negative situations. The self-perpetuating forces, in this instance, can be changed only by a deliberate process which sets something new in motion.

It is further important for you to understand and visualize that the spheres of consciousness operate exactly according to the directions that we have discussed. In other words, the positive principle and direction is the sphere of reality, the sphere in which there is unlimited self-perpetuation in whatever respect consciousness is aware of the existence of such wholeness and inexhaustible abundance.

The personality level that wants the negative and pursues that direction creates a new world, or psychic sphere, covering the original positive one. Images and forms—the product of attitudes, thoughts and feelings—create this negative world. There are many variations, degrees, and possibilities, according to the strength of the negative desires, the awareness of both positive and negative desires, and the balance between the two. You may gain an inkling of this by comparing your own change in awareness with your previous unconscious denial of positive experience, or even your direct desire for the negative. You will see that this difference constitutes another sphere of consciousness, a different world, with its own distinct flavor and atmosphere.

The physical, material world you live in manifests the positive and the negative, and presents a combination of the two. All these exist in and outside of you—in timelessness and spacelessness. You can and must reach these worlds within your psyche by becoming acutely aware of them. They are a product of your own self-expressions, of your various spheres of consciousness. You must go through them, layer by layer, within yourself. Where you are relatively free from negative desires, it will be fairly simple and easy to grasp, to feel, to experience the world of truth, where all good exists and is self-perpetuating. Therefore there is no need for struggle, for doubt, for fear, or for deprivation. In these areas you will find that you fearlessly open your heart to the positive, dynamic experience, which moves eternally toward further unfoldment, greater happiness, more inclusion, since you do not stop this movement with your fearful mind, holding it in check and bringing it to a standstill. These spheres are there; they not only exist deep in your psyche where you can sense the eternal life of all existence, but they manifest in your outer life too. To become aware of them is also useful, so you can compare them properly.

And then, of course, there is always the main problem, the area in your psyche where the fear of the positive, hence its negation, exists. Consequently, deprivation and suffering manifest in your outer life. You must fully experience this sphere within your consciousness so you can transcend it by transforming yourself. You must live it through, not by denying it or struggling away from it, but by seeing and accepting it, learning to understand its nature. This is what is meant by going through it. When it is affirmed and ascertained as a temporary reality, only then can the underlying world of self-perpetuating good be reached, where you no longer have to reach and grasp and want, but know that it is already yours, even before you have attained it.

Whenever you are separated from others, from your fellow creatures, you must be in the negative world, in a self-perpetuating negativity that you sow through your destructive wishes. You must therefore suffer because you deny and ignore the full significance of the thus evolving struggle. The struggle varies from individual to individual, and with a given individual from phase to phase, and even at times from hour to hour, because at different times different wish-directions come up. They alternate in predominance at any given moment.

So there must always be in you an unceasing struggle in which one side strives toward wholeness and union with your fellow creatures in many different ways: toward love and understanding, toward consideration, toward giving and receiving. But always there is still this other side that negates and denies the former direction, that fears and resists it. Therefore a particular pain exists, and the greater the denial, the greater the pain.

The pain is aggravated by the struggle that sets in with the other person. For do not forget, my friends, that it is painful enough that you want and do not want, alternately, to relate and love on the one hand, and to hate, reject, and withdraw on the other. It becomes infinitely more complicated when this conflict is multiplied by a second individual whose parameters you enter into, and who wages a similar fight within.

Negatively Oriented Pleasure

Both the positive and negative directions are attached to the pleasure principle. It is this attachment that makes it so difficult to give up the negative direction and change. The positively and negatively oriented pleasure principle tears you apart. It inflicts pain on you by itself, but it does not exist in you alone. It also exists in those with whom you are involved in this conflict, and about whom you cannot decide whether or not to love or to reject them. If they were perfectly in balance and free from such an inner division, they would surely be unaffected by your struggle. Their harmony with the universal forces and the high degree of awareness would protect them from your negativity and the resulting tension between the positive and negative pulls. If it were possible, for the sake of argument, that such an evolved being could enter into a relationship with an ordinary person who is wracked by this fight, the latter would still be in pain because of his or her own division. But how much more complicated it becomes when the other person is in a similar position, for then the struggle is not twofold, but a compounded fourfold one. Imagine the many mathematical possibilities that arise from such a situation, with all their psychological consequences of misunderstanding, misjudgment, and hurt, which, in turn, create further negativity.

Let us imagine two people, A and B. A momentarily expresses the positive direction toward union. B is frightened of it and therefore withdraws and rejects A. Consequently, A again becomes convinced that the healthy soul movement toward union was risky and painful and so reverts to the negative and the denial. Since this is so painful, the negative pleasure principle attaches itself to it, making the pain more bearable. A will then revel in the negative situation. In the meantime, the pain of isolation in B becomes unbearable, and B ventures out while A is in a dark hole. Now, this goes on and on, sometimes in crass opposition, although at times there is a fleeting conjunction. At times A's positive direction meets B's negative one; at other times they are reversed; at still other times, both negative currents are out, both withdraw or antagonize one another. At still other times, both temporarily venture into the positive, but since the negative principle still exists in them, the positive position is only tentative, so uncertain, so fearful, so divided, so defensive and apprehensive that these negative emotions about the positive direction produce negative results sooner or later. These are then attributed to the positive venture, rather than to the problematic emotions about it. It is inevitable that the negative direction must again take over after such periods of mutual positiveness, until the negative, destructive, and denying side is fully understood and eliminated.

The negative and destructive direction would not be as fierce and as difficult to overcome if the pleasure principle were not attached to it. You find yourself in the position of not wanting to part from the precarious pleasure you derive from indulging in destructive feelings and attitudes. This may evolve subtly, insidiously, and inadvertently when an individual starts out in a healthy and constructive direction.

Let us take the following example, which might prove useful for all of you. Suppose, on your road toward self-realization, you gain strength and self-confidence. Where you felt uncertainty and guilt as you experienced friction with another person, you now experience a new inner calm, certainty in yourself, and a strength and resilience you never knew existed. In the old way, you might have responded submissively to assuage your guilt, or with hostile aggression to assuage your self-contempt for your uncertainty. Whatever you did, however you responded with your negativity and self-doubt, you were attached to the negatively oriented pleasure principle. You enjoyed your woes. Now, you have progressed. You experience yourself in a new way. Instead of choosing the nagging self-doubt, you gain insight into why the other person behaves that way. For the moment this understanding sets you free, makes you strong, and gives you more objective insight into yourself and into the other person. In other words, the self-perpetuating principle of insight and understanding has been set in motion.

But then the still existing, because not yet fully recognized, negative pleasure principle attaches itself to your understanding of the other person's negativity. You begin to talk yourself into dwelling more and more on that person's faults and blindnesses, and you inadvertently begin to enjoy this. You do not immediately distinguish between the two different kinds of joy. The first comes when you see with detachment what exists in the other, and this sets you free; the second appears when you pleasurably indulge in the other's wrongness, and this blinds you. What you first noticed in the other you build up until the old negative pleasure principle has reappeared in a new guise. This is where you lose your harmony and freedom because you again indulge in the negative pleasure. This is an example of how insidiously this can happen whenever the old roots still exist unobserved.

Here, my friends, the continuation of the path becomes clearer and more concisely defined. You have the immediate tools to set out and discover what I explained here.

Be blessed, every one of you. Receive this warm stream of love that is all around you. Open yourself. For this love is truth, and this truth is life. And this life is yours for the asking. The courageous steps all of you undertake have a meaning. May you always know this. Every admission of something negative that exists in you contributes more toward the universal process of wholeness than any other thing imaginable. So proceed this way. Be blessed. Be in peace. Be in God!

ॐ

POSITIVITY AND NEGATIVITY: ONE ENERGY CURRENT

Greetings, my dearest friends. May the blessings of the creative intelligence, existing all around and within you, strengthen and enlighten you so that these words will echo in you and will serve as material to help you continue successfully your path toward finding your real self.

Many of you have now found a layer within your selves where you are face to face with your own destructiveness. And I am referring to more than the discovery of a mere emotion, the acknowledgement of a momentary hostility; I mean an overall, pervasive, essential, lingering destructiveness that has been dormant all along and merely covered up. You are now in a state in which you can observe yourself thinking, feeling, and acting destructively, while before you were at best only theoretically aware of such destructiveness and could merely surmise its presence by the unpleasant manifestations in your life. Now you are coping with the problem of how to get out of this condition.

You are puzzled because you do not like being this way. You even know and comprehend quite profoundly that this condition is totally useless and senseless, that destructiveness does not serve one good purpose. Nevertheless, you find yourself in the situation of being unable to let go of this destructiveness.

The Nature of Destructiveness

It is not easy to reach an awareness where you can see yourself think, feel, and act destructively; where you are furthermore aware that this causes you misery, but are still totally unable and unwilling to give up this way of being. I might say that it is a great measure of success, if this word can be used, to be aware of being in this state. But to accomplish the second part of this phase of your evolution, namely the letting go of destructiveness, the nature of destructiveness must be better understood.

The whole human problem of a dualistic concept of life has a great deal to do with humanity's lack of comprehension of its own destructiveness. Human beings are geared to think of a destructive force as something opposed to a constructive force. Even those of you who theoretically know quite well that there is no such division tend to think, "Here are my negative feelings. I wish I could have positive feelings instead." Or you think that after the negative emotions are dissipated, a new set of feelings will follow, as though this new set of feelings consisted of an entirely different energy or psychic material. When you speak of the two forces, the two sets of feelings, it is merely a figure of speech, a way of expressing two different kinds of experiences. However, this figure of speech is an expression of the dualistic misconception operative within all human consciousness.

Actually, there is only one power. This is very important to understand, my friends, particularly when you come to deal with your own destructiveness and negativity. There is one life force which energizes every expression of life. The same life force can flow in a constructive, positive, affirming way, or it can turn into a destructive, negating current. In order to understand this process in a specific and personal way, I will discuss it from the point of view of an individual looking at his or her life. I will not give a discourse on general spiritual principles here, but only touch upon them when it is necessary to the understanding of the whole topic.First I will repeat that the life force as such, when untampered with, is totally constructive, totally positive and affirming. Therefore it produces total pleasure for any living, feeling, or perceiving consciousness. The more fully this consciousness is developed, the fuller the pleasure it can experience from and through the pure life force, in whatever way this may find expression.

Every life organism—a newborn baby, a plant, a cell—tends to realize this potentiality in nature. When this natural flow is interfered with, the energy current seeking expression is blocked and prohibited from flowing to its destiny; the natural flow is stopped by conditions. These may be either outer or inner conditions—or both. When young children encounter conditions in the outer environment that prohibit the natural flow of the life force, the extent of the damage depends upon how free they are from inner blockages. If inner blockages exist and lie dormant because they have not been eliminated in previous existences, the outer negative conditions will create a severe blockage, freezing the floating energy current and petrifying it into a hardened psychic mass. When no previous blockages exist, the outer negative conditions will create only a temporary disturbance in the flow of the life force. People's persistent problems in life result from such blocked energy. Unblocking can occur only when the relationship between the inner and the outer negative conditions responsible for the blockage are thoroughly understood. The child's immature ego faculties make adequate dealing with the negative condition impossible. An outer negative condition can therefore never be totally responsible for the condensation of energy and for the paralysis of the life stream. It can only be the final activating factor, bringing the dormant negative inner condition to the fore.

The place in the soul where outer negative conditions activate the dormant inner negative condition is the very point at which the positive life force turns into a destructive non-life force. Feelings turn from love to fear and hostility, from trust to distrust, and so on. Finally, the negative power becomes so unbearable that the feelings connected with it are numbed altogether.

When human beings find themselves on a path of self-recognition, it is very important for them to understand specifically that a negative emotion cannot be replaced by a different positive emotion. It must be reconverted to its original state. How do we go about this, my friends? Each individual must find the way to reconvert this energy flow into its original state. Each life manifestation you experience that is unpleasant, problematic, or anxiety-producing is the result of a repetition of the original event in this life, when the positive pleasure force was blocked, hindered, or prohibited and has therefore turned into unpleasure.

The Pleasure of Negativity

Now, it cannot be stated accurately that in this unpleasure, pleasure is totally absent. When you find yourself stymied in your attempt to overcome negativity, it is extremely important to sense deep within yourself the pleasurable aspect of this negativity, regardless of how much pain you feel in your surface consciousness. The difficulty of ridding yourself of destructiveness is, of course, also due to other reasons which you have already verified: the desire to punish or to use the forcing current that says, "If I am sufficiently unhappy, that will show the world how wrong it is not to give me what I want." But these reasons do not constitute the deepest difficulty in dissolving negativity. It is necessary to sense intuitively, and then to feel very specifically, that in your negativity, paradoxically, both pleasure and unpleasure are simultaneously present.

This is very understandable when you look at the process in terms of the explanation I have given. The pleasure principle cannot possibly be completely absent even though it appears in its distorted form. Its basic ingredients must always remain, no matter how distorted the manifestation is and consequently how difficult it is to detect the original nature of the life current. This is precisely why negativity seems so difficult to transform. The pleasurable aspect of it always exists. When it is understood that only the form of expression must be changed, so that the identical life current can reconvert itself, negativity can be left behind. When you have understood that the painful aspects of the negative expression can be abandoned, while the pleasurable aspects grow stronger, negativity can transform itself. When you have understood that a new set of emotions will not come from out of nowhere, but that the same current will manifest differently, then what seems hard will happen by itself.

When you meditate on this, it will become possible for you to be aware of the pleasure attached to your destructiveness. Instead of feeling guilty about this pleasure and consequently repressing it, you will be in a position to allow the destructive current to unfold, express itself and reconvert itself. The attachment of or connection between pleasure and destructiveness has been instrumental in the widespread guilt human beings feel about all experiences of pleasure. This in turn is responsible for numbing all feelings. For how can pleasure be liberated from destructiveness if both are considered equally wrong? And yet, human beings cannot live without pleasure even if they have to have it in secret, for life and pleasure are one and the same. When pleasure is linked to destructiveness, destructiveness cannot be given up. It feels as if life were given up. This brings about a situation where, on one level of your inner life, you hold on equally to pleasure and destructiveness, feeling guilty and at the same time afraid of both. On a more superficial conscious level, you are numbed and feel little or nothing.

It is not sufficient to know this generally; the knowledge must be brought back to your specific circumstances. What is the outer manifestation at this moment that causes you continuous anguish? It is not a momentary experience caused by a one-time condition that then dissolves when new conditions arise. No, these are the problems in your life you cannot come to terms with. To truly resolve these conditions which we call images and which forever recreate similar conditions and new situations, the blocked and paralyzed energy must be made fluid again. And this can only happen when you begin, as the first step in this particular phase of your development, to ascertain the pleasurable aspect in your destructiveness. You must feel the pleasure attached to the unpleasure of the problem.

Blocked Sexual Energy

Since the pleasure current in the life force primarily manifests itself in your life in what is referred to as sexuality, destructive, blocked energy contains blocked sexual energy. It follows that outer problems must be symbolic or representative of how sexual energy was first blocked by outer conditions. The pain of this blockage has caused destructiveness which at the same time contains aspects of the pleasure principle. Therefore, every difficult situation in life represents a sexual fixation in the innermost psyche that you fear and run away from. Because you do not face up to this and continue to live with it, the outer conditions become unresolvable; you become more and more alienated from the inner cause where it is still enlivened by the pleasure aspect.

You on this path must therefore go back in, as it were, and permit yourself to feel the pleasure in the destructiveness. Then and only then will you truly comprehend the painful outer situation which, offhand, may have nothing to do with your emotional life or with any sexual problems. I have often mentioned that *in your most secret sexual fantasies lie the secrets of your conflicts*, as well as the key to their resolution. When you find the parallel between the outer problem and the pleasure current in your sexuality, you will be able to make the frozen energy fluid again. This will enable you to dissolve the negativity, the destructiveness, and this of course is essential for the elimination of the outer problem in your life.

Your inability to feel the pleasure in the unpleasure is the result of your fighting against yourself and not liking yourself for this particular distortion. Consequently, there is denial, repression, and further alienation from the nucleus where these conditions can still be experienced and gradually altered.

Every problem must have such a nucleus, where the original current has been blocked and is therefore distorted, and where the pleasure/unpleasure dichotomy produces an unconscious fixation of the pleasure experience on a negative situation. You then fight against this for any number of reasons, with the further consequence that outer problems begin to form and then repeat and repeat. They cannot be overcome until this nucleus is experienced. This applies to all stubborn problems, whether or not they seem to have anything to do with sexuality.

All this may sound very theoretical if you are still far from this point, but it can eventually be a turning point in your inner and consequently your outer life, after which it will no longer be a problem to abandon destructiveness. For one cannot succeed by forcing it away with the surface will, without a deep comprehension of the forces within that constitute this very destructiveness. Yes, the will must of course be there in principle, but at the same time, as I have said in so many other contexts, the outer will should only be used for the purpose of liberating the inner powers that make the development a natural, organic, harmonious process. Thus destructiveness dissolves itself. It is not deliberately dropped like a cloak, nor are constructive feelings produced by a similar act of will. It is an evolutionary process within yourself, right here and now.

Are there any questions?

QUESTION: What makes the perception of pleasure so unique and specific in relation to the unpleasure?

ANSWER: It is known that you fear pleasure when you are still full of conflicts and problems the nature of which you do not understand. Any of you on this path who go deeply enough to probe your reactions discover this startling fact: you are more afraid of pleasure than of pain. You who have not verified this fact in yourselves may find this unbelievable, for you consciously resent the unpleasure and wish it away. And to a degree this is right, for the unpleasure cannot really be wanted. You cannot resolve this dichotomy unless you go deep into your psychic processes to feel the pleasure in the unpleasure.

Total pleasure is feared for a very important reason: the pleasure supreme of the cosmic energy current must seem unbearable, frightening, overwhelming, and almost annihilating when the personality is still geared to negativity and destructiveness. To put it differently, to the degree that the personality has impaired its integrity, and impurity, dishonesty, cheating, and malice still exist in the psyche, pure pleasure must be rejected. Hence the negative pleasure is the only way the entity can experience a modicum of pleasure at all. When you who are on your path find that deep within yourself you fear pleasure as a danger, you must ask yourself, "Where am I not honest with life or with myself? Where do I cheat? Where do I impair my integrity?" These areas show precisely where, why, and to what degree pure pleasure must be rejected. When you ascertain in yourself that you fear and reject pleasure, and it is not that life deprives you of it, you can do something by asking yourself the pertinent questions and subsequently finding the elements of impairment in you. This is the way out. When you find where you violate your sense of decency and honesty, you can unlock the door which has closed your access to transforming the negative pleasure and forced you to reject pleasure that is unhampered by pain.

May your understanding grow so that you sense your own distortions and how these distortions are a valuable life energy that can be activated in the specific way I showed here.

Be blessed every one of you; receive the strength and the power that flows into you. Make use of it, travel this path to the very nucleus of your own inner being. Be in God.

ॐ

OVERCOMING NEGATIVITY

Greetings and blessings for everyone of my friends.

In recent lectures we have been talking about negative creation, which is an on-going process in every human being. For, if you were free from negative creation, you would not be a human; you would not live on this plane of consciousness, which expresses a certain degree of development. Humanity is to some degree free, so that people create quite constructively also. But to varying degrees negative creation is still ongoing in the psyche. This means that it is humanity's task on this earth to struggle out of its negative creation and become more and more free of its snares. This is not easy, for the fascination with any creative process takes hold of people, so that they want to remain in it. It is my task now to help you step by step to further loosen the hold of your negative involvement with distorted creative processes.

There is a world of difference between an intellectual belief in this philosophy, and the clear-cut realization that you create negatively, that the very unhappiness you deplore is caused by negative attitudes you secretly enjoy and want to maintain. This does not mean that the ills you see in society do not actually exist. They do exist. But they could not really affect you if you were not deeply and still unconsciously contributing to those very ills of society you so much deplore.

This truth may be hard to believe when you are still at the very beginning of such a path as this. But once you are really involved in it, you must come to see that it is just that way. You are never an innocent victim, and society itself is but the sum total or product of your and many other people's constant negative production and creation. This realization is at first shocking and painful, but only as long as you remain unwilling to give up the negativity. If you will not give it up you do need the illusion that others do it. You hope to come to bliss without meeting that aspect in you that makes reaching bliss impossible. You hope to become a truly self-accepting and self-respecting human being without giving up all that which truly impairs your integrity. Thus you live the illusion that others are doing it to you, others whom you can blame for supposedly victimizing you. This is one of the very frequent games of pretense that have been uncovered by many of you in various forms.

Three Steps for Working Your Way Out

I would like to discuss the various steps of working your way out of the maze of your own illusion and negative creation in which you seem to be so inextricably and inexorably caught. Evidently, the first step must be for you to find, determine, acknowledge, accept, and observe your own negative attitudes.

The second step is that, deep inside, you question your particular feelings and reactions to this negative production, and your own deliberate and chosen intent. You will then see that you like it, find some sort of pleasure in it, and do not wish to give it up.

The third step is to painstakingly work through the exact consequences and ramifications of your negative production, without glossing over any detail, any effect, or side-effect. The realization and precise understanding of the harmful effects on you and on others must become very clear. It will not do if you assuage your guilt for your negative creation by telling yourself you only harm yourself. It must be seen that you cannot harm yourself without also harming others, no more than you can harm others without also harming you. It is unthinkable that anything that adversely affects you does not affect others as well. Self-hate, for example, always manifests also as the inability to love, or even the compulsion to hate others.

The third step also consists of seeing that the pleasure you derive from your negative production is never worth the exorbitant price you pay for it, because all you deplore most in yourself and in your life experience is a direct result of it. You sacrifice joy, peace, self-esteem, inner security, expansion and growth, pleasure on all levels of your being, and a meaningful and fearless existence.

Still another aspect of step three is to reach for the understanding that the pleasure you derive from being destructive in your feelings and attitudes is not what has to be given up. In fact, the same pleasure will be transferred to positive creation, where you can expand joyfully and guiltlessly without paying the heavy price you now pay for negative creation. Exact working through of cause and effect, and seeing results and connections, is what makes wanting to give up negativity possible. It is not sufficient to be aware of being deliberately destructive. It must be admitted that you do not want to give this up.

At step two you are still separated from the effects. You may see that the cause is your destructiveness and admit it, but you do not yet see the connection with all you deplore in your life. The connecting link between cause and effect is still absent. As long as this connecting link is not established, you cannot really want to give up the negativity. You must see the heavy price you pay to be truly motivated to want to give it up. Step two may be the most difficult to reach; it certainly constitutes the most drastic change in self-perception and the perception of life processes. But working through step three is equally important, for without it the motivation to change is lacking. However, step three is not half as difficult, and never meets with as much resistance as step two.

When you begin to discover the same fascination with creating in a positive way as in the negative, but this time unmarred by suffering, guilt, fear, and self-blame, the world opens up before you with such beauty and light that there are no words to describe it. You will taste the freedom of being creator of your chosen life.

Roles and Games

To facilitate the discovery of this connecting link of positive fascination with creation, you will need to recognize the destructiveness and negativity behind facades of various kinds: the pretenses, the defenses, the games and ploys, the idealized self-images, the specific forms of denial you use in order to conceal your destructiveness. All these masks are hypocritical. They always display the opposite of what you reject and dislike in yourself.

In order to hide from others—and primarily from yourself—you produce something that appears to be the opposite of what you wish to be hidden. The role becomes like second nature, but it has nothing to do with you. It is merely a habit you cannot shed as long as you are unwilling to look behind it. It is of specific importance that you disillusion yourself concerning the image you project into the world and of whose genuineness you try arduously to convince yourself. The artificiality of this role you indulge in must be unmasked. It always appears to you to be good in some way, even if only by pretending you are a victim. But you must analyze it exactly and comprehend it in detail to see that it is none of what you pretend it is.

Yet the pretended role contains the same aspects you so busily try to conceal. If you hide and your role is that of being persecuted by the hate and unjust accusations of others, in this pretense lies the hate itself. The front or the role is never innately different from what it covers. It is a hating attitude to pretend being a victim of the hate of others. This is only one example. The game itself must be exposed not only to reveal what it hides, but also to lay bare its actual aspects and what they really mean. The negative creative energy is totally involved in this presented image. I suggest that you take some time now to identify the various roles you have chosen. Name these roles in simple sentences that describe what they are meant to convey. See if you can detect how the role which is supposed to be quite angelic is as destructive as what is concealed behind it. Indeed, it could not be different, for you cannot hide the energy of soul currents, you cannot make them different by pretending, no matter how busily you try.

The role or game you adopt in the illusion that it eliminates your deliberate destructiveness is the first layer that must be confronted. Then you can begin to take the steps I have outlined. Sometimes these steps overlap.

The Fourth Step

The more insight you have into the absolutely losing game you play with life when you hold on to the false role that covers up destructive attitudes, the more you will be motivated to give up all of this. You will strengthen your will. This will lead you to the fourth step, which is the actual process of recreating soul substance. By your meditation, by prayer, by formulating deliberate thoughts of truth about this entire matter and impressing them onto your psychic material, recreation begins and continues as you become more adept. You will become aware of your attempt to exaggerate and drag out old injuries, to quite deliberately punish others for what your parents did to you or what you think they did to you, and of your refusal to see their failures as anything but a deliberate act of hate against you. When you then perceive that it gives you pleasure to dwell on all this within yourself and not change your outlook and attitude, or your feelings, you can begin to recreate. When you see the falsity of your pretenses, you can then remind yourself to want to see what is underneath your particular facade of blame and victimization, in whatever guise it may appear.

Your feelings of being injured first appear as quite real and it requires deeper probing to discover that they are not real at all. They are cultivated habits. So are the roles you play. Each objective acknowledgment of your pretenses enables you to want to be in deeper truth, to abandon those falsities and to meet life with real and honest attitudes. The issuing of this intention and the calling upon the higher powers in you to help you is step four.

Another part of step four is to ask a concise question of your innermost being: "What approach can I use to live my life without a pretense? How does it feel to bring forth better ways of responding to life's experiences?" In answer to these questions something new will evolve. In this recreating process healthy, resilient, adequate, and truthful reactions will come easily from your real nature, which needs no concealment. When you create, formulate your sentences very concisely. State that what you do does not work, why it does not work, and that you wish to operate in a different way. These statements, if truly meant, have great creative power.

These are the steps of purification in the deepest and most vital way. Purification is unthinkable without going through these four steps. Purification is also unthinkable without receiving active help. It is too difficult to do alone. It is utter illusion to hope—consciously or unconsciously—that facing these aspects of your being can be avoided, skipped, bypassed or whisked away by some magic "spiritual" means. Self-realization, or self-actualization, or reaching your spiritual center, or whatever other name you wish to use in order to describe the goal of all living, cannot occur unless you face your deepest negativities and hypocrisies. Many are the people who want to reach spiritual heights but who harbor the unexpressed illusion that to face what I am discussing here can be avoided. They run from pillar to post, and whenever they are confronted with their own unpalatable truth, they run away.

Whenever destructive attitudes remain unfaced and untouched, you live in painful ambivalence. For you cannot ever go in one direction when you want to be negative. There is always the real self clamoring for ultimate reality and pulling in the opposite direction. Unification of inner direction can only happen when the personality is truly and genuinely constructive without hidden destructiveness.

In order to experience yourself as that eternal you which you essentially and ultimately are, you have to consider and test the possibility of positive creating. You will then see that to create positively is really so much more natural and easy: it is an organic process. Negative creating and destructive attitudes are artificial and contrived, even though you are now so used to them that they seem more natural. The positive is effortless. Offhand it seems that to abandon the negative that has become so much second nature to you is too great an effort. It seems too great because you still believe that by giving up negativity you create a positivity that is something completely new. If this were so, to create it would indeed be quite impossible in most instances. But the moment you realize that the positive creation is already there within you and that it can unfold and reveal itself the moment you allow this to happen, abandoning negativity becomes a relief from a heavy burden that has pulled you down all your life—and in many lives before this one.

When we say that God is within you, we mean precisely this. Not only is the greater consciousness with infinite wisdom of the most personal order available to you at whatever moment you need it, not only are there powers of creative strength and energy, feelings of bliss, joy, and pleasure supreme available to you on all levels, but also, right underneath where you are ill with your negativity, a new life exists in which all reactions to all possible contingencies are clear, strong, and entirely satisfying and right for each occasion. A resiliency and creativity of reacting already exists now behind the false roles of pretense, beyond the grip of destructiveness. Underneath your outer deadness a bubbling aliveness already exists. At first it will shine through at moments only. Eventually it will manifest itself as your steady inner climate.

I think most of you can sense the importance of this lecture especially if you use it as referring to your own life instead of as a mere theoretical discussion. Then it will prove of vital significance in your personal evolution. Be blessed. Love and strength are given forth for everyone here.

ॐ

TRANSFORMATION

There is one great and universal wish of mankind expressed in all religions, in all art and philosophy, and in all human life; the wish to pass beyond himself as he now is.
                                        Beatrice Hinkle [1]

Many people enter a path such as the Pathwork for the same reason that others go into some from of psychotherapy—due to unhappiness and dissatisfaction with their life. Others begin the path because they are seeking answers to ultimate questions. All who walk such a path must deal with both sides, the psychological/emotional, and the spiritual. Psychological work, pushed far enough, must become spiritual work. Spiritual work, to be truly effective, must also deal with the psyche of the seeker. This truth is not a new one; here is an expression of it by the fourteenth-century theologian and mystic, Meister Eckhart:

> *To get to the core of God at his greatest, one must first get into the core of himself at the least, for no one can know God who has not first known himself. Go to the depths of the soul, the secret place of the Most High, to the roots, to the heights: for all that God can do is focussed there.[2]*

So the ultimate goal of the Pathwork is not merely to gain self-knowledge; it is to change, to *transform* oneself; and this change is both psychological and spiritual. The preceding sections of this book have taught us how to examine ourselves, and how to penetrate beneath the mask of our idealized self-image. If we then have the courage to begin feeling all our repressed feelings, we will eventually come to *know* that it is our own unconscious negativity that causes our life problems. Such knowledge is necessary if there is to be a chance for true, deep change to occur; and in Part III we now turn our attention to how we can effect self transformation.

The change process takes place on two levels. The first is principally psychological and emotional, in which we learn to become a different sort of human being—having seen through and given up our self-defeating and self-sabotaging attitudes, beliefs, fears, and behaviors. The second level is predominantly spiritual; it involves a radical shift in identity, beyond the personality, even, one could say, beyond human-beingness.

A great deal of psychological and emotional change comes about simply in the course of acquiring self-knowledge. Some of our self-defeating behavior comes to be seen so clearly, and the pain of it felt so strongly, that it is simply given up; it vanishes. Or, more precisely, the energy that had been tied up in negativity once again becomes available for positive life expression.

But the later Pathwork lectures focus on how to deal with negative patterns that stay stuck and resistant, even though they seem to have been fully analyzed and understood, completely felt, owned, and repudiated. This final stage of the work depends greatly on the proper use of a specific kind of meditation. In Pathwork meditation, one must first have learned how to drop below the usual level of the mind's chatter, and how then to reside in a place of deep stillness. In this place of stillness, one can learn to hear clearly the voice of the lower-self child, and can dialogue with it. Here one can also contact and call upon the wisdom and strength of the higher self. It is in this phase of the work that one's sense of identity begins to shift.

The Guide has said: "The Pathwork is not psychotherapy, although aspects of it must necessarily deal with areas psychotherapy also deals with. In the framework of the Pathwork, the psychological approach is only a side issue, a way of getting through obstructions. It is essential to deal with confusions, inner misconceptions, misunderstandings, destructive attitudes, alienating defenses, negative emotions, and paralyzed feelings, all of which psychotherapy also attempts to do and even posits as its ultimate goal. In contrast, the Pathwork enters its most important phase only after this first stage is over. The second and most important phase consists of learning how to activate the greater consciousness dwelling within every soul." [3]

What is the "greater consciousness"? Or, what really is meant by the phrase "one's sense of identity begins to shift"?

There are different levels of human consciousness and different kinds of work are required at these different levels, in the long process of waking up, of becoming more and more aware, of becoming enlightened. When we first begin to come out of our waking sleep, our consensus trance, we must penetrate our self-delusions, and reintegrate those parts of ourselves that we have pushed into the shadow. It could be said that this is a process of becoming "bigger", for we are integrating and claiming more of ourselves. We have *re-identified* as ourselves aspects that we had unconsciously denied.

As the work continues one finally arrives at the stage that Abraham Maslow termed self-actualization. Most therapies seem to believe that this level is as far as anyone can go; that fully attaining this represents the successful end of the growth process. But there are two levels beyond this: the *transpersonal* and the *unitive.*

At the transpersonal level, one begins to experience that

there are realms beyond the human, and that one can contact those realms. As Ken Wilber says, "the average person will probably listen in disbelief if it is pointed out that he has, nestled in the deepest recesses of his being, a self that transcends his individuality and connects him to a world beyond conventional space and time." [4] But indeed one can, at moments of peak experience, or self-transcendence, or deep meditation, actually experience oneself as a being that lives on this spiritual plane of existence. It is from this level that the Guide transmitted the Pathwork to Eva Pierrakos, and from which all true revelation comes. For the spiritual seeker, the most practical result of reaching this level of consciousness is that one can begin to live one's life by *guidance;* one can tap into this level of greater wisdom and receive from it instruction in how to live one's life in such a way as to achieve greater fulfillment.

Working at this level more and more becomes a process of stepping back from one's individual personality concerns and of learning how to calmly witness them. One finds a still calm center within, which exists all the time, even when the personality self is having temper tantrums or anxiety attacks. So a subtle shift has occurred. No longer am I working on re-identifying parts of myself that I had disowned. Rather, I am now engaged in a process of *dis-identification;* discovering more and more clearly that, even though "I" have "problems", there is a deeper self that exists below the level of the problems, that precedes the problems, that calmly exists all the time, even through life and death.

As the amount of time that I live at this level continues to increase, the experience of receiving guidance begins to change in quality. No longer do I feel so much that "I" am being spoken to by somebody else. Rather, I have a growing sense that one part of me is speaking to another part of me. It's not that some "Greater Consciousness" is sending me a message, but rather that I more and more seem to be that Greater Consciousness. This can be quite confusing, even spooky, for a while. But in time it is no longer upsetting; in time it feels like a wonderful, marvelous, pleasureful coming home.

The lectures in this section deal with meditation, dissolving fears, identifying with the spiritual self, and making the transition to positive intentionality. Then, after this close examination of personal negativity, we end with a lecture which opens out into the vastness of inner space, and describes how this inner space can be filled with the Holy Spirit.

D. T.

1. Beatrice Hinkle, *The Re-creating of the Individual*. Harcourt, Brace, 1923.
2. *Meister Eckhart*. Trans. R. Blakney.
3. Pathwork Lecture #204. "What is the Path?"
4. Ken Wilber, *No Boundary*. Center Publications, 1979. p.123.

ಎಲ

MEDITATION
WITH THREE VOICES:
EGO, LOWER SELF, HIGHER SELF

Greetings, all my friends here. Love and blessings, help and inner strength are coming forth to sustain you and help you open up your innermost being. I hope you will continue and cultivate this process, so that you bring to life your entire being—creating wholeness in you.

There are many different kinds of meditation. Religious meditation consists of reciting set prayers. There is meditation in which the main emphasis is put on increasing the powers of concentration. In another type of meditation spiritual laws are contemplated and thought through. There is also meditation in which the ego is made totally passive and will-less and the divine allowed its own flux. These and other forms of meditation may have more or less value, but my suggestion to the friends who work with me is rather to use the available energy and time for confronting that part of the self that destroys happiness, fulfillment, and wholeness. You can never create the wholeness you truly aspire to, whether or not this aim is articulated, if you bypass this confrontation. This approach includes giving voice to the recalcitrant aspect of the egotistical, destructive self that denies happiness, fulfillment, and beauty for any reason.

To really understand the dynamics, the meaning, and the process of meditation and derive the maximum benefit from it, you must be clear about certain psychic laws. One of those is that if meditation is to be truly effective, three fundamental layers of personality must be actively involved in it.

These three fundamental personality levels we may call:

(1)   the *conscious ego level,* with all conscious knowing and willing;

(2)   the *unconscious egotistical child level*, with all its ignorance, destructiveness, and claims to omnipotence; and

(3)   the *supraconscious universal self,* with its superior wisdom, power and love, as well as with its comprehensive understanding of events in human life.

In effective meditation the conscious ego activates both the unconscious, egotistical, destructive self and the supraconscious, superior universal self. A constant interaction among these three levels must take place, requiring great alertness on the part of your conscious ego self.

The Ego as Mediator

The conscious ego must be determined to allow the unconscious egotistical self to reveal itself, to unfold, to manifest in awareness, to express itself. This is neither as difficult nor as easy as it may seem. It is difficult exclusively, my friends, because of the fear of not being as perfect, as evolved, as good, as rational, as ideal, as one wants to be and even pretends to be, so that on the surface of consciousness the ego becomes almost convinced of being the idealized self-image. This surface conviction is constantly counteracted by the unconscious knowledge that this image is untrue, with the result that secretly the whole personality feels fraudulent and terrified of exposure. It is a significant sign of self-acceptance and growth when a human being is capable of allowing the egotistical, irrational, destructive part to manifest in the inner awareness, and acknowledges it in all its specific detail. This alone will prevent a dangerous *indirect* manifestation of which the person's consciousness is not aware because it is not connected with it, so that the undesirable results seem to come from outside.

So the conscious ego has to reach down and say, "Whatever is in me, whatever is hidden that I ought to know about myself, whatever negativity and destructiveness there is should be out in the open. I want to see it, I commit myself to seeing it, regardless of the hurt to my vanity. I want to be aware of how I deliberately refuse to see my part wherever I am stuck, and how I therefore overconcentrate on the wrongs of others." This is one direction for meditation.

The other direction must be toward the universal higher self, which has powers that surpass the limitations of the conscious self. These higher powers should also be called upon to expose the destructive little self, so that resistance can be overcome. The ego-will alone may be incapable of accomplishing this, but your conscious self-determining ego can and must request the higher powers to help. The universal consciousness should also be asked to help you to understand the expressions of the destructive infant correctly, without exaggeration, so that you do not go from ignoring it to making it a monster. A person can easily fluctuate from an outer self-aggrandizement to a hidden inner self-deprecation. When the destructive infant reveals itself, one could fall prey to believing that this destructive self is the ultimate, sad reality. For a complete perspective on the revelation of the egotistic infant, one needs to ask constantly the guidance of the universal self.

When the infant begins to express itself more freely because the ego allows it and receives it as a non-judgmental, interested, open listener, collect this material for further study. Whatever reveals itself should be explored for origins, results, further ramifications. Ask yourself what underlying misconceptions are responsible for the hate, spite, malice, or whatever negative feelings come to the surface? When the misconceptions are recognized, guilt and self-hate diminish proportionately.

Another question to ask is, what are the consequences when for the sake of a momentary satisfaction you give in to the destructive impulses? When questions like these are clearly worked out, the destructive aspects weaken—again in proportion to the understanding of the particular cause and effect. Without this part of the pathwork, the task is only half done. Meditation must deal with the entire problem of unconscious negativity step by step.

The interaction is threefold. The observing ego must initially want it and commit itself to reaching in and exposing the negative side. It has also to ask for the help of the universal self. When the infant reveals itself, the ego should again ask for the help of the universal self to strengthen the consciousness for the further work which is the exploration of the underlying misconceptions and the heavy price paid for them. The universal self can help—if you allow it—to overcome the temptation to give in again and again to destructive impulses. Such giving in does not necessarily result in action, but may manifest in emotional attitudes.

The Meditative Attitude

Such meditation requires a great deal of time, patience, perseverance and determination. Remember that wherever you are unfulfilled, wherever there are problems, wherever there is conflict in your life, your attitude should not be to concentrate with woe on others or circumstances outside your control, but to reach into yourself and explore the causes embedded in your own egocentric childish level. Meditation is an absolute prerequisite here: it means *ingathering yourself,* calmly, quietly wanting to know the truth of this particular circumstance and its causes. Then you need to quietly *wait for an answer.* In this state of mind, peace will come to you even before you fully understand why you have a particular negativity. This truthful approach to life will already give you a measure of the peace and self-respect you lacked as long as you held others responsible for what you had to suffer.

If such meditation is cultivated, you will discover a side of yourself that you have never known. In fact, you will come to know two aspects: the highest universal powers will communicate themselves to you to help you discover your most destructive, ignorant side, which needs insight, purification, and change. Through your willingness to accept your lower self, the higher self will become more of a real presence in you. In fact, you will increasingly experience it as your real self.

Many people meditate, but they neglect the two-sidedness of the endeavor and therefore miss out on integration. They may indeed actualize some of the universal powers that come into play wherever the personality is sufficiently free, positive, open, but the unfree, negative, closed areas are neglected. The actualized universal powers will not, by themselves, enforce an integration with the undeveloped part of the self. The conscious ego-self must decide for this integration and fight for it, otherwise the universal self cannot get through to the blocked-off areas. Partial integration alone with the universal self may lead to even greater self-deception if the consciousness is deluded by the actually existing partial integration with divine powers and becomes even more prone to overlook the neglected side. This makes for lopsided development.

The Changes Effected by the Pathwork Meditation

When you go through the entire process, a tremendous strengthening of your whole self takes place. Several things begin to happen within your personality, my friends. In the first place, your conscious ego-personality itself becomes stronger and healthier. It will be stronger in a good, relaxed sense, with more determination, awareness, meaningful directedness and a greater power of concentration with one-pointed attention. Second, you will cultivate a much greater self-acceptance and understanding of reality. Unreal self-hate and self-disgust will go away. Equally unreal claims for specialness and perfection also stop. False spiritual pride and vanity as well as false self-humiliation and shame disappear. Through the steady activation of the higher powers, the self feels less and less forlorn, helpless, lost, hopeless, or empty. The whole sense of the universe in all its marvelous possibilities reveals itself from within, as the reality of this wider world shows you the way to accept and change your destructive inner child.

This gradual change enables you to accept all your feelings and let the energy flow through your being. When your small, petty, mean side is accepted without thinking that it is the total, final reality, then the beauty, love, wisdom and infinite power of the superior self become more real. Dealing with your lower self leads to balanced development, integration, and a deep, reassuring sense of your own reality. Realistic, well-founded self-liking must result.

When you see the truth in yourself and it becomes second nature to want and commit yourself to this truth, you will detect an ugly side in you, which until this point you were too resistant to see. Simultaneously, you also detect this great, universal, spiritual power that is in you and that in fact is you. Paradoxical as it may seem, the more you can accept the ignorant little infant in you without losing your sense of self-worth, the better you will perceive the greatness of your innermost being, provided you truly do not use your discoveries about the little self to beat yourself down. The lower self wants to seduce the conscious ego to stay within the narrow confines of neurotic self-beating, hopelessness, and morbid capitulation, which always cover unexpressed hatred. The conscious ego must prevent this stratagem using all its knowledge and resources. Observe this habit of self-beating, hopelessness, and capitulation in yourself and counteract it—not by pushing it underground again, but by using what you know. Talking to this part of yourself you can bring to bear on it all the knowledge of your conscious ego. If this is not sufficient, request the powers beyond your consciousness to come to your help.

As you get to know both the lowest and the highest in you, you discover the function, the capacities, but also the limitations of the conscious ego. On the conscious level the ego's function is wanting to see the full truth of both the lowest and highest in you, wanting with all of its strength to change and give up destructiveness. The limitation is that the ego-consciousness cannot execute this alone and must turn for help and guidance to the universal self and wait patiently without doubting or impatiently pushing. This waiting needs an open attitude about the way the help might manifest. The fewer preconceived notions one has, the faster help will come forth and be recognizable. Help from the universal consciousness may come in an entirely different manner than your concepts may make room for.

The Reeducation of the Destructive Self

So far we have discussed two phases of the meditation process: first the recognition of the unconscious destructive egotistical self and then the understanding of the underlying misconceptions, the causes and effects, the meaning and the price to be paid for the present destructive attitudes. *The third phase is the reorientation and reeducation of the destructive part of the self.* The destructive infant is now no longer entirely unconscious. This infant with its false beliefs, its stubborn resistance, must be reoriented. Reeducation, however, cannot take place unless you are fully aware of every aspect of this destructive infant's beliefs and attitudes. This is why the first part of meditation—the revealing, exploratory phase—is so fundamental. It goes without saying that this first phase is not something one gets over with, so that then the second, and later the third phase can begin. This is not a sequential process; the phases overlap.

What I will say now must be taken with great care, otherwise the subtleties involved will not be communicated. Reeducation might very easily be misunderstood and lead toward a renewed suppression or repression of the destructive part that is beginning to unfold. You have to take great care and deliberately aim to avoid this, without, however, allowing the destructive part to engulf you. The best attitude toward the unfolding destructive part is one of detached observation, of unjudging, unharried acceptance. The more it unfolds, the more you must remind yourself that neither the truth of its existence, nor its destructive attitudes, are final. They are not the only attitudes you have, nor are they absolute. Above all, you have the power inherent in you to change anything. You may lack the incentive to change when you are not fully aware of the damage the destructive part of you does to your life when it goes unrecognized. It is therefore another important aspect of this phase of pathwork meditation to look deeply and widely for indirect manifestations. How does unexpressed hate manifest in your life? Perhaps by feeling undeserving and afraid or by inhibiting your energies. This is only one example; all indirect manifestations have to be explored.

It is important here to remind yourself that where there is life, there is constant movement, even if this movement is temporarily paralyzed: matter is paralyzed life-stuff. The frozen blocks of energy in your body are momentarily hardened, immobilized life-stuff. This life-stuff can always be made to move again, but only consciousness can do it. For life-stuff is filled with consciousness, as well as energy; whether this energy is momentarily blocked and frozen or whether this consciousness is momentarily dimmed does not matter. Meditation must mean, above all, that the part of you that is already conscious and moving actually intends to make blocked energy and dimmed consciousness moving and aware again. The best way to do this is to allow the frozen and dimmed consciousness first of all to express itself. Here you need a receptive attitude, instead of a reaction that what comes forth is devastating and catastrophic. The panicky attitude toward one's own unfolding destructive infant does more damage than the destructive infant itself. You must learn to listen to it, to take it in, to calmly receive its expressions without hating yourself, without pushing the infant away. Only with such an attitude can you come to understand the causes of its underlying destructiveness. Only then can the process of reeducation begin.

The denying, panicky, frightened, self-rejecting, and perfection-demanding attitude you usually have makes every part of this meditation impossible. It does not permit unfoldment; it does not permit exploration of the causes of what might be unfolded; and it certainly does not permit reeducation. It is the accepting and understanding attitude that enables the conscious ego to assert its benign dominion over violently destructive and stagnant psychic matter. As I have said many times, kindness, firmness, and deep determination against your own destructiveness are necessary. It is a paradox: identify with the destructiveness and yet be detached from it. Accept that it is you, but also know that there is another part of you that can say the final word if you so choose. For this you need to widen the limitations of your conscious ego expressions to include saying at any moment: "I will be stronger than my destructiveness and will not be hampered by it. I determine that my life will be at its best and fullest and that I will and can overcome the blocks in me that make me want to remain unhappy. This determination of mine will bring in the higher powers that will make me capable of experiencing more and more bliss because I can let go of the doubtful pleasure of being negative, which I now fully recognize." This is the task of the conscious ego. Then and then only can it also call into play the powers of guidance, wisdom, strength, and a new inner feeling of love that comes from being penetrated by the universal self.

For reeducation, too, has to proceed through the relationship of the three interactive levels, just as it was necessary for making the destructive side conscious and exploring its deeper meaning. Reeducation depends on the efforts of both the conscious ego, with its instructions to and dialogue with the ignorant egotistical child, and on the intervention and guidance of the universal, spiritual self. Each in its own way will effect the gradual maturing of this infant. The ego determines its goal to change the consciousness of the negative inner child by wanting this and committing itself to it. This is its task. Full execution of this task is made possible by the spiritual influx from the deeper personality that has to be deliberately activated. Here the consciousness must again adopt a twofold approach: one is activity that asserts its desire to transform the self-defeating aspects, leading the dialogue and calmly but firmly instructing the ignorant child. The other is a more passive, patient waiting for the final, but always gradual, manifestation of the universal powers. It is they who bring about the inner change when the feelings lead to new, more resilient reactions. Thus good feelings will replace those which were negative or dead.

Rushing and pressuring the resisting part is as useless and ineffective as accepting its direct refusal to budge. When the conscious ego does not recognize that there is a part of the self that actually refuses every step toward health, unfoldment, and the good life, a counteractive movement may be one of hurried, impatient pressure. Both derive from self-hate. When you feel stymied and hopeless, take it as a sign for you to search for that part in you that says, "I do not wish to change, I do not wish to be constructive." Set out and find this voice. Use the meditative dialogue here again, to explore and let the worst in you express itself.

This is the only meaningful way in which meditation can move your life toward the resolution of problems, toward growth and fulfillment, and toward unfolding your best potential. If you do this, my friends, the time will come when trusting life will no longer sound like a vague, faraway theory that you cannot put into personal action. Instead, your trust in life, as well as self-love in the healthiest sense, will fill you more and more.

These are very important concepts to understand, to use, and to observe within yourself. When the three-way interaction within yourself takes place, there is always a harmonious blend between desire and desirelessness; between involvement and detachment; between activity and passivity. When this balance becomes a steady state, *the destructive infant grows up.* It is not killed or annihilated. It is not exorcised. Its frozen powers resolve themselves into live energy, which you will actually feel, my friends, as a new, *living force.* This infant must not be slain. It must be instructed so that salvation can come to it, liberating it, bringing it to growth. If you work toward this goal, you will steadily move closer to unifying the ego level and the universal self.

This is powerful material. Be blessed, be in peace, be in God.

ès

SELF-IDENTIFICATION
AND THE STAGES
OF CONSCIOUSNESS

Greetings and blessings are poured forth unto all of you in a great and magnificent spiritual force which you can partake of and assimilate to whatever degree you truly open yourself to it with your heart and your mind.

In this lecture I will discuss consciousness from a new and different approach. It is perhaps difficult for human beings to understand that consciousness permeates the entire universe. Consciousness is not simply dependent on the personality of an entity. It permeates everything that exists. The human mind is geared to think of consciousness as exclusively a byproduct of personality and even associated exclusively with the brain. This is not so. Consciousness does not require a fixed form. Every particle of matter contains consciousness, but in inanimate matter consciousness is consolidated, just as energy is petrified in inanimate objects. Consciousness and energy are not the same, but they are interdependent aspects of life manifesting.

As evolution progresses, this static condition decreases as consciousness and energy become increasingly more vibrant and mobile. Consciousness gains in awareness; energy gains greater creative power to move and to make forms.

Every trait familiar to human understanding, every attitude known in creation, every aspect of personality is just one of many manifestations of consciousness. Every manifestation that is not yet integrated into the whole needs to be unified and synthesized into one harmonious whole.

It requires a leap of your imagination to comprehend the concept I am trying to convey here. Can you imagine for a moment that many familiar traits, which you have always assumed could only exist through a person, are not the person *per se,* but are free-floating particles of an overall consciousness? It does not matter whether these traits be good, or evil; for example, take love, perseverance, sloth, laziness, impatience, kindness, stubbornness, or malice. They all need to be incorporated into the manifesting personality. Only then can purification, harmonizing, and enrichment of the manifesting consciousness take place, creating the preconditions for the evolutionary process of unifying consciousness.

The human being is a conglomeration of various aspects of consciousness. Some are already purified. Some have always been pure and are thus part of the individual, forming an integrated whole. Other aspects of consciousness are negative and destructive and thus separate, like appendages. It is the task of each human being in each incarnation to synthesize, unify, and assimilate these various aspects of consciousness. If you truly try to comprehend what I say here, you may find that this is a novel way of explaining human existence. Naturally this not only applies to the level of human consciousness, but also to higher states of consciousness where the struggle is no longer as severe or painful. Increased awareness of higher states of consciousness facilitates the synthesizing process immeasurably. The human predicament is the general lack of understanding of what is going on, the blindness of many individuals involved in the struggle, and their deliberate attempts to perpetuate their blindness.

To the degree that struggle and tension exist in a personality, the various aspects of consciousness will be at odds with one another. The entity is unaware of the meaning of the struggle and is trying to identify with one, or several, of these aspects, without knowing which or what is the true self. Where is it located? What is it? How can it be found in the maze of this discord? Are you your best? Or are you your worst? Or are you any of the many aspects in between? Whether individuals know it or not, there is this on-going inner struggle and search. The more conscious the struggle is, the better, of course. Any path of self-development must sooner or later come to terms with these questions—with the deep problem of self-identity.

You are the Integrator

It is a human distortion to identify with any of the above-mentioned aspects. You are neither your negative traits nor your self-punishing superimposed conscience, nor even your positive traits. Even though you have managed to integrate the latter into the fullness of your being, this is not the same as identifying with them. It is more accurate to say that you are that part of you which managed this integration by determining, deciding, acting, thinking, and willing, so that you could absorb into your self what was previously an appendage. Each aspect of consciousness possesses a will of its own, as those of you who do the pathwork know. As long as you are blindly involved in the struggle and therefore submerged in it, each of these various aspects will control you in turn because the real self that could determine your identification differently has not yet found its power. Your blind involvement enslaves you and inactivates your creative energy. This missing sense of self leads to despair.

If the personality blindly believes it actually is nothing but its own destructive aspects, it becomes embroiled in a special kind of inner battle. On the one hand there will be self-annihilation, self-punishment, and violent self-hate as a reaction to perceiving the self as only the negative parts. On the other hand, how can you truly want to give up these negative traits or even fully face and investigate them when you believe that they are the only reality of the self? You are thrown back and forth between the attitudes of, "I must remain as I am, unchanged and unimproved, for this is my only reality and I do not want to cease to exist," and, "I am so terrible, so bad, so despicable, that I have no right to exist and therefore I must punish myself out of existence." Since this conflict is too painful to face when it is believed to be real, the entire issue is put to sleep.

You then lead a life of "as if," or pretense, which then shifts your sense of identity to your mask. You struggle against exposing the pretense, let alone giving up the pretense, for the only other alternative is the painful struggle I have just described. No wonder human beings have so much resistance. And yet, what a waste it is. For none of it is the true reality. There is a real self that equals neither your negative aspects, nor your adamant self-annihilation, nor the pretense that covers everything up. Finding this real self is our main concern.

Before the universal self can fully manifest in you, there is already one aspect of it available right now which you can immediately realize: your conscious self at its best, as it exists right now. It is a limited present manifestation of your spiritual being, but it is truly yourself; it is the "I" you need so as to make order out of all your confusion. This already manifest consciousness exists in many realms of your life, but you take it for granted. You have not yet brought it to bear on this area of conflict where you continue to be blindly controlled by a false self-identity, or rather by its consequences.

The "I" that is able to make a decision, for instance, to truly face this conflict and to observe its various expressions is the self with which you may safely identify. To the degree the personality awakens and self-consciousness is gained, such decisions and choices of attitude are possible. Conversely, to the degree such decisions and choices of attitude are made, consciousness awakens and expands. The immediately available consciousness of every living human being is usually not fully put to use right where the greatest sufferings and conflicts exist. The full scope of its power is not put into the service of this struggle about identity. When the entity begins to do this systematically, a major change will take place, and a new stage of development is reached. To the extent your conscious self can use its already existing knowledge of truth, its already existing power to execute good will, its already existing capacity to be positive, committed, truthful, courageous and persevering in the struggle to find your identity, and its already existing ability to choose with what attitude it should deal with the problem, to exactly that degree your consciousness expands and becomes increasingly more infiltrated by spiritual consciousness.

Spiritual consciousness cannot manifest when your already existing consciousness is not fully put to use in the conduct of your life. When you can put existing consciousness to use, new inspiration, new realms of vision, understanding and profound wisdom all well up from your depths. But as long as you follow the line of least resistance, giving in to blind involvement, giving up on finding true self-identity and settling blindly for a would-be existence, you remain stuck in the old rut of reacting from habit and easily justifying it. You indulge in compulsive, negative, hopelessly circular thinking, and your present consciousness cannot be fully put to use. Consequently, consciousness cannot possibly expand, nor can it transmute and synthesize the negative aspects with which it falsely identifies itself. It also cannot bring in deeper aspects of the spiritual self. As long as existing values are not fully put to use, additional values cannot possibly be realized. This is a law of life that applies to all levels of being. This is a very important thing to understand, my friends.

When you identify with one or even a cluster of aspects and believe that these aspects are you, you become submerged in them. At the very beginning when I started giving lectures, I used the terms higher self, lower self, and mask self. These are very abbreviated terms which comprise, of course, many subdivisions and variations. As a convenient frame of reference, one may classify certain aspects as belonging to one or the other of these three basic categories.

The genuine will for good is, needless to say, an expression of the higher self. But there is also another will for good which can easily be confused with the former, though it is by no means the same. It is the will to be good for the sake of appearance, for the sake of denying the lower aspects, because the conscious, determining, choosing self does not take up the challenge to confront the negative aspects. The demoniacal, destructive aspects are obviously an expression of the lower self. But the giant guilt that threatens to punish these destructive aspects with total annihilation is not an expression of the higher self, although it may easily pose for it. It is, in fact, more destructive than the destructiveness itself. It comes entirely out of the false self-identification mentioned above. If you believe you are your demon, you seem to have no other choice but to annihilate yourself; yet you dread annihilation and thus hold on to the demon. But if you observe the demon, you can begin to identify with the part of you which observes.

You must never forget that no one is totally involved in this struggle, else it would be impossible to rise out of it. There are many aspects of your being where you do use the power of your creative thinking, where you expand your mind and thus build productively. But we are now focused on those areas where you are not expanding and productive.

As long as human beings are unable, or rather unwilling, to recognize their destructive aspects, they must be lost in them, and therefore cannot attain proper self-identification. Although your desire to hide the destructive aspects is more destructive than whatever it is you hide, at the same time it indicates that you wish to be free from destructiveness. Thus the desire to hide destructiveness is a misplaced, misunderstood, and misread message of the higher self. It is a wrong way of applying and interpreting the longing of the spiritual self. Now let us discuss further how the conscious self can be more activated and utilized, so that you can expand it and make room for spiritual consciousness to infiltrate it.

Everyone on the path who has worked diligently and conscientiously to shed the mask, to give up defenses, and to overcome the resistance to exposing apparently shameful liabilities, has experienced how acknowledging negative traits creates a new freedom. Why is this so? The obvious answer is that the mere fact that you have the courage and honesty to do so is in itself a relieving and liberating factor. But it goes beyond that, my friends.

The Shift in Identification

Through the very act of acknowledgement, a subtle but distinct shift in identification occurs. Before such acknowledgement, you were blind to some or all of your destructive aspects and were therefore helplessly controlled by them, indicating that you believed them to be you. You could not afford to even acknowledge these unacceptable aspects, because you identified with them. But the moment you acknowledge the hitherto unacceptable, you yourself cease to be the unacceptable; instead, you become identified with that part of you which can and does decide to make the acknowledgement. Then some other part takes over which can do something about them, even if, to begin with, it can merely observe and grope for some deeper understanding of the underlying dynamics. It is a totally different situation when you identify yourself with the ugly traits than when you identify them. The moment you identify them, you cease being identified with them. This is why it is so liberating to acknowledge the worst in your personality after having battled the ever-present resistance to do so. It will become even easier once you can make this clear distinction.

The moment you identify, observe, and clearly articulate your destructive aspects, you have found your real self with which you can safely identify. This real self can do many things—the first being what you are doing now: identifying, observing, and articulating. Now you no longer need to persecute yourself so mercilessly with your self-hate. There seems to be no way to avoid hating yourself as long as you have neglected this all-important process of identifying yourself with the real self, which also has the power to recognize and adopt new attitudes, without devastating self-judgement. It is also possible to judge negatively in a truthful spirit, but there is all the difference in the world between believing that what you judge is the only truth of your being, and realizing that the part of you which can acknowledge the presence of destructiveness has other options and is closer to your ultimate reality.

How different your attitude to yourself must be when you realize that it is the task of human beings to carry negative aspects with them for the purpose of integrating and synthesizing them. This allows for truthfulness without hopelessness. What a dignity it lends you when you consider that you undertake this important task for the sake of evolution.

When you come into this life, you bring negative aspects with you for the purpose just mentioned. There exist certain meaningful laws which determine what aspects you bring with you. Every human being fulfills some immense task in the universal scale of evolution. This task gives you great dignity, which is so much more important than the momentary suffering that accrues from not knowing who you are. Only when you first take responsibility for them can you come to the wonderful realization that you are not them, but that you carry something in you for which you have taken responsibility for an evolutionary purpose. Only then can come the next step: that of integration.

The Four Stages of Awareness

Let me recapitulate the four stages of awareness mentioned thus far:

(1) the half-asleep climate where you do not know who you are and blindly battle against what you hate in yourself—either consciously, semiconsciously, or unconsciously;

(2) the first state of awakening, when you can acknowledge, observe, and articulate what you do not like; when you can feel that this is just an aspect of you, rather than the secret ultimate truth about you;

(3) the awareness that the "I" or real self which observes, articulates, can also make new decisions and choices, and can look for hitherto undreamed-of options and possibilities—not by magic, but by trying out attitudes that were totally negated and ignored before. Some examples of new attitudes are: setting a positive goal of self-acceptance without losing a sense of proportion; groping for new ways; learning from mistakes and failures; refusing to give up when immediate success fails to arrive; putting faith into unknown potentials which can manifest only as these new modes are adopted by the consciousness.

The attitude of adopting the new modes of perception which your consciousness is capable of right now leads directly to

(4) the eventual comprehension of those previously negated and hated aspects, which means their dissolution and integration. Simultaneously, the ever-expanding consciousness merges with more of the spiritual reality which can now unfold to ever greater degrees. This is what is meant by purification. To the extent you lead your life in such a way, the overall consciousness permeating the universe becomes less split off into separate particles and more unified.

When you assimilate what I have said here, you will understand several all-important facts. First of all you will see the tremendous overall importance of recognizing the distorted demonic traits. You will take full responsibility for them which will paradoxically liberate you from being identified with them. You will know your real self and recognize that these negative aspects are just appendages, which you can incorporate into yourself as you dissolve them. Their basic energy and undistorted nature can become part of the consciousness that you manifest.

Thus, no matter how undesirable the reality may be, you can

deal with it, accept it, explore it, and no longer be frightened by it. This capacity to observe, articulate, evaluate, and choose the best possible attitudes for dealing with what is observed—that is the true power of your real self as it already exists right now. Freedom, discovery, and knowledge of self are the first steps toward realizing the greater universal, divine consciousness in you. As long as this is not done, your innermost spiritual consciousness remains a principle, a theory, and a potential to be realized only in the future. You may believe in it with your intellect, but you cannot truly ascertain it within you until you use the consciousness already available to you now, but which you leave unused wherever your so-called problems exist. As these four stages are recognized and worked through in the way I outlined in this lecture, your conscious mind can expand sufficiently to let in the as yet unmanifest wisdom, truth, love, energy, strength of feeling, capacity to transcend painful opposites that will enrich and reorient your life toward creating more joy and pleasure.

Terror Disappears

The moment self-identification takes place, a deep and apparently bottomless terror of the human soul disappears. Often this terror is not experienced consciously. Only when you are on the threshold of these states, making the change from being lost, blind, and confused about what and who you are to having the first inklings of identification with your real self, do you become aware of the terror. This is a transitional period which may last for weeks or for many incarnations. You may hide the terror from yourself or face it. To the degree you do the latter, you will come out of it sooner. When you hide it, you have gained nothing, for the terror will still leave its indelible marks on your life. The hidden fears are not one iota less painful and limiting than the actual experience of the terror. In fact the truth is just the opposite.

The terror exists only because you do not know there is a

real you beyond those aspects of you which you hate. Because of this terror, you consistently hesitate to even identify what you hate. As long as you lack the courage to explore whether your fear is justified or not, you cannot find out that it is not, and that you are much, much more than what you fear you are. The human personality is often on the brink of wanting to make this step. But this brink feels like a precipice, and therefore you hesitate and prolong a pseudo-existence. When this point is not dealt with, terror remains in the soul; then the terror is denied and repressed—and the repressed terror has additional adverse effects on the personality, which becomes more and more alienated from its true nucleus.

When you finally make the full decision and commitment to face your fears, the terror disappears and you realize that you can find out who you truly are. You also find that life is full, rich, open, and infinite. The moment you experience yourself as being that part which observes, and not that which is being observed, there is no need any more to annihilate yourself, or to limit your identity to the fraudulent mask or the hateful demon or the petty, selfish egotist. So, identification with the real self removes the terror of annihilation—not just death, but annihilation, which is different.

We shall now return to your conscious mind as it already exists in you at this moment. It is now in the state of being able to acknowledge and observe the self, or an aspect of the self, and it has many choices. Your chosen attitude toward your undeveloped, undesirable traits is the key to expanding your consciousness.

Expanding Consciousness

You hear so much today about the concept of expanding consciousness. Often this is believed to be a magical process that suddenly occurs. It is not. To attain true spiritual consciousness it is necessary to first pay attention to the not yet fully utilized material within you. Every minute of depression or anxiety and every hopeless or otherwise negative attitude toward a situation contains various options. But it requires an act of inner will on your part to awaken your dormant forces and make them available to you. When the already available potentials are being used, a much greater power of spiritual consciousness unfolds gradually and organically.

People will often go through various spiritual practices and wait for a miraculous manifestation of the greater consciousness, while their immediate mind and thought power is ensnarled in the same negative attitudes, feelings, and thoughts. They must either be disappointed or experience delusions. No exercises, efforts, or hope for grace intervening from outside can bring you genuine awareness and genuine manifestation of your spiritual self.

The creative energy that is inherent in thoughts and thought processes is totally underestimated by most human beings. Hence, your processes for creating and re-creating life are neglected. Making use of this creative power is a challenging and fascinating undertaking. Right now you can explore the recesses of your conscious mind to search for new, better, and more creative ways of meeting difficulties, for more realistic and constructive ways of reacting. You do not have to react the way you do; you have at your disposal many possibilities of thinking, of directing your thoughts, thought processes, and attitude patterns to a new goal. To whatever degree identification with your real self has not taken place, and you find yourself still secretly identified with the aspects of you which you most hate and therefore resist even observing, to that degree your consciousness is unable to avail itself of its options and possibilities.

When you begin to pose the question to yourself, "What attitude do I choose toward what I now observe in me and what I do not like?" you have made one of the most significant discoveries in this present phase of your evolution. This does not require a subliminal breakthrough of the profounder spiritual self. It simply means using what you already have made available to yourself in the course of centuries and millennia of evolution.

What are your choices as you observe the destructive attitudes and intents within you? You can either choose—which you have done until now, only without awareness—to be totally dismayed and hopeless, or you can choose to think that it is impossible to ever be different and that this is all there is to you. You can also choose to think that you have the power to make an immediate and drastic change. This last attitude is no more positive than the previous one. Because it is based on unreality, it must lead to inevitable disappointment and to an apparently even more justified negativity. Unrealistic hopelessness and unrealistic magical hope are the two extremes which lead to a vicious circle.

But do you not have other options available? Isn't it possible, with your mind as it is now, to choose other modalities? Say, "It is likely and predictable that I will forget and become involved again in the old blindness and its conditioned reflexes. But this need not deter me. I will have to struggle again and grope to find, over and over again, my key. But I can do this, and I will do this and thereby gradually build new strength, resources, and energies. I will not be deterred by the fact that building a beautiful edifice requires patience. I will not be childish enough to expect this to be done at once. I want it and will use all my powers to do it, but I will be patient and realistic. I would like the spiritual powers in me to guide me, but if I cannot perceive the guidance yet because at the beginning of this undertaking my energies are too dense and my consciousness too dulled, I will trust and wait and persevere. I want to give my very best to the venture of living. I will try over and over again to identify, observe, and articulate what I do not like, without being identified with it. I will grope for new ways of understanding it all, so that I will eventually grow out of it."

Such an attitude is at your disposal. It is not magic. It is an immediately available choice. You can start now with the attitude that you would like to observe and identify, rather than be submerged in what you hitherto did not even wish to acknowledge. These and other attitudes and options exist in every possible dilemma and difficulty. Knowledge exists in you which you can bring to bear upon what you observe. If you use this available knowledge you expand the knowledge as well as the scope of your attitudes and feelings.

The more you do this, the more the infinitely greater and unlimited consciousness of your as yet submerged spiritual self will integrate itself into your conscious mind, and you will become it. As I said previously, this happens best in a threefold dialogue: the dialogue of the conscious self with the demonic aspects, the dialogue of the conscious mind with the divine self, and the dialogue between the divine self and the demonic self. In all three of these possibilities, both sides alternately speak and listen, as in every meaningful conversation. Therefore, the more you can perceive and observe in this way, the easier it will become to make the next leap: the realization of your true spiritual identity. You will then truly know that this incredible, beautiful, limitless conscious-ness is the real you, where all the power lies and where there is nothing to fear.

My friends, once again this lecture requires working through diligently. Much of the material cannot be taken in at first because it is difficult. It requires you to concentrate your mind and use your good will, and also contact through meditation higher realms of spiritual reality and power to help you absorb and put to use what I have said.

Be blessed, be in peace, be in God.

સ

DISSOLVING YOUR FEARS

Greetings, my dearest friends here.

We all know how important and essential it is to face and accept those aspects, feelings, convictions, and attitudes in you which are either not at all conscious or not sufficiently so. Unless this awareness is cultivated, it is impossible to free the innermost center of your being, the nucleus from which all life springs. Let us now try to see where you are with respect to the ground still to be covered within yourself. How much have you unearthed? How much are you aware of what is really going on in you, as opposed to the superficial explanations you have so handy?

To remove self-illusions seems at first insurmountably difficult, since all human beings vaguely believe that the underlying truth is unacceptable and that therefore they themselves are unacceptable. Thus a double illusion must be removed: the underlying belief in question, as well as the cover you put over it. And this is always the most arduous part of the pathwork.

Evil As Defense Against Suffering

To continue this phase of the work on yourself, it is necessary for you to comprehend on a deeper level where the negative attitudes and destructiveness come from. What is the real origin of evil? You know and have often heard me say that the denial of your vulnerabilities, your shame of feeling helpless, and your feeling of being unlovable create evil and destructive attitudes and feelings. In other words, evil is a defense against suffering.

It is therefore obvious that your further direction on the path can now be more directly concerned with the hurts and sufferings you have endured in your early life and have defended against so far. You who have learned to emotionally reexperience past feelings can corroborate as a felt reality what I have reiterated for so many years: the denial of the original experience compels you to reexperience it over and over again. You recreate the denied experience, and thus increase the accumulated pain and hurt. More of this reexperiencing must still be done, and now it can be done safely.

Too much of what you suffered as children, especially the extent of your unhappiness, is still only intellectual knowledge for you. You do not feel how unhappy you really were as a child, and for a long time many of you believed just the opposite about your childhood. Gaining this knowledge first intellectually is the necessary preparation to experiencing it. Without such intellectual awareness of the truth of your childhood the defenses cannot be sufficiently weakened for safe reexperiencing on the emotional level. When the defenses are still strong they block the path to the emotional experience so that the attempt to get to the feelings is choked off. You are now truly ready, my friends, to venture into the depths of your being. There you can let go, and give yourself freely to all the accumulated feelings which up to now could never leave your system. They could not be transformed before now into their natural energy-stream precisely because you had locked the gates against feeling your feelings.

The Problem of Laziness

Some time ago, I was asked to discuss the problem of

laziness. There is an intimate connection between the problem of laziness and feelings that have not been fully experienced. Do not look at laziness as an attitude to be given up at will, if only the person would finally come around to being reasonable and constructive. This is not a moralistic issue at all. Laziness is a manifestation of apathy, stagnation, and paralysis, a result of stagnant energy in the soul substance. Stagnant soul substance is the result of feelings that have not been fully experienced or expressed, and have therefore not been totally understood as to their significance and true origin. When feelings are not thus experienced, understood, and expressed, they accumulate and stop the flow of the life force.

It is not enough to deduce that you must have in you certain past feelings which must have logically brought about the present circumstances. Such deductive knowledge is often the necessary opening to allowing yourself the deeper experience. However, the knowing, by itself, can be a barricade when you replace the feeling with knowing. In this case the unity of these two functions is interrupted in the same way as when you feel and do not know what the feelings mean, why and how they came about, nor how they still direct your life now.

There still exist many defenses against the full experience of accumulated feelings in you, my friends, in spite of all your progress. Keeping this in mind will help you to focus your attention and awareness upon these defenses to overcome them more and more. You can systematically lower the threshold of defending against your deep accumulated experiences which have become poisonous from not being released. These painful experiences cannot be released if they are not felt, known, expressed, and lived through as fully as possible.

To recapitulate: all that is evil, destructive, and negative in human nature is a result of defending against experiencing painful, undesirable feelings. This denial stagnates energy. When feelings stagnate, energy stagnates; and if energy stagnates, you cannot move. As you know, feelings are moving energy currents. They transform constantly from one set or type of feeling into another, as long as the energy flows freely. Not experiencing feelings stops the movement of those currents and therefore stops the living energy. When the natural energy flow is halted within your soul substance, you find yourself in the position of feeling laziness, that state where movement is possible only when it is forced painfully by the outer will. So, my friends, when you find yourself stagnating, lazy, passive, or inert, and when you desire to do nothing, which is often confused with the spiritual state of just being, you have a good gauge that there are feelings in you which have created psychic toxicity because you were loath to experience and acknowledge them.

The stagnation of energy currents traps not only feelings but concepts as well. You generalize from single occurrences and hold on to the resulting false beliefs. It is rare that stagnant feelings do not also include stagnant conceptualizations of life. These may exist in the deepest recesses of the soul, totally hidden from consciousness. This is what I called years ago the "images" that are held within the psyche. I helped you find these images, and you saw how you were compelled to reexperience misconceptions and stagnant feelings. Over and over again you are entrapped in the cycle of reproducing the past in one way or another until you can summon the courage to choose to live through now what was not lived through before because of your defenses. You cannot come out of these repetitive cycles, no matter how good your intentions are and how much effort you use in other ways, unless you really fully reexperience your earlier feelings. We mentioned many times that the human predicament is the dualistic split, which is nothing but a delusion of perception. This delusion has many facets, one facet being a split in the human consciousness itself. Human beings may feel one thing, believe another, and act without knowing how both these functions govern them. Lack of awareness of what you feel and what you really believe creates another manifestation of the split. When you unify knowing and feeling, you work toward mending and integration, which manifests as a wonderful new awakening and sense of wholeness.

When feelings are not experienced in their full intensity, the inner life flow must become stagnant. People will find themselves inexplicably paralyzed. Their actions will become ineffectual; life will seem to obstruct all their goals and desires. They find closed doors to realizing their talents, their needs, their selves. So-called laziness may be one manifestation of this paralysis. A lack of creativity or a feeling of general despair may be another. In this latter instance, people may often use a current event or difficulty to explain away their inner state. The truth is that a sense of futility and confusion about life and your role in it must envelop you when you resist living through the feelings you harbor; you go on harboring them because you delude yourself that avoiding the feelings will hurt you less than exposing them. There are many other manifestations. The inability to feel pleasure or to fully experience life is one of the most widespread general effects.

The Fear of Feeling All Feelings

The total experience of a feeling is as available as your willingness and readiness to venture into it. These feelings are often accumulations of centuries or millennia—not just decades. Each life incarnation presents the task of cleansing yourself by experiencing and understanding them. You are purified when there is no more waste material. After you terminate this life cycle, the conditions, circumstances, and environment of your next life into which you are drawn by an inexorable law of life, will afford you the opportunity to bring to the fore any previously accumulated waste material. But memory of previous incarnations is blotted out, so that you have only this life's past experiences to draw on.

The dimming of memory is a byproduct of the life/death cycle in which everyone is caught who denies feeling experience. When you go on denying awareness and refusing to feel the experience of what you have lived through in this very life, you perpetuate the process of dimming memory. Thus you perpetuate the cycle of dying and being born, and this process always manifests as a break in the continuity of awareness. Conversely, you eliminate this discontinuity of awareness, and with it the entire cycle of dying and being born, by living through whatever has accumulated from this life wherever it is possible to re-establish the links of memory. If all the feelings of this lifetime are fully experienced, all residual matter of previous lives will automatically be dealt with because the trauma of the now is only a trauma because the previous pains had been denied.

You can do this, my friends, if you trust in the process and in the venture of letting go, truly letting go. And here again is the problem. You cannot let go if your innermost being defends against feeling your feelings, which you know exist inside of yourself. Actually you defend against establishing a connecting link between those feelings, your inner knowledge, and your current action patterns. The paralysis that is often deemed laziness, and about which you moralize as if it were that, is therefore to be viewed as a very indirect symptom.

Laziness is a protection against the movement of the soul substance which threatens to bring up the feelings you think you can go on avoiding without blocking your very life. Thus laziness is simultaneously an effect as well as a defense. Movement stirs up what lies stagnant. By fully understanding this, you can redirect your inner will and intent toward overcoming this self-induced protective stagnation, by mustering the courage to feel what is there to feel.

The true, serene state of being which every soul unconsciously longs for is not cautious passivity which must avoid movement and makes movement appear undesirable. The true spiritual state of being is a very active state, although it is a calm and relaxed state at the same time. It is joyous movement and action. It is only the passivity of the fearful self that creates frenzy as a counter-action against the stagnation. It is as though the personality fought hard against the stagnation by superimposing compulsive action, and then became more alienated from the truth of its stagnation, and from the reason for the stagnation, which is the fear of feeling all feelings including fear. Only when this truth is fully felt and understood, when you stop fighting against it and dissolve what causes it by feeling your feelings, can you come out of both the frenzy of overactivity and the paralysis. In other words, you must come to feel the fear that lies in laziness and in all types of stagnation.

This fear sits in everyone, even in those of you who are not overtly lazy, or who are not aware of other symptoms which this denied fear creates. This basic human condition of fear must be allowed to express itself outwardly. You must allow it to take over, in the right setting of course. And when you experience this fear, you will find two basic elements within it. The first is the childhood conditions which were so painful that you thought you could not let yourself feel them, so you cut yourself off from them. And the second even more important and significant element is the fear of the fear; the fear of experiencing the fear. This is where the real harm lies.

A number of years ago I spoke to you in a lecture on the phenomenon of self-perpetuation,[1] and I illustrated how a denied feeling compounds itself so that it multiplies. For example: denied fear creates fear of fear, and then the fear of feeling the fear of the fear, and so on. The same is true about other feelings. Denied anger creates anger at being angry. Then when this is denied, one becomes even angrier for being unable to accept the anger, and on and on. Frustration itself is bearable when you fully go into it. But when you are frustrated because you "ought" not to be frustrated, and then are even more frustrated because you deny it, the pain extends. This process is

1. See Lecture No. 140

so significant because it points clearly to the necessity of feeling directly, no matter how undesirable feelings may be. If you compound your pain because you deny feeling your pain, this secondary pain must become bitter, twisted, and unbearable. If you accept and feel the pain, a dissolving process begins automatically. Many of you have experienced this truth a number of times in your pathwork. The same is true with fear, anger, frustration, or whatever the feeling may be.

Thus, when you feel the fear of your fear and can let yourself drop into the fear itself, this fear will very quickly give way to another denied feeling. The denied feeling—whatever it may be—will become easier to bear than its denial, the fear. And the fear itself is more bearable than the fear of the fear. In that way, you can progress to the nucleus of the accumulated waste energy of denied feelings. Fighting your feelings and defending against them creates a whole extra layer of experience that is alienated from your core and therefore artificial and more painful than the original experience it fights against.

Commit to Going In and Through

Your whole conscious self has to gather all its faculties, all its resources, and use all the ground you have gained in order to be fully determined to experience the fear of deep, painful, hurtful, frightening feelings in you. As I have often said to you, "The only way out is in and through."

It is important now to focus your meditation. Those of you who have become convinced of the great power you thus generate have learned that the specific focusing and conscious direction you give to your meditations evokes an inner guidance in the right and balanced measure, which you can then apply to your life. The proper direction is twofold. First you need a commitment to go in and not around yourself. This voluntary commitment to going in and through your feelings should be the driving force in this specific meditation. Your declaration and statement that this is what you want and intend to do must create a new condition in your soul substance. You can then request specific guidance which will immediately loosen up some of the stagnant matter. The laziness that makes you avoid, postpone, and procrastinate will disappear sufficiently at this point to set a new energy influx in motion. The voluntary attitude of commitment will create an involuntary energy influx and activate the guiding wisdom of your spiritual self. Stating in your meditation your intent and wish to experience all accumulated feelings and rid yourself of waste is the best and most effective beginning.

In addition to right balance and timing, inner and outer guidance will be set up in just the way you need it for your personal situation. You will learn to become attuned to this guidance and sense it, rather than miss out and be blind and deaf to it. For it always exists as a waiting potential—not just for this phase of the path, of course, but for every single, specific phase that is necessary for you to go through. The outer, volitional self must voluntarily play its part so that the involuntary self can then take over.

This involuntary self manifests in two entirely different ways: the higher wisdom and guidance just mentioned, and the surfacing of the self that often writhes in pain but denies the experience of the residual pain of long ago. The first helps and guides the latter.

Through this meditational approach, energy is released that can be directed to this all-important purpose. You often persuade yourself that you lack the energy and the time to go into the depths of your feelings. At the same time you spend a lot of energy on other activities which may well seem more important at the moment. No matter how vitally important the other activities are, they can never be more important than this exploration, for attending to this life task is your true reason for living. In addition, it is the key to productive living for you right now.

The second important aspect of meditation is to summon your faith that "going in" will not annihilate you. Without this act of faith you will not have the courage to do it. To put it differently, if the safety and validity of this course is not clearly conceived at the outset, your disinclination to experience painful feelings will inadvertently lead you to manufacture an artificial doubt about the safety of the process. Together with this comes an artificial illusion that "going in" can be avoided and still permit you to achieve integration, health, and a full life. Avoidance of feelings always creates such dualistic paradoxes of false doubt and false hope.

Many years ago in a lecture called "The Abyss Of Illusion" I said that the path of self-realization and unification contains many junctures where it is necessary to let the self fall into what appears to be a bottomless abyss. Falling into it threatens to annihilate the entity. I said that up to a certain point in the individual's evolution, he or she crouches in front of this abyss, holding on and not daring to jump. The individual is very, very miserable in this state, but still believes that the pseudo-safety of this cramped, fearful position is preferable to annihilation. Only after finally summoning sufficient trust to risk the jump can the person find out that he or she actually floats. Many such junctures are necessary for making the discovery all over again that it is safe to jump.

The same applies to letting yourself fall into the apparent abyss of your blocked feelings—painful, frightening feelings. Unless you do so, you will remain in the crouched, uncomfortable position in which it is really quite impossible to live and enjoy yourself. The necessary faith to take the jump can be activated by confronting the issue squarely and examining what is at stake. You have to give consideration to the fundamental question which can be summed up as follows: "Is there really a bottomless pit of negativity, destruction, and evil at the foundation of the human condition? Or are these aspects of a distortion that need not exist?" There are many junctures where a human being's faith is put to the test. You have to face the discrepancy between what you claim to believe and what you actually do believe. If you believe in humanity's ultimate spiritual nature, then you have nothing to fear. If you do not, it is necessary to be aware of this underlying doubt and confront its real nature. Having your doubts in the open will, at least, protect you from the illusory nature of your faith in humanity and its spiritual destiny. If you then come out with the conviction that you really believe human nature is ultimately bad, destructive, fearsome, and chaotic, the true motive and reason for this belief must also be examined. Such confrontation with what one truly believes versus what one thinks one believes must always be honestly worked through. This is true for any single issue of importance. Help and guidance can and should also be activated through meditation for this specific purpose.

Also state in your meditation that you wish to be aware of your special methods of avoidance, and that you no longer want to deceive yourself in this regard. It is better to go on avoiding the jump into the abyss and knowing that you do so and why, than to deny your fear of it and pretend to be unafraid. By freely admitting your fear, you are more in touch with yourself than when you deny the fear. By confronting the validity of the fear, you may often find that the real reason behind the fear is shame and its partner, pride. Denied pride and shame often create fear. The idea that it is humiliating to have certain feelings or be in certain vulnerable states, along with the idea that you ought not to be where you are, and the feeling that your past suffering as a child is due to your being unacceptable and unlovable, all create the tendency to deny the state you are in. The pressure of this denial then creates fear, and the fear in turn requires the person to concoct theories to justify the fear. If people convince themselves that it is indeed dangerous to feel their feelings, this conviction may bring about a breakdown and a crisis that is merely a result of this deep conviction. Terror can bring the person into an acute state of crisis. But the true underlying core feeling is often merely shame/pride and the misconception that the childhood pain existed because of personal inadequacy which the individual is too ashamed to expose.

Crossing the barrier of embarrassment, humiliation, shame, and pride will often dissolve fear. You must confront and squarely face these issues. Only thus can the way be smoothed to let yourself go into yourself. *Meditation is a requirement without which the way becomes unnecessarily difficult.* Such an approach and attitude will build the climate you need to go into the abyss of fright, loneliness, helplessness, pain, and the anger generated by the suffering you had to endure. Every tear not shed is a stoppage. Every protest not voiced sits in you and makes you express it where it is inappropriate. All these feelings seem like bottomless pits, but once you jump into them you are bound to find that there is deep inside of you that divine nucleus which dwells in you and of which you are an expression. It is a light, a warmth, an aliveness, and a security. All these are stark realities but can be experienced only when you go through the heretofore denied reality of avoided feelings.

Through the Gateway

Your spiritual self with all its joy, safety, and peace is right behind the sadness and pain. It cannot be activated by a direct act of will, nor by practices and actions that leave out the necessity to experience all your feelings. But your spiritual center does manifest inexorably as a byproduct, the result of the direct act of will to go through your denied feelings.

I will end this lecture by telling you that the fear is not real. It is truly an illusion, but you must go through it by feeling it. Through the gateway of feeling your weakness lies your strength; through the gateway of feeling your pain lies your pleasure and joy; through the gateway of feeling your fear lies your security and safety; through the gateway of feeling your loneliness lies your capacity to have fulfillment, love and companionship; through the gateway of feeling your hate lies your capacity to love; through the gateway of feeling your hopelessness lies true and justified hope; through the gateway of accepting the lacks of your childhood lies your fulfillment now. When you experience all these feelings and states, it is essential that you do not delude yourself into believing they are caused by anything you experience or fail to experience now. Whatever the now brings forth is only the result of the past which still resides in your system.

Through these gateways you will find true life. All the many temptations that beckon you to follow paths which imply that it is possible to find the spiritual reality of yourself without going through these gateways are wishful thinking. There is no way around what has accumulated in you and has poisoned your whole system—your spiritual, your psychological, and often also your physical system. This poison can be eliminated only by feeling what you hoped you could avoid feeling. Then a new energy influx comes in ever greater measure. Many of you have experienced to some degree what I am saying here, and therein lies your growth. But you all have to go further in this regard. The self-punishment for hatred and spite, for cruelty and greed, for selfishness and one-sided demands upon others must be released so you can go into the terror of your fear, your shame, your pain. When you stop fighting this, you will become real, open, and truly alive.

Blessings to you all.

ॐ

IDENTIFICATION WITH THE SPIRITUAL SELF TO OVERCOME NEGATIVE INTENTIONALITY

Blessings and greetings for everyone of you here. Let the power of spirit enliven you, live and manifest through you. Then you will be in the real world and your life will have meaning. Every step you take in this direction generates new energy. You who truly want to find out who you are, and are prepared to make the sacrifice of giving up old destructive patterns of thinking and reacting, will discover the incomparable treasure within you. Then the word sacrifice becomes indeed ludicrous, for you give up nothing to gain everything.

As you become more perceptive and attuned as a result of your accelerating development, you know that the reality of spirit is much greater than that of the things you touch and see. The spiritual energy that is generated by you becomes self-perpetuating. This is noticeable in your personal lives as well as in your undertakings with others. Of course, even after making great progress you still have to deal with your defenses and undissolved negativities, your resistances, distortions, and darkness. As usual, these aspects must first be fully acknowledged and accepted before you can give them up. It is impossible to let go of something you do not know you have or will not express.

Negative Intentionality
Now I should like to speak about the need to be aware of

your previously concealed but now conscious negative intentionality. In the past you may have accepted the theory that you, too, have a lower self, that you have faults and character defects. You may have even faced many of them and dealt with them honestly and constructively. But this is not the same as finding your negative intentionality.

It is an important fact of human psychology that whatever people fear, they unconsciously want; that whatever they experience, they also unconsciously want. The entire pathwork is based on this true fact of life. Now many of you are truly face to face with a basic negating attitude toward life: an attitude that expresses no desire to give, to love, to contribute, to reach out, to receive, or to live well and fruitfully. This may sound preposterous to the conscious mind that wishes for nothing more than any and all fulfillments imaginable. But there is this other part of the soul, in a hidden corner of the psyche, which says just the opposite. It wants to hate, to be spiteful, to withhold—even if this causes suffering and deprivation.

Recognizing this part of the soul is of paramount importance. It need not be the major part of the self. In fact, it may be that a relatively small part of your consciousness is locked into negation, while a much more substantial part of the self strives for the opposite. But no matter how small in relationship to the liberated, positive aspects of self, the negative part holds a magnetic power over the life of the individual precisely because it is not being consciously recognized.

When you become aware of this negative intentionality, you begin to perceive what a devastating grip this attitude has on you and your life. In spite of your knowing how destructive and how senseless it is, you still find yourself unable—that is, unwilling—to abandon this attitude. A great effort in overcoming resistance is necessary before you can accept this, at first shocking, realization about your life. As a matter of fact, much of the resistance you encounter in yourself and your companions is based precisely on not wanting to see the existence of such senseless destruction and negation within you.

But when you finally do see it, it is a blessing. You can then deal with this negation of life. There are a number of "reasons" for negativity, if we may call them that, of which you are already quite conscious. Nevertheless, you may find that you still cannot move from this point. Yet the mere fact that you know that *you* are the one who wants isolation, loneliness, lovelessness, hate, and spite, instead of blaming some fate that befalls the innocent you, is a key to finding the next link in the chain of your evolution.

At this point, it would be useful to make a clear distinction between *negativity* and *negative intentionality*. Negativity comprises a wide range of feelings including hostility, envy, hate, fear, pride, and anger, to name a few. But when we speak of negative intentionality, we mean expressly the intention to hold on to the state of negating life and the self. The mere word intention connotes that the self is in charge, and makes a deliberate choice, intending to do, act, and to be in a certain way. Now even when you own up to the most destructive, cruel, and brutal attitudes, you always give an impression that you cannot help being the way you are. However when you ferret out your negative intentionality, you can no longer deceive yourself that negativity just "happens" to you. You must sooner or later come to terms with the fact that your life is the result of your choices. And choice implies the possibility of adopting another attitude. In other words, you can truly discover on a deep level that you are free. Even your present narrow confines are the result of a freely chosen course you follow and will continue to follow until you choose to change this course.

To the conscious mind, such negative intentions may appear preposterous, but rest assured that negative intentionality indeed exists. To admit and to deal with this fact extensively and profoundly takes considerable struggle, effort, and patience as well as an inner overcoming of resistance. I do not talk about an occasional vague hint of a recognition that is then left to itself.

Truly dealing with one's negative intentionality is a major crisis in one's life and signifies a basic transition. It is not something that anyone can easily come by.

Let us now look at certain fundamental stages and progressions of this transition. You can start out on such a path without any awareness of your stubborn negative intentions. As I said before, if you were to be confronted with this fact, you could not believe it, let alone feel and observe it within you. You might be aware of some faults and destructive attitudes, of some neurotic behavior and feelings, but I cannot sufficiently emphasize that this is not at all the same as being aware of your negative intentionality.

When your pathwork progresses well and you gain deeper and more honest insight into yourself you can accept more of your good as well as your painful feelings. You gain strength and objectivity. By your renewed commitment to facing the truth in yourself over and over again, which activates the purest spiritual energies, you finally come to discover your intentional negation of all the good things in life. You will find that the more frustrated you feel for not attaining what you so ardently desire, the greater your inner negative intention and the less inclination you have to deal with it. This correlation is extremely important. The same applies to doubts: the more you fear that what you want will not materialize, the less faith you have in your life, and the less connected you are with your own negative will.

A New Hope

That the self deliberately chooses a course of denial, spite, and hate even at the price of suffering is tremendously difficult to admit. But once this is done, the door opens to freedom, even before one is actually ready to step through it. Even before the self is ready to make a new choice, the mere availability of another road, another approach to life and to reinvesting one's energies and resources, brings hope—not false hope, but realistic expectation.

You pin so much on false hopes, my friends. You actually invest your best energies into neurotic solutions based on unrealizable hopes or on sheer illusion. But there exists a real, realistic and realizable hope: a hope that is not bound to wind up in disappointments and disillusionments. This hope slowly but surely grows into manifest reality and fact, resulting in self-fulfillment and the realization of the best within you, and therefore access to all that life has to offer. Just think of all the potentialities life has to offer. They are endless and they are yours for the asking.

However, important as it is to discover the existence of your negative intentionality, awareness is not the same as giving it up. Sometimes it can happen that realizing a destructive or distorted attitude automatically eliminates it, but this is not always true. It becomes evident again and again in almost everybody's work that in spite of knowing how senseless and destructive one's negative intentionality is, more than just recognizing it is required before the mind, the will, and the intention can be changed.

We have already gone into many of the beliefs and misconceptions, motives and reasons why this is so. We have worked on many of them. There is the fear of the unknown; the fear of being hurt and humiliated; the fear of and refusal to experience pain, past and present. A negative attitude is thus a defense against real feelings. Holding on to a negative will direction is also due to a refusal to assume responsibility in life; or to deal with less than ideal circumstances. It is an inner insistence on forcing your "bad parents" to become "good parents" using your misery as a weapon against them. Negative intentionality is also a means to punish life in general. Some of you may have amply explored, verified and worked through these feelings, reactions and attitudes, yet you still insist on holding on to them. Why?

We have also worked on the origin of this negation. It is often the only way a child has to preserve its selfhood. If the inner resistance is not maintained, the personality feels threatened: the child equates giving up the resistance with capitulation, with giving up his individuality. Many of you are aware of this and know the inappropriateness of carrying a once valid position into the present where it is no longer valid and downright destructive.

It may seem almost inconceivable to those of you who have not yet made the self-discovery that one can admit to a senseless, wasteful attitude that does nothing but bring undesirable results, and yet insist on maintaining it. Why does this apparently senseless refusal exist, even though you know it only causes you and others pain? There must be a powerful reason that obviously goes beyond any of the aforementioned causes—true as they are in themselves. Many of you are stuck at this particular point and need help to get beyond it.

What Part Do You Identify With?

In order to deal with this bottleneck, the question of identification has to be focused on. What part of yourself do you identify with? Such identification is not something the conscious ego chooses. Once again, it is something that must be discovered by your observing mind. In what way are you identified with the different parts of your being?

For example, if you exclusively identify with the ego—that conscious, willing, acting part of you—it is automatically impossible to bring a change that lies beyond the province of the ego. Inner change of the deepest attitudes and feelings of an individual cannot be brought about by the very limited functions of the ego. One must be identified with a deeper, broader, and more effective aspect of the self in order to even believe in the possibility of such a change. Any profound change comes about by the ego committing itself to wanting the change, and trusting in the processes of the involuntary spiritual self to bring it about. If there is no identification with the spiritual self, such trust and the necessary climate of unpressured positive expectation cannot exist. And if it does not exist, the person cannot even want it, for the conviction of failure would drive home the powerlessness of the ego in too unpleasant a way. Thus it is preferable for the limited ego to say, "I do not want" than to say, "I cannot."

Identification can exist in a most positive and constructive way or in a most negative, obstructive and destructive way. The difference is not determined by your identification with one or the other of the various personality aspects—as if one would be good, the other bad. Identification with any aspect of yourself can be either desirable, healthy and fruitful, or the opposite. For example, you might think, "How can it be destructive to identify with the higher self?"

If you identify with the higher self without truly being aware of your lower self, mask self, your defenses, your dishonest devices, and your negative intentionality, then your identification with the higher self becomes an escape and an illusion. Under these circumstances it is not at all a truthful or a real experience. It is much more like paying lip service to a philosophy you believe in on the purely intellectual level. It is all very well to know that you are a divine manifestation with potentially limitless power to change yourself and your life, that you are the very spirit of the universe in manifest form. This is true. And yet it is a half-truth when this kind of identification overlooks the part of you which needs your scrutiny and candid attention.

By the same token, it is one thing to identify with your lower self or your mask self, but to observe and identify it is another. When you are identified with the lower self, you believe that this is all there is to you. When you identify it, observe, admit, and tackle it, you do not believe that this is all there is to you. If it were, you could not identify, observe, evaluate, analyze and change it. For that part of you which is doing all this watching is certainly more in charge, has more power, and is more active and real than the part that is being observed, evaluated, or changed. The moment you identify something, good, bad or indifferent, the identifying part is more you than whatever is being identified. In other words the observer is more real and in charge than the observed.

This is the vast difference between identifying something and being identified with it. When the mask and lower self, or the negative intentionality, are being identified, there is room for real feelings, including pain, to be honestly experienced, and the pain no longer needs to be denied. This is so because the energy no longer invested in denial will bring you to the truth. And when you can truly feel your feelings, you can then identify with the spiritual self.

The lower self should be identified; the spiritual self identified with. The ego makes the identification, but gives itself up voluntarily so that it is integrated into the spiritual self.

Giving Up Negative Intentionality

When giving up negative intentionality, the person experiences himself already as something more than this lower self that should be dissolved. That is, its energies are being dissolved in their present form, and are being reconverted, altered, and channeled in a new and better way. The senseless refusal to give up negative will exists because the person is completely and totally identified with this aspect of the self, regardless of other developed aspects of the self where this may not hold true at all. In other words, this is not a total condition. It is not true to say that the person is either entirely identified with the lower self or not at all. It is invariably a combination: some aspects of the self are free, and in those areas a deep spiritual identification may be sensed. At the same time, the as yet unidentified lower self aspects, the as yet unfelt feelings, create, in part, a fearful submersion into the lower self, which the self believes to be its only reality. Also at the same time, a third identification, one with the ego as the only valid, reliable function, can exist too. This is the way people are split in regard to identification.

When a secret, albeit partial, identification with the lower self exists, giving it up is like self-annihilation. To that part of the self that is destructive, cruel, hateful, and spiteful, this seems the real self. Anything else seems unreal, perhaps even phony, especially when an actual phony veneer is used to cover up the reality of the lower self. Giving up hate, spite, negative intentions seems like giving up one's very being. Such apparent self-annihilation cannot be risked, even if the promise beckons you that joy and fulfillment accrue from this sacrifice. At best, this joy appears to exist for someone other than the familiar you. What good do joy, fulfillment, pleasure, self-respect, abundance do if they are to be experienced by someone other than you? This is the unarticulated feeling and climate.

This is the most difficult part to overcome. Or, perhaps, I should correct this and state that it is the second most difficult part. The first is to make the initial commitment to find out the truth about yourself. This includes the mental observation and admission of your real thoughts, the experiencing of all feelings, and owning up to them on all levels. The second is to extricate yourself from your identification with your lower self.

When you experience yourself as real only in the lower self, to whatever degree this may hold true, you cannot give up the lower self. The refusal to do so is the misplaced will to live. You live in the illusion that beyond your most negative aspects nothing of you exists. You feel real and energized only when negativity and destructiveness manifest, no matter how much the environment curtails it and forces you to experience this energy as existing only inside of yourself. The outer deadness and numbness seem the result of having "given up" evil; but it has not been given up at all.

My friends, let this sink in: your resistance to giving up what you hate most in yourself is due to a false identification.

The Way Out

How are you going to find your way out? The first thing to

do would be to question yourself, "Is this really all I am? Is it true that my reality ceases to exist when I give up my negative intention and will? Is this all there is to me?" The mere fact that you raise these questions honestly will already open a door. Even before the answers come—and they will eventually pour forth—the fact that these questions are raised will permit you to come to the second stage in this progression where you realize that the part which asks the question is already beyond your assumed identity. Thus you already establish a new bridge. From there on it will not be quite so difficult to find a voice in you that answers in a new way, beyond the limited scope of the lower self which you used to protect so jealously.

Reach out with tentative questions, questions asked with good will and in good faith. This is the very first step to find your way out of your prison of unnecessary suffering. When you do this, you are no longer identified with the lower self which knows nothing beyond these confined walls and derives its identity, or reality, from being negative. Instead, you come to the point when you can identify it and be its observer. Identifying with the observer then becomes a first step away from and a first extension beyond your familiar self-experience.

Let us assume, for example, that you have grown accustomed to experience yourself as haughty, cold, and contemptuous. Giving up this attitude seems like dying. But dying into what? Dying into your true self where your real feelings and your real being are. If you are willing to feel your feelings regardless of their nature, you will know who you are. If you are not willing, you must remain that hard, stiffened, limited "self." Here lies your choice.

It cannot be claimed that when you give up your negative intentionality you will instantly experience bliss. You will experience your real feelings, some of them quite painful. But the pain will be so much easier to bear than the position you now maintain. In its flowing nature it will carry you into new and better states, like the river of life itself.

The commitment must always be to the truth of the self—what it really feels and thinks and is. If commitment to the self is the aim, then you cannot fail to realize yourself. You will experience new depths of feelings. You will even welcome the pain for it is real, it is moving and is totally you.

The first answers you will receive to your questions may not even come from your deeper, spiritual self as yet. The first answers may come from your conscious mind. Your ability to formulate new possibilities and answers and to use the knowledge of truth that is already integrated into your consciousness will feel safe and very real. At the same time, it will give you a new key to use the equipment at your disposal in ways other than your habitual old groove.

Such new thoughts may take into consideration that trying out a positive intentionality could be interesting and desirable for you. You could play at first with forming new thoughts, weighing new possibilities and alternatives in the way you set your thinking apparatus. This is an exciting endeavor and one that does not in principle oblige you to follow any course of action. It merely means giving a new scope to a very set mind. You can always exert your right to go back where you were, you are never coerced by life or anyone else. It is always your choice. This knowledge will make the apparent risk of trying out a new thought-direction seem less final. Just investigate how it feels to set a positive intentionality in motion. As you avail yourself of this new freedom, you build another bridge to a greater expansion of the self. Little by little you can become calm, and listen into yourself. You will perceive the ever present, ongoing voice of truth and God. It will increase in intensity and frequency until you realize that you are everything that exists. There is nothing you are not, my friends. This may sound very far off, but it is not as far away from you as it may now seem.

You who make yourselves available to new possibilities in conceiving, perceiving, and forming new inner attitudes will experience the richness of the universe, the richness of its innermost being. New action and new outer experience stream forth from that. You who stay confined within your old possibilities must stay in an unsatisfactory condition no matter how developed you may be relative to others. There is no standing still. If you stand still you confine yourself. Only when you continue to expand can you truly become yourself.

A beautiful golden force wants to work its way through the clouds. The clouds disperse more and more. To whatever degree you take a step toward merely wanting it, the clouds become thinner. To whatever degree you hide behind negation and doubt, which are the strongest defenses against coming out of your hold, the golden sun and force cannot come through. But it is there. Do not believe that you have to become a different person. You become the best that you already are. When you become it you will recognize it, you will experience its familiarity and you will feel how safe it is, how much you it is! It is the best of you. You do not betray your reality, you do not become something that you need be ashamed of. Try to believe this. Let go a little. Let the light come into you and accept that reality is not dismal. Reality is beautiful. The universe is full of love. Truth is love and love is truth. The freedom of your own spirit will be found in truth and love. Be blessed, all of you!

ࢍ

TRANSITION TO
POSITIVE INTENTIONALITY

Greetings, and God bless everyone of you here. Focus on the dimension which now wants to communicate its fullness and richness to you. You can be enriched by it if you so choose. It is a question of focus and intent. Ask inner guidance to help you in this endeavor so that this lecture will again be helpful as a further step in your search.

I would like to discuss again—this time on a deeper level and with a new approach—your attempt to change negative intentionality into positive expressions. Many of you who are doing this pathwork are finally aware of what you previously ignored, denied, or repressed. How important and vitally essential this is on any path of self-knowledge, self-confrontation, and purification. But it is not enough, my friends, to be aware; more must come.

I have also said that a fundamental reason for the difficulty in changing negative to positive intentionality is that secretly the self identifies almost totally with the destructive part. Hence, giving up this part of the personality appears hazardous, dangerous, and annihilating. The question then is how to proceed in order to shift that subtle, inner sense of identity. When negative expressions are not admitted to the self they congeal into a festering sore of guilt and self-doubt which, translated into concise words, would mean: "If only the truth were known about me, it would be that I am all bad. But since this is the real me, and since I do not want to cease existing, I cannot want to give up me. All I can do is pretend that I am different."

This is a devastating soul climate in which confusion grows and the genuine sense of self gets more and more lost. Theoretical correct knowledge in the intellect does little to alleviate this painful and disturbing condition. In this lecture we shall deal in more detail with the process I recommend in order to create a change.

Examine All Thoughts

The first step is to realize that your negative intentionality is really not unconscious in the strict sense of the word. It is not at all deeply repressed material. It is really a conscious attitude and expression, only you have chosen to ignore it, until you have finally "forgotten" that it is there. Sustained, deliberate looking away from something eventually results in really not seeing what has been there all along. The moment the eye begins to focus again, the material immediately becomes discernible. Such material is not truly unconscious. This difference is quite important.

By now, most of you accept, face, and admit some of this negative intentionality, but not all of it; you still choose to ignore some. In order to make the remaining aspects completely conscious, and also in order to bring about the change from negative to positive intentionality, it is necessary that you peruse those "little, unimportant" everyday thought patterns which have become so much part of you that it hardly occurs to you to pay attention to them. Yet all the thought processes have tremendous power and must be checked out. So many thoughts and automatic reactions are taken for granted and glossed over. Their significant power is ignored. Thus you can ignore a reaction of ill will, envy, or blaming resentment in spite of being aware of your negative intent in other respects. But it is those little habitual reactions and thoughts that must be explored.

For example, you may admit an irrational anger or hate. You may outwardly assert that these reactions are irrational, but a part of you still feels entitled to have these feelings because that part feels unjustly treated. You still react to the past and bring your reaction into the present. The past pain and anguish may really be repressed in the true sense of the word. In order to make the real direct experience accessible, it is necessary to deal with the defense in a most thorough way. The defense is always a negative intentionality in one form or another that is not truly unconscious. Your past pain, the experience of which you deny to yourself, becomes a present distorted reaction. And these reactions must be seen for what they are.

Let us assume you find yourself angry and resentful in a present situation. As I said, generally you may know and admit that this is your negative feeling, but emotionally you still feel right about the issue. There may be a painful confusion here: one part of you senses that your demands and responses are unjustified; another part feels so deprived and demanding that it reacts as though the world ought to revolve around you, and prevents you from seeing the entire picture objectively.

What is necessary at this stage is to draw out the thought that festers in you, and examine it with that part of you which is mature. You have to follow this confused thought all the way and use all your resources and attention to go further in your self-understanding. Then your negative feelings with the distorted thoughts behind them will be met by truthful, mature and realistic thoughts. The latter must not push the former into hiding again. This ought to be strictly avoided—and you on this path know enough by now not to be tempted into this pitfall. The process must be a conscious dialogue. It is an integrative process that will eventually unite the split and establish an identification with your mature, constructive, genuine self.

It is not only necessary to admit the existence of the mistaken, destructive, mean and unrealistic attitudes. The next step is that you must know exactly why these attitudes are negative, and in what way they distort truth. You then can intelligently consider the realistic situation instead of your childish, distorted view of it.

If you can first express the totally irrational desire and intent behind the destructive attitude, and then express in what way this intent opposes reality, fairness, and truth; then whatever the negativity, you will have made another major step toward changing it into positive intentionality. You will have removed an unnecessary defense or brittle wall, which keeps you from experiencing life.

Your adult thinking has to express itself alongside the childish destructive thinking about the issue in which you are so emotionally involved. This you can do, if you really want to. Your thinking processes usually function quite well if and when you so desire. The thinking processes are usually the most highly developed and can be put into the service of the purification process.

It is absolutely necessary for you to know the ramifications and the significance of your faulty attitudes; for instance, why your anger, your hostility, your jealousy, your envy, and your unfair, one-sided demands are truly unjust. Only then will you also understand that healthy anger can be justified. When this is understood, you can experience it cleanly, without guilt, self-doubt, weakness, and lingering ill-effects. Though feeling anger and hurt can be justified, as long as you do not clearly know whether your anger is justified or not, you will always be confused. You will always fluctuate between guilt and resentment, between negation and rejection of self, of others and of life, and between fear and blame. You will, on the one hand, attempt to assuage your self-doubts by strenuously building cases; on the other hand, you will be paralyzed by fear and weakness and unable to assert yourself. You will be equally weak and confused in situations where you express your irrational, childish demands, and then your destructive intent once those demands are not met, or in situations where you should protect your rights for the sake of the truth. Often both these expressions exist in one and the same situation, which makes it all the more confusing. Your mind alone cannot solve such conflicts. The destructive elements must be admitted first; but then the mind must confront and counter them, understand and correct them.

If the adult intelligence is used merely to rationalize the painful confusion, to build defensive cases, to justify one's own situation, or to protect oneself from admitting the destructive intent, then nothing is ever gained. But if the adult mind is used to shed light on the irrational demands, making it clear that they are unrealistic and unfair and showing that the resulting emotional reactions prove destructive for all concerned, then a lot will be gained and the truth of the situation will emerge.

Going All the Way

This is the work that awaits you for your next phase on the path. You have made good progress in admitting partial negative intentionality. But sometimes such admission becomes in itself a subtle escape. By merely admitting a destructive feeling over and over again, without going further and examining it to find out why and how it is wrong, you merely open yet another little back door. You seem to do the right thing, but you refuse to really go further, to go all the way.

The temptations of evil are so very subtle. Every truth can be put into the service of a distortion. This is why so much vigilance is needed. This is also why doing the right thing is in itself never a guarantee of being truthful and in harmony with universal law. There is no one formula that can protect you from evil; only sincerity of heart can do so. This sincerity of the heart and this good will must be cultivated again and again. It comes from the spiritual cleansing of doing daily review and meditation and from commitment to God's world of truth, love, honesty, and integrity. When the willingness exists to honor decency, truth, love and fairness more than the apparent advantages of the fearful, holding, vain little ego, your liberation will truly proceed in no uncertain way. When this is being done on the inner levels you are now contacting through this work, not just superficially on the level of the outer being, purification becomes very deep.

Bring the level of feelings and the level of mind together. Probe the meaning of your feeling experience, and the validity and reality behind the feeling. Find out if the assumption that underlies a feeling reaction is valid. Any destructive attitude is an expression of an underlying value judgment, and these value judgments must be very clear as to their accuracy or fallacy.

Doubt can only be eliminated when you make room for and try out a trusting attitude. If you merely admit your distrust, without going further to find out what it means, why it is wrong, and how it could possibly be otherwise, you must remain in the status quo. You have to examine the thinking and the conclusions inherent within spite, distrust, jealousy, hostility, and so on, because these conclusions are only in your mind.

Human beings have all kinds of little thoughts every day and every hour of their lives. They do not pay attention to them, but these thoughts mean a lot. Thoughts have such power. All thought creates. Your thoughts, just as much as your feelings, create your actions and your experiences. They create your state of body, mind, soul and spirit.

The time has come, my friends, when more and more of you can take these steps of transition, by taking the realistic steps by which the evil becomes transformed. You will allow yourself full experience of all feelings and give the power to your own consciousness to govern the life you want to have.

This is positive creation at work. This can be done. Request your inner guidance every step of the way to give you alertness and awareness, so as not to push underground what must be dealt with. As you do this, you will not only know in every fiber of your being, but you will feel and experience that what you fear is illusion and that the universe is a rich and joyous place.

In your meditation after this lecture express your trust in the universe; think that you can indeed have abundance, joy, and the fulfillment of your life, of your incarnation—and that fulfillment brings deep peace. Be blessed, all of you, my dear ones.

ई

VISUALIZATION PROCESS FOR GROWING INTO THE UNITIVE STATE

Greetings and blessings. This lecture is another step to help you in a very specific way. The individualized personality in the process of growth and expansion must always evolve toward new states of consciousness and experience. Each stage deepens in scope and releases new creative substance with which to create desirable life experiences and worlds. In this way more of the abundance of the universe becomes available to the individual.

You all know that visualization is quite essential to the creating and recreating work you do in meditation. Unless you can visualize the state you are to grow into, it is hardly possible to reach it. However, it is extremely difficult to visualize a new state to grow into unless an example of some sort exists.

In this lecture I wish to give you some clear-cut pointers and initial concepts of what to look for, what to be attuned to, and what to be prepared to recognize as your own as yet dormant potentials. I will draw a picture of what it is like, inwardly as well a outwardly, to come to the point where the personality truly unites with the inner divine self, with the inexhaustible wealth that is every human being's inner nucleus: the center of one's very being. This lecture is just an outline that describes certain very basic conditions and expressions which can safely be generalized and applied to all of you who have reached the state where your divine self is being continuously expressed and actualized. I will try to give you a concept and a vision so that you can begin to see with fresh eyes, and perhaps recognize in others what you have previously been blind to.

Making a Whole-Hearted Commitment

When individuals come to the state of deliberately and consciously choosing to commit themselves to the divine will and reality, then the groundwork has been laid for certain vital changes to occur in their inner and outer lives. This is a commitment to the all-consciousness indwelling in every creature. It can be called by any name you choose: God, universal consciousness, the real self, the inner self—whatever name you give to that which transcends the little ego. When this whole-hearted commitment is made totally, then certain things begin to happen in one's life. Obviously, one reaches this state not by crossing a sharply defined line, but through a gradual process. Before describing this process, I wish to say that you must not be misled by the fact that you may consciously have made such a commitment, and yet find no greater inner or outer change occurring in your life.

Some of you may be very committed to God on a conscious level, but you may not realize at all that there are other levels in you where this is not the case. You may find it very easy to believe on a merely conscious level that this commitment to God is what you want. Consciously you may be full of good will and really mean it. But unless you have really come to experience the contradictory levels within you where you do not wish that, or where you only wish it on your own ego terms which defeats the very act of self-surrender, you will want to balk. Unless you acknowledge your contrariness, fear, selfwill, and pride, your conscious commitment will always be blocked. Unless you own up to the contrary ego level hidden behind your good will, you may not even understand why certain results are still lacking despite your conscious commitment to truth, to God, to love.

This awareness is extremely important, and the Pathwork deals with it in a very intensive way in order to help you avoid one of the most insidious obstructions: self-deception.

We search for and bring out that negative part of the self which says, "I will not." You will learn the courage, humility, and honesty to expose this part—the part that even says, "I want to resist. I want to be spiteful. I want to have it all my way, or else!" Only when the secret crevices of your psychic substance yield up and expose these areas can you begin—often with a lot of struggle—to change this very negative level, this darker part of the personality. When this part remains hidden, you are split and do not understand why your positive endeavors fail to go further.

Then there comes a point when you have won this particular battle. At this stage you can wholeheartedly embrace and trust the surrender to divine consciousness. But again, this does not come in one fell swoop. At first this surrender must be fought for every time. You need self-discipline to remind yourself. Although resistance is gone, the outer self is still conditioned to the old functioning and automatically forges ahead on the top level of the mind. At this stage you need to acquire a new habit pattern. It takes time. Perhaps when you are really in trouble, in a state of crisis, you will remember to let go and let God. But in ordinary life, in you everyday chores, this does not yet occur to you. Perhaps you can do it where you are relatively free, but you still find your old obstinacy, distrust, and forgetfulness where problems persist. Only little by little do you reach the state where a new habit pattern is instituted, where the act of self-surrender to the all is actualized, where it manifests and where it permeates all your thoughts and perceptions, your decisions and actions, your feeling and reactions. We shall come back to this.

Inner Life and Outer Life

First let me speak about the relationship between your inner and outer life. A lot of confusion exists among people about this topic. There are those who claim only the inner life is important. They prohibit the inevitable movement from the inner to the outer life because they do not see the limitation and actual falsity of this idea. If unification and divine process are truly in movement, the inner content must express itself in outer form. In short, the outer life must mirror the inner life in every possible respect. But if your consciousness ignores this truth, or even strongly embraces the opposite belief, that the outer does not matter, then you prohibit the flow of the whole process. If this happens, the more radiant energetic matter cannot express itself on the levels of coarser matter and thereby refine the latter.

The false concept that the outer level does not matter encases the inner spiritual truth and beauty behind a wall, separating it from the material reality. The individual with this false concept begins to see a dichotomy between the two which are really one. Many movements and spiritual schools of thought preach asceticism and the denial of the outer life under the guise that this furthers inner spiritual life. This distortion is a reaction to the equally distorted opposite extreme, which position claims that outer form is more important than inner content, and may even negate that an inner reality or content exists at all. Instead, it asserts that only outer form matters. True inner growth must eventually also manifest outwardly, though not necessarily with the speed designated by the outer-oriented person, who in expecting an instant change is making mistakes in judgment. It is certainly possible to express outer form without it being a direct expression of inner content. You must therefore be careful in your evaluations.

These two distortions are faulty counter-reactions, each one attempting to eliminate the other by misunderstanding its own. This phenomenon can occur on all subjects as long as consciousness is entrapped in dualistic illusion. During different eras and civilizations, and under different cultural conditions, one of these opposite distortions may be adopted until the pendulum swings to the other. Only a truly connected, self-actualizing, and unified person expresses outer form as an inevitable sequence of inner content.

When the outer form exists without the inner content, it is a temporary cover that must break down, even though it resembles the glorious perfection of divine reality and its expressions. Again, this is a process that repeats itself in many areas throughout human development. However, it is an ongoing law that all false covers must crack and crumble. When outer form exists unconnected with an organic inner content, it must disintegrate. If it exists on faulty premises based on appearance, on confusing the outer life with the inner, then the outer form must first crumble before it can be rebuilt as an organic expression of the inner movement and content. Only when the outer form has crashed and the inner chaos been exposed and thoroughly eliminated, can inner beauty build outer beauty, inner harmony build outer harmony, and the inner abundance build outer abundance. A clear vision of this principle is also necessary for creating a visualization of your own movement which can then manifest in your outer life as a result of your inner process.

Actualizing the Divine Life

I shall now discuss specific manifestations that take place in a person who is already deeply anchored in the process of actualizing the divine life into his or her ego consciousness. What are the inner and outer attitudes, manifestations, and expressions of such a person? All decisions, big or small, are made on the basis of self-surrender, where the little self surrenders to the godself. It steps aside and allows the inner wisdom to permeate it. In this process the personality realizes that there is nothing that is unimportant. Every thought, every opinion, every interpretation, every mode of reacting is given a chance to be permeated by the greater consciousness.

At this stage the resistance to pay attention to everything

that occurs is overcome; a new habit has been formed so that the divine process is now self-perpetuating. It is so much part of the whole person that it operates even on those rare occasions when the personality forgets to establish the contact, when, perhaps, an old raw area might still flare up and push the personality in the wrong direction. The inner self is sufficiently freed to manifest so that it can send forth warnings, disagreement, advice—and then leave the decision of whether or not to follow such advice to the outer personality. This is already a state of grace. Confidence and trust have been established as a result of repeated proof that divine reality brings truth, wisdom, goodness, and joy. At first, the divine will is not trusted. It is confused with untrustworthy parental authority, which may often have proclaimed something as good for the child that really proved not to be so. At the stage in question this confusion no longer exists. The self is fully aware that divine will is truly in accordance with all that the heart may possibly desire. This trust grows gradually every time you overcome your resistance and go into the apparent abyss of surrender, giving up narrow selfwill.

This self-perpetuating divine process brings a vital revolutionary change into the entire person. I can touch upon only a few of its manifestations. Thoughts of truth will be sent forth into your being, notwithstanding the limited thoughts you still habitually follow. You will hear an inner voice instructing you with a wisdom and a unifying spirit that your outer self cannot possibly produce. According to this wisdom, there is never any need to hate, to feel self-rejection or to reject others. The answers and revelations will show the oneness and unity of all, which will completely eliminate fear, anxiety, friction, and despair.

Surrendering the knowledge of the limited ego to the knowledge of the deeper self, so as to exert all energy, courage, honesty, and self discipline toward making the deeper knowledge self-perpetuating, leads to ultimate fulfillment.

Without this as the essential foundation, no joy, pleasure, or fulfillment can exist for long. Even while they do exist, the fulfillment becomes unbearable and finally cannot be accepted. Give up your stake in your negative reaction, in the stubborn opinions of your little mind, in the laziness that forces you to succumb to the old habits of your separated self. You will thus gain true life. Wait patiently, but be ready to receive divine wisdom which you can activate if you so desire. When this state has been instituted, or is in the process of being continually deepened and strengthened, then certain other manifestations begin to appear, inwardly and outwardly.

You will find an immense security. This is a security you can only gain when you discover the reality of the spiritual world within you and operative around you. You will then know the deep peace of the meaning of your life and of all life. You will intuitively know the connections and be permeated by a sense of fulfillment and safety that surpasses all words. All this will then no longer be a theory of belief that you cling to or deny, but an experiential fact which you can recognize again and again. There is always a way out of every darkness and therefore never a reason to despair. You will know that you are always capable of using whatever you experience to heighten your blissful life. Dark spots become opportunities for further light and no longer need to be avoided, whether they be pain, guilt, fear, or whatever. Again and again you will experience the wide open system of creation.

You will know and make use of your own creative powers, rather than feeling a helpless object in a fixed world. Peace and knowledge of the rightness of life come from realizing that your world, your experience, your life is your creation. This opens many new doors. You no longer live in the two-dimensional world of either/or. You avail yourself of the many-faceted reality at your disposal.

The confidence and fearlessness in which you then live necessarily release an immense amount of energy and joy. As you lose your fear of anger and hate because you can accept your own anger and hate, they no longer exist. The energy is now free for other, better expressions. You now become capable of pleasure and joy and no longer need to reject them. Instead of creating loneliness, you can create relationships: the bliss of the most intimate relationship with one mate, and the satisfaction of deep, open friendships. Pleasure will no longer frighten you because you now know in every pore and cell of your being that you deserve it. Your every pore and every cell are expressions of a consciousness which is now in harmony with your god-consciousness.

Many of you find yourselves in an interim state where you experience new joys and pleasures you never knew existed. Life opens up for you as it never did. But you also find yourself in the position where you cannot yet bear too much of it. This is because you have not totally surrendered to the god-consciousness, or you have not sufficiently faced negative aspects in you and still cling to them. Hence, you fear pleasure, which becomes more frightening than the grayness you still wish for and create, a grayness of neither pleasure nor pain. You often want to painstakingly preserve this state of grayness without knowing that you do so. It is a grayness which gives you comfort, but in the long run leaves you empty.

An inevitable manifestation of the continuous process of actualizing your deep self is the incredible creativity that blossoms out from your inner life. You are creative in ideas, alternatives, talents, richness of feelings, and the ability to live with and relate to others. You find the treasure of your creative powers, the wealth of your feelings, and the fullness of your own being. Only as you go through the emptiness can you find that fullness. And that requires courage which comes when you pray or meditate for it. You must want the fullness and commit yourself to it. This fullness of feelings, this wealth of creative ideas, and the ability to live in the now with all its excitement and peace, will deepen and widen. It will not consist of mutually exclusive opposites but of different facets of the same fullness. The times when you seem to lose it will come less often and be less severe.

Since you now have the power to create, you can create a deeper intuitive understanding of yourself, others, and life. Your total attitude of relaxation about every part of yourself eliminates the need to cover up and escape from anything in you and therefore must make you aware of other people on their deepest levels. You read their thoughts and understand the deeper connections within and between them so that you can help them, have empathy for them, and love them. You need never fear and defend against others with your destructive ego defenses.

Inner unity with your eternal self makes it possible to use your creative ability to explore any area of universal truth you truly wish to comprehend. You now know the power of thought and consciousness and you can focus it as a result of the self-discipline you have learned. Thus you can cultivate a creative receptivity to experience the eternal state beyond physical death. This perception is not reliable as long as you seek it out of your own fear of death. It is reliable only when you do not fear death because you now can die, just as you can be in pain. Whenever you want something because you fear its opposite, the result cannot be reliable. You can create only out of fullness, not out of need and poverty.

So the difficulty is in initially creating fullness. Seeking the opposite of what you fear is an escape and leads to a split rather than to unification. Exactly the opposite road must be taken. You must die many deaths, right now, every day in your life, in order to discover the eternality of life. Only then will you live fearlessly.

How can you die all these little deaths? Follow exactly the process I described: let go of the little ego, the little opinions, the negative reactions you have such an investment in. You have to die to those. The little ego with its little investments must die. In that way you can transcend death and intuitively experience the reality of life ongoing.

When you live without fear of death because you experience it so many times, you will know that in principle physical death is the same. You find it to be so by temporarily letting go of the smaller self, only in order to find a larger self wakening, which then unifies with the little self. So you see, not even the little self of the ego really dies. It is enlarged and united with the larger self, not given up. But it appears to be given up and you must be ready to take the plunge.

When this happens, a measure of eternality will manifest in your life right now. It manifests not only by eliminating fear of dying but also in a more immediate practical sense. It will keep you vital and youthful, giving you as it were a foretaste of the timelessness and agelessness of the true life.

Another outward manifestation is abundance. Since real spiritual life is limitless abundance, to some degree you must begin to manifest that when you actualize your divine self. If you can make room in your consciousness for outer abundance as a reflection of universal abundance, you will create and experience it. If you want to experience it because you fear poverty, you also create a split. The abundance you create out of fear is not built on reality, and its flimsy structure must be crushed again so that you can then let yourself be poor and dissolve the illusion of poverty. Only after this can the real, unified richness grow. Only when you first can be poor can you allow yourself to be rich as an outer expression of inner content. Then you will not want to be rich for the sake of power or for outer gains in the eyes of others, or out of greed and fear, but in order to be a true divine expression of the abundance that is the nature of the universe.

Another outer manifestation of the continual process of actualizing divine life is the proper balance of everything: the balance of assertion and giving in, for instance. The spontaneous knowing when one or the other is appropriate comes from within. Or consider the proper balance of right selflessness and wrong selfishness. All these balances and dualities will become elements in a spontaneous unification and harmony. The intuitive knowledge of when, what, and how will come not because you decide it with your mind, but as an expression of inner truth and beauty that reaches expression on the outer level, appropriately and beautifully.

There will be a poise and beauty in your whole bearing—a courtesy and chivalry that never needs to fear being ridiculed or being taken advantage of. There will be order without a trace of compulsiveness, order in all things of your life. Order and beauty are related and interdependent. There will be generosity, a giving and receiving in one ongoing stream. There will come a deep ability to be grateful and to appreciate others, yourself, and the whole creative universe.

A new freedom to be soft and vulnerable will make you truly strong and take away false shame. Concurrently, you will experience a new freedom to be strong and assertive—even angry—without false guilt. You will know and act from within because you are in constant contact with the wisdom, love, and truth of your inner divine reality.

The emotional loneliness that is the self-chosen lot of so many people gradually begins to disappear among you, my friends. In your development you learn to be real, to function without your masks and pretenses. Consequently you begin to feel comfortable in closer intimacy. As you simultaneously cease to fear the pain/pleasure syndrome, true ecstasy and deep fusion on all levels must give you the deepest fulfillment a human being can experience. You will progress to new heights and depths of experience, where you explore the inner universe in unison. Loneliness and the torture of conflict about the need for and fear of closeness will no longer exist. Such relationships fuse on all levels. The abundance of the universe expresses itself in all areas of life. You will feel it in the sharing, the respect, the warmth, the ease and comfort with which you can be intimate and fused with another person, or in giving to and receiving from another person. The security of your own feeling will make you equally secure about being loved.

You will experience the deep satisfaction of giving, helping, fulfilling a task, and of being devoted to doing so. You will rejoice in the ongoing creative process that is at work in it.

All of these are gauges for you, my friends. These gauges are not to be used to put yourself down in impatience and intolerance. They are gauges you can use in order to create deliberate inner visualization about any and all of these life expressions. And then you will perhaps be more strongly motivated to search further for what still stands in the way. This lecture will give you many tools for your work.

The love of the universe spreads over all of your and reaches deep into your hearts, my dearest friends. Be blessed, be God.

૨ર્

INNER SPACE,
FOCUSED EMPTINESS

My beloved friends, you are blessed in body, soul and spirit. Your path is blessed, every step of the way. You may at times doubt this when the going gets rough. But when this is so, it is not because blessings are withheld from you. It is because you encounter parts of your inner landscape that need to be successfully traversed. To traverse difficult inner terrain it is necessary to understand its meaning for your own being and thus to dissolve the roadblocks you find on your way.

We have occasionally discussed this inner landscape. I have made mention of the *inner space* that is the real world. The term "inner space" is used quite frequently in your world these days, as opposed to outer space. Most human beings think of inner space as merely a symbolic description of a person's state of mind. This is not so. Inner space is a vast reality, a real world. It is in fact the real universe, while outer space is merely a mirror image, a reflection of it. This is why outer reality can never be quite grasped. Life can never be truly understood and experientially absorbed when it is viewed only from the outside. This is why life is so frustrating, and often so frightening, for so many people.

I can see that it is hard to understand how inner space can be a world in itself—*the* world. The reason for this difficulty lies again in the limited time/space continuum of your three-dimensional reality. Everything you see, touch, and experience is perceived from a certain very limited angle. The mind is focused, accustomed, conditioned to operate in a certain direction and is therefore incapable at this juncture of perceiving life in any other way. But this way of perceiving reality is by no means the only way, or the correct way, or the complete way.

Finding the Inner Reality

In every spiritual discipline the goal is to perceive life in this other way, the way that goes beyond the outer reflection, the way that focuses on new dimensions to be found in inner space. In some disciplines this goal may be directly mentioned, or it may never be mentioned as such. But when a certain point of development and purification is reached, the new vision awakens—sometimes suddenly, sometimes gradually. Even the suddenness of the vision is only an illusion, because it actually is the result of many arduous steps and inner battles.

It has been recognized that every atom is a duplication of the outer universe, as you know it. This recognition is very meaningful. Perhaps you can imagine that just as time is a variable, dependent on the dimension from which it is experienced, so is space. Just as there is really no objective, fixed time, so there is no objective, fixed space. Your real being can live, breathe and move, and cover vast distances within an atom according to your outer measurement. When the spirit withdraws to the inner world, the relationship of measurement changes, just as the relationship to time changes. This is why you seem to lose contact with and awareness of so-called "dead" people. They live in the inner reality which, for you, is as yet only an abstraction. Yet the actual abstraction is the outer space. In physical death, the spirit, that which is alive, *withdraws* into the inner world, not as is often erroneously assumed, into heaven. It does not lift out of the body; it does not float into outer space. If, at times, an extrasensory perception seems to reveal such a sight, it is again only after the mirror image of the inner event.

In the same way, a majority of humans have, for the longest time, looked for God up in heaven. When Jesus Christ came, He taught that God lives in the inner spaces and He must be found there. This is also why all meditational practices and exercises focus on inner space.

A long time ago I suggested a meditational exercise in which you do not think, in which you make yourself empty. Those of you who occasionally try this exercise experience how difficult it is to do so. The mind is filled with its own material and to still it is not an easy undertaking. There are several ways of doing it. Eastern religions usually approach it by long practice and discipline. This, in conjunction with solitude and outer stillness, may eventually produce inner stillness.

Our approach on this path is different. These teachings do not want to take you out of your world. On the contrary, the aim is to be *in* your world, in the best possible way. To understand, to accept, and to create in it in the most productive, constructive way. This can only be done when you fully know and understand yourself and when you traverse, as I said, the difficult spaces, which must make you better equipped to function in this three-dimensional reality. Then there is no split between the inner and outer spaces. As inner truth reigns, perception of outer truth increases. As understanding of self grows, so does understanding of the world. As you learn to re-mold that in you which is imperfect, faulty, so do you learn to restructure—transform—your outer life. As you learn of your eternal beauty as a divine manifestation, so does your vision expand to a greater appreciation of the beauty of the Creator's creation. As peace within yourself comes to be, so do you become at peace with this world, even when you are surrounded by undesirable experiences. In other words, you do not require outer conditions of absolute seclusion in order to reach inner space. You take the other route in which you go right through what seems the greatest of obstructions: the imperfections within and around you. You approach them, you deal with them, until they lose their fearsome aspect. This is your path.

Focusing on the inner emptiness is an additional exercise that is very helpful, but it must never be the sole approach to self-realization, just as dealing with the outer adverse conditions in your world must never be the sole approach to your own and your world's salvation.

Focused emptiness grows, both deliberately and spontaneously, as you remove inner obstacles. At the early stages, you experience just that: emptiness, nothingness. If your mind can quiet down, you encounter the void; this is what makes the attempt so frightening. It seems to confirm the suspicion that there is nothing within you; that you are indeed only your outer, mortal self. This is why the mind makes itself so busy and so noisy—in order to blot out the quietness that appears to herald nothingness.

Once again you need the courage to go through a tunnel of uncertainty. You need to take the risk to allow the great quietude that is, at first, empty of meaning, devoid of anything that spells life or consciousness.

I believe most of you have already experienced how the voice of your higher self sends its inspirations through your mind not necessarily immediately after a meditation or a prayer, but sometime later, often when you least think of it. It is then that your mind is relaxed enough and sufficiently free from self-will to allow the higher self to manifest. The same is true in regard to experiencing the inner universe—the real world.

Focused emptiness will bring you in touch with all the levels of your being. It allows the emergence of what was hidden—the distortions, the errors, the lower-self material, and eventually, the reality of your higher self and the vast world of eternal life in which it dwells. There are many stages and phases to go through. The latter stages can take place only when a certain purification and integration has taken place. Unfocused emptiness is a lessening of consciousness. Focused emptiness is a heightening of consciousness. The former is a tuning out, a vague wandering of the mind that may lead to mindless emptiness. Sleep, or other states of unconsciousness are the final stages. Focused emptiness is extremely concentrated, aware, and fully there.

If you focus on the inner world to the exclusion of your outer world, you not only create a split, but also a condition in which you forfeit the purpose of your incarnation. How can you fulfill your task, whatever it may be, if you do not utilize your outer world for that purpose? You would not have come into this dimension if it had not been a necessity for you. So you need to make use of it and always bring outer and inner conditions into a meaningful relationship with each other. You are learning to do this on this path. All your outer experiences are related to your personality, your various levels of self. Your inner being always creates your outer conditions, a truth you soon learn to recognize on this path. If relating the outer to the inner is not a constant way of life, the imbalance must create unfavorable conditions. You can see how sometimes in your world people who do a lot of good works outwardly lose their way just as easily as those who never give others a thought. The outer good intent and good works must have an inner focus in order to avoid a disharmonious condition and a dangerous split.

The Stages of Focused Emptiness

Focused emptiness brings you eventually to the light of the eternal. Maybe we can categorize certain basic stages, even if somewhat oversimplified. In reality these stages often overlap and do not come neatly in the succession outlined here for the purpose of clarification.

1) You experience the noise and the busyness of mind.

2) You succeed in quieting this noise, you encounter emptiness, nothingness.

3) Recognitions about the self, connections between some aspects of the self and outer experiences become clear. New

understanding and with it heretofore unrecognized levels of lower self material appear. This stage is really a ray of divine guidance, and not merely an experience of the lower self. Recognition of the lower self is always a manifestation of higher-self guidance.

4) Direct manifestation of higher-self messages, or what you call the opening of your channel. You receive advice, encouragement, words intended to give you courage and faith. In this phase divine guidance still operates primarily through your mind. It is not necessarily a total emotional and spiritual experience. The manifestation may excite and gladden you, but this reaction is a result of the knowledge your mind has absorbed and has found convincing.

5) In this stage a direct, total, spiritual and emotional experience occurs. Your whole being is filled with the Holy Spirit. You *know,* not indirectly through your mind, but directly through all of your being. Knowing through the mind is really always an indirect knowledge. It is a relayed knowledge. The mind is the instrument necessary for human beings to function on this level of consciousness. Direct knowledge is different.

This phase has many subdivisions, many stages within itself. There are many, no, limitless, possibilities in which the real world can be experienced. One is simply *total knowing,* which affects every fiber of your being, every level of your consciousness. Experience of the real world can also occur through visions of other dimensions, but such visions are never merely things one sees. They are always a total experience that affects the total person.

In the real world, as opposed to your fragmented world, every sense perception is total. Seeing is never only seeing, it is simultaneously hearing, tasting, feeling, smelling—and many other perceptions you know nothing about on your level of being. In this fifth stage, seeing, hearing, perceiving, feeling, knowing are always all inclusive. They encompass every capacity God has created. And you can hardly imagine the richness, the variety, the limitless possibilities of these capacities.

Focused emptiness is the ideal state to be filled by the Holy Spirit. The Holy Spirit is the whole world of God in all its splendor, in its indescribable magnificence. Its richness cannot possibly be conveyed in human language. There is no way of describing what exists when fear, doubt, distrust—and therefore suffering, death and evil—are overcome. Focused emptiness is therefore nothing but a threshold to a fullness that exists only in the world of spirit.

The practice of focused emptiness must never be undertaken in an attitude of immediate expectations. In fact, it is necessary to have *no expectations* whatever: expectations are a tension, and tension prevents the necessary state of total inner and outer relaxation. Also, expectations are unrealistic, for it may take many incarnations of development before a human being can come anywhere near these experiences. So to have any kind of expectations will cause disappointments which, in turn, set off a chain reaction of further negative emotions, such as doubt, fear, and discouragement.

I am talking about this topic because I want to prepare you for an important practice within meditation. I have discussed this in the past in connection with the various ways of meditation, particularly in regard to *impressing* and *expressing*. Many of your meditations have dealt with impressing, and should continue to do so. This aspect of impressing is a cleansing of the mind and serves to make the mind into a constructive tool. Then the tool becomes a creative agent.

The aspect of expressing has begun to manifest to some degree with those whose channels are open, perhaps only occasionally. But you need to know that there are further stages, further phases and possibilities, and you should approach them with patience, awe, and humility. You should understand that these experiences will open the vast inner spaces in which many worlds, many universes, many spheres exist, endless plains, mountains, seas of indescribable beauty. You should know that these inner spaces are not abstractions or symbolic expressions; they are much more real and accessible than your outer, objectified world that you believe to be the only reality. Inner space is based on different measurements, on a different relativity between time/space/movement and measurement. Even a vague and hazy consideration of this concept on your part will change your outlook and will create a new approach to your further work on your path.

You need not spend hours practicing focused emptiness. Such is not the purpose. But you may attempt it to some degree every time you pray and meditate, after you use your mind to impress your soul substance and align it with divine intent.

The Real You That Lives in the Real World

Spirit can penetrate matter to the degree that spiritual truth, spiritual law, spiritual health are being established. And the individual's self-responsibility is indeed the key to this. When the self becomes stronger, more of life can penetrate matter; more of the spirit can be born in the flesh. So, you will see, as you grow in stature through gaining selfhood, more of your real being is born into your physical manifestation. More talents may come to the fore of which you had known nothing before. Suddenly a new wisdom manifests, a new understanding and capacity to feel and love; a hitherto unsensed strength unfolds from you. All these manifestations are the real you that lives in the inner space—the real world. As you make room for these aspects, they will push into the life of matter and you will fulfill your part in the evolutionary scheme. These attitudes do not grow from outside; they are not being added on to you. They are a result of your outer manifest being making room for the inner, as yet unmanifest being. This happens by the growing process, the hard work you undertake on this path. And, after a certain point in your development, it can be helped along by focusing on the inner emptiness until you discover that the emptiness is illusion. It is a fullness, a rich world of glory. You can receive all you need from this inner source, and translate it into outer experience.

By approaching the void without fear, you also remove an obstruction to life. Focusing on the inner space means, to begin with, approaching what appears as emptiness. Through this void you reach the fullness of spirit, the totality of life in its pure, unobstructed form. This stuff of life contains all possibilities of expression, of manifestation. The joy of experiencing this reality is greater than any other. In this joy is your oneness with the Creator, where you are indeed one.

You can see, my friends, that nothing in your personality, no aspect of it, is insignificant in terms of creation and evolution. There is no such thing as a "merely psychological aspect." Every attitude, every way of thinking, feeling, being, and reacting reflects directly on your participation in the greater scheme of things. By knowing this you will perhaps, once again, find it easier to give your life, your pathwork, your endeavors, greater value. You will learn, once again, to unify an arbitrary duality—spiritual versus worldly concerns.

Make room for unobstructed life, for unencumbered spirit! Let it fill every part of your being, so that you will finally know who you really are. You are all blessed, my very dearest ones.

છે

EVIL TRANSFORMED;
EVIL TRANSCENDED
THE UNITIVE STATE

*Know that, by nature, every creature seeks to
become like God. Nature's intent is neither food
nor drink nor clothing, nor comfort, nor
anything else in which God is left out. Whether
you like it or not, whether you know it or not,
secretly nature seeks, hunts, tries to ferret out the
track on which God may be found.*
Meister Eckhart [1]

It may be tempting to think that work on the lower self is
only required at the earlier stages of the spiritual path, and that
as one explores the transpersonal realms and moves toward the
unitive, considerations of the lower self may be left behind. But
such is not the case.

The Guide has explained how self-will, pride, and fear are the
principal roots of personal evil. Of these three, it is fear that has
been the most difficult for people to connect with as a source of
evil. But with only a bit of reflection one can see how fear of
being hurt by others so easily leads to hurting others. As the
Guide has said, evil is a defense against suffering; whether real
suffering or feared suffering.

Beyond this, fear is a root of evil because it is so totally at
variance with ultimate reality. In truth, the universe is benign,

and therefore there is nothing to fear. In truth, the universe is one, and therefore there is no one outside of me who can hurt me.

In the later stages of spiritual growth fear is the greatest obstacle. At this level the fear is not of being hurt by others. Rather, the fear is of surrendering one's sense of being a separate self. As Meister Eckhart says, all of nature yearns for, strives for, the experience of becoming like God, of achieving a state of oneness with all that is. "Enlightenment" is the experience of totally and completely realizing that God-oneness.

Strange though it may sound, enlightenment need not be sought; it is already here and so one need not travel in order to find it. Rather, we must more and more clearly see the ways in which we are constantly running away from enlightenment. No matter what may be our methods of running away, the cause of the running is fear. We fear what we desire. We fear the loss of our sense of separate identity; we fear the death of the ego, mistakenly believing that such will mean an end to existence.

The Guide has pointed out that most spiritual paths attempt, by way of various spiritual practices, to take the seeker to an experience of the unitive state; and he acknowledges that they sometimes succeed in attaining this goal. He also points out a danger inherent in such paths: That it is possible to achieve this goal of *transcendence* of the human state while still leaving parts of oneself mired in the lower self. There are many examples in our own century of spiritual teachers who have attained a substantial *transcendence,* but who turned out to have still a great deal of *transformation* of the lower self yet left undone.

The Guide's position is that most spiritual seekers attempt a premature transcendence, caused by a failure to see one's lower self clearly, and a desire to be beyond where one truly now is. The Guide continues to stress, therefore, the need for the horizontal movement of transformation; the need for a continual examination of oneself in order to find the lower self, and on then *working through* this material, and *transforming* it, rather than attempting to *transcend* it.

But, as has also been pointed out in many of the lectures in this volume, after a certain point the work cannot be done unless the worker learns to shift his/her sense of identity. To shift, that is, from the personal to the transpersonal; from the small ego-consciousness to the greater consciousness. And once that shift has been fully made, it is correct to say that a transcendence has occurred. This is working in a vertical direction, rather than horizontal. Clearly, both are required; and finding the proper balance between the horizontal and the vertical, between transformation and transcendence, is one of the subtlest and most important aspects of the work on oneself.

So, to use their dictionary definitions, "to change in composition or structure, character or condition" (transformation) *and* "to rise above or go beyond the limits of" (transcendence) are both required. We need to fully accept our human condition, and then bit-by-bit discover that we are more than simply human.

To be human is to be flawed and imperfect, but this is not cause for despair. We live in an intermediate realm, neither in heaven nor in hell. That is the condition of our existence. Within that condition we have a nobility and a purpose. Our purpose is precisely to learn to examine ourselves honestly, see our imperfections clearly, resolve to change, learn how to change, and then to proceed, diligently and courageously, with the work of self-transformation. This is our nobility. This is what the human state is for.

As we proceed on the path of self-transformation, we become progressively more loving and more wise. Our clarity increases, as do our courage and our joy and our compassion. Life opens up, becomes both wider and deeper. Pain and grief and challenge we will still have, but we learn to not be crushed by them.

But, you may say, are we not all eventually crushed by death? Death is experienced as a crushing defeat only if one is still so totally identified with one's skin-encapsulated ego. For even death will lose its sting as we come to know that the alternation of death and life is no more fearsome than the alternation of sleep and waking.

In other words, as we accept our human state with its flaws and imperfections, and we have the courage to face and transform our lower self, we strengthen to the point where we can realize that we are more than human. Birth and death are prime ingredients of the human state, but one's true essence precedes birth and death. In other words, continued work on transformation of the lower self ultimately leads to an ability to transcend the lower self. And the final transcendence is into the state of God-oneness of which Meister Eckhart speaks.

The path is a challenging one. As Christ said, the pearl of great price must be purchased at the cost of *all that you have.* But the journey is ultimately a totally safe one.

As the Guide has said, in many lectures and in many different phrasings: "You have nothing to fear."

Donovan Thesenga

---

1. *Meister Eckhart.* Trans. R. Blakney.

Textual Note

Each chapter in this book is an edited version of a Guide lecture. Some have been shortened only slightly; some substantially. Since chapter titles are not always the same as the original titles of the lectures, we give here a listing of chapter numbers and the equivalent lecture numbers and titles.

Chapter 1 is a portion of lecture 11 – *Know Yourself.*

Chapter 2 is lecture 14 – *The Higher Self, the Lower Self, and the Mask*

Chapter 3 is lecture 25 – *The Path.*

Chapter 4 is lecture 26 plus a portion of lecture 28 – *Finding One's Faults* and *Communication with God-Daily Review.*

Chapter 5 is a condensation of lectures 38 through 41 – *Images, Image-Finding, More on Images* and *Images–the Damage They Do.*

Chapter 6 is lecture 50 – *The Vicious Circle.*

Chapter 7 is lecture 73 – *Compulsion to Recreate and Overcome Childhood Hurts.*

Chapter 8 is lecture 83 – *The Idealized Self-Image.*

Chapter 9 is lecture 84 – *Love, Power, and Serenity.*

Chapter 10 is lecture 100 – *Meeting the Pain of Destructive Patterns.*

Chapter 11 is lecture 124 – *The Language of the Unconscious.*

Chapter 12 is lecture 125 – *Transition from the No-Current to the Yes-Current.*

Chapter 13 is lecture 132 – *Function of the Ego in Relationship to the Real Self.*

Chapter 14 is lectures 134 and 135 – *The Concept of Evil* and *Mobility in Relaxation – Attachment of the Life Force to Negative Situations.*

Chapter 15 is lecture 140 – *Attachment to Negative Pleasure as the Origin of Pain.*

Chapter 16 is lecture 148 – *Positivity and Negativity: One Energy Current*

Chapter 17 is lecture 176 – *Overcoming Negativity.*

Chapter 18 is lecture 182 – *The Process of Meditation.*

Chapter 19 is lecture 189 – *Self-Identification Determined through Stages of Consciousness.*

Chapter 20 is lecture 190 – *Experiencing All Feelings Including Fear.*

Chapter 21 is lecture 195 – *Identification with the Spiritual Self to Overcome Negative Intentionality.*

Chapter 22 is lecture 198 –
Transition to Positive Intentionality.

Chapter 23 is lecture 210 –
*Visualization Process for Growth into
the Unitive State.*

Chapter 24 is lecture 256 –
Inner Space, Focused Emptiness.

For further information about the Pathwork:

There are a number of very active Pathwork Centers in North America and Europe, and a network of many groups which study and work with the Guide lectures.

We welcome the opportunity to support you in connecting with others who are interested in exploring this material further. To order any Pathwork lecture, or to receive an index of all lecture titles, or for further information please contact any of the regional centers below.

Sevenoaks Pathwork Center*
Route 1, Box 86
Madison, VA 22727
(703) 948-6544

Great Lakes Pathwork*
305 Pineridge
Ann Arbor, MI 48103
(313) 585-3984

Philadelphia Pathwork
c/o Carolyn Tilove
901 S. Bellevue Ave.
Hulmeville, PA 19047
(215) 752-9894

Northwest Pathwork*
811 Northwest 20th
Suite 103-C
Portland, OR 97209
(503) 223-0018

Phoenicia Pathwork Center*
Box 66
Phoenicia, N.Y. 12464
(914) 688-2211

Pathwork of California*
1355 Stratford Court, #16
Del Mar, CA 92014-2327
(619) 793-1246
Fax (619) 259-5224

Padwerk - c/o Johan Kos
Boerhaavelaan 9
1401 VR Bussum, Holland
02159-35222

Il Sentiero
Raffáele Iandolo
Via Campodivivo, 43
04020 Spigno Saturnia (LT)
Italy
39-771-64-463

Additional copies of *Fear No Evil* may be ordered from centers marked with an asterisk (*).